Conflict, Security and Development

This textbook draws on academic theory, field research and policy developments to provide an overview of the connections between security and development before, during and after conflict.

Academics and policymakers increasingly argue that security and development are closely related and therefore cannot be achieved independently of each other. This book uniquely combines academic teaching and approaches with practical policy experience in three key ways:

- using the best of recent academic theory, field research and policy to provide an overview of the connections between security and development;
- exploring the implications of these connections for the theory and practice of development;
- investigating the challenges that arise for post-conflict reconstruction when we recognise that security and development are mutually contingent.

The authors are experienced in both the theory and the practice of development and conflict and illustrate the theory about the links between conflict, security and development with practical examples, drawing on key case studies from the past twenty years. Each chapter is informed by student pedagogy, and the book will be essential reading for all students of development studies, war and conflict studies and human security, and is recommended for students of international security and IR in general.

Danielle Beswick is a Lecturer in the International Development Department at the University of Birmingham.

Paul Jackson is the Director of the International Development Department at the University of Birmingham. He has been the Director of the UK's Global Facilitation Network for Security Sector Reform and is on the Advisory Board of the Geneva Centre for the Democratic Control of Armed Forces.

Conflict, Security and Development
An introduction

Danielle Beswick and Paul Jackson

Routledge
Taylor & Francis Group

LONDON AND NEW YORK

First published 2011
by Routledge
2 Park Square, Milton Park, Abingdon, Oxon, OX14 4RN

Simultaneously published in the USA and Canada
by Routledge
711 Third Avenue, New York, NY 10017

*Routledge is an imprint of the Taylor & Francis Group, an informa
business*

© 2011 Danielle Beswick and Paul Jackson

The right of Danielle Beswick and Paul Jackson to be identified as
author of this work has been asserted by them in accordance with
sections 77 and 78 of the Copyright, Designs and Patents Act 1988.

All rights reserved. No part of this book may be reprinted or
reproduced or utilised in any form or by any electronic, mechanical,
or other means, now known or hereafter invented, including
photocopying and recording, or in any information storage or
retrieval system, without permission in writing from the publishers.

Trademark notice: Product or corporate names may be trademarks or
registered trademarks, and are used only for identification and
explanation without intent to infringe.

British Library Cataloguing in Publication Data
A catalogue record for this book is available from the British Library

Library of Congress Cataloging-in-Publication Data
Beswick, Danielle.
Conflict, security, and development: an introduction / Danielle
Beswick and Paul Jackson.
    p. cm.
1. Security, International. 2. Political violence—Economic aspects
3. Economic development—Political aspects. I. Jackson, Paul, 1968
Apr. 24– II. Title.
JZ5588.B47 2011
355'.033—dc22   2011000597

ISBN13: 978–0–415–49984–2 (hbk)
ISBN13: 978–0–415–49983–5 (pbk)
ISBN13: 978–0–203–81018–7 (ebk)

Typeset in Times
by Book Now Ltd, London

Printed and bound in Great Britain by
TJ International Ltd, Padstow, Cornwall

Contents

Acknowledgements

Danielle Beswick would first of all like to thank her parents, Debbie and David, and her brother, Andrew, for the incredible emotional and practical support they have shown over the years. She wouldn't be the first Dr Beswick in the family if it were not for their faith in her. She would also like to thank her husband, David, who has always provided encouragement when it is most needed, not to mention much appreciated company (and humour!) during difficult periods of fieldwork overseas, and endured many hours of proofreading and listening to her ranting about politics! Finally, sincere thanks are due to her grandparents and particularly her grandfather, Paul Maurice D'John, for his tireless support and encouragement of her research, for pushing her not to accept things at face value and always to ask more difficult and challenging questions of those in positions of power. She couldn't have done this without all of you.

Paul Jackson would like to thank everyone he has worked with over several years and especially his colleagues in the International Development Department. In particular, he would like to thank his family – his wife, Anne, and two children, Sam and Andrew, for their patience. He would also like to thank his parents, who always encouraged him in whatever ridiculous thirst for knowledge he was exhibiting at the time.

Both authors would like to thank Ndubuisi Nwokwolo for his work in collating materials for the book and the University of Birmingham School of Government and Society for providing financial support.

Abbreviations

ACOTA	African Contingency Operations Training and Assistance
AFRICOM	United States Unified Command for Africa
ANC	African National Congress
ASEAN	Association of Southeast Asian Nations
AU	African Union
BAPSC	British Association of Private and Security Companies
CRC	Convention on the Rights of the Child
DAC	Development Assistance Committee
DDR	Disarmament, Demobilisation and Reintegration
DFID	Department for International Development (UK)
DPKO	Department of Peacekeeping Operations (UN)
DRC	Democratic Republic of the Congo
ECOMOG	Economic Community of West African States Monitoring Group
ECOWAS	Economic Community of West African States
ICC	International Criminal Court
ICISS	International Commission on Intervention and State Sovereignty
ICRC	International Committee of the Red Cross
IDP	Internally Displaced Person
IMF	International Monetary Fund
IPOA	International Peace Operations Association
IR	International Relations
IRC	International Rescue Committee
ISAF	International Security Assistance Force
LRA	Lord's Resistance Army

MDGs	Millennium Development Goals
MONUC	United Nations Mission in the DRC
MONUSCO	United Nations Organization Stabilization Mission in the DRC
NGO	Non-Governmental Organisation
OECD	Organisation for Economic Cooperation and Development
ONUMOZ	United Nations Operations in Mozambique
PMC	Private Military Company
PSC	Private Security Company
PSO	Peace Support Operations
R2P	Responsibility to Protect
RUF	Revolutionary United Front (Sierra Leone)
SALW	Small Arms and Light Weapons
SSR	Security Sector Reform
STD	Sexually Transmitted Disease
TRC	Truth and Reconciliation Commission
UNAMID	African Union–United Nations Mission in Darfur
UNAMIR	United Nations Assistance Mission for Rwanda
UNAVEM	United Nations Angola Verification Mission
UNDP	United Nations Development Programme
UNEF	United Nations Emergency Force
UNHCR	United Nations High Commissioner for Refugees
UNICEF	United Nations Children's Fund
UNITAF	United Nations Unified Task Force
UNMIL	United Nations Mission in Liberia
UNOSOM	United Nations Operation in Somalia
UNRWA	United Nations Relief and Works Agency for Palestine Refugees in the Near East
UNTAG	United Nations Transition Assistance Group

Introduction

The end of the Cold War heralded a shift from a bipolar world order, characterised by superpower competition, to a multipolar world, characterised by considerable turbulence and an enhanced awareness of global inequality. Since the 1990s the considerable disparities between states and societies in terms of wealth, development, security and stability have become increasingly obvious, leading to a range of international initiatives to combat poverty and underdevelopment and to resolve conflicts within and between states.

In the context of the post-Cold War world, theorists and practitioners have progressively come to recognise the impact of conflict and insecurity on the success of development initiatives. At the same time, they are more aware than ever of the need for development strategies, and those attempting to deliver them, to be sensitive to the environment in which they operate, particularly in regions experiencing conflict or in the context of failed or collapsed states. During conflict, a range of actors, from citizens, aid workers, members of local civil society, governments and warlords to soldiers – including child soldiers – pursue their own agendas, which ultimately impact on the character and duration of the conflict and prospects for lasting security and development. Studies of individual contexts have highlighted the importance of economies of conflict, which must be taken into account by those seeking to improve security and development. Strategies are emerging which seek to replace them instead with economies of peace, which can facilitate development whilst tackling poverty and insecurity.

In an interdependent world, the challenges of underdevelopment and insecurity have global implications. Vast sums of aid are distributed by bilateral and multilateral donors, and a host of non-state organisations, for development and reconstruction. There are protracted debates about which actors are responsible for peacekeeping, peacemaking and even peace enforcement. Refugees from the civil wars in the South inevitably impact the states and regions to which they move, regardless of their level of development. The trafficking of resources such as diamonds and timber through international networks funds conflict in the developing world but can also have implications for global security; the activities of groups designated as terrorist organisations, such as Hamas and al-Qaeda, are believed to be partly funded through these illicit transactions. Given that these instances are by no means an exhaustive account of the challenges being faced, the need for a holistic understanding of the relationship between conflict, security and development has never been more apparent or more urgent.

Development and security

This book seeks to introduce some of the core ideas surrounding development and security in the contemporary world. The truism that development requires security and security requires development has become firmly entrenched in the lexicon of state-building. The idea that providing basic needs to populations in countries that have been ravaged by conflict requires a fundamental level of security is an obvious one, but it has become similarly accepted that the long-term security of peoples and states relies on their having access to sufficient resources to enable their survival but also their development. As a colleague once put it to one of these authors, 'The best way to prevent a conflict is to give everyone a job.'

It has also become common to hear this type of statement on the ground in those areas where conflict has taken place. Ask an army officer in Sierra Leone from either the Sierra Leonean Army or the British military team, and they will tell you that they are progressing well and improving security infrastructure, but that what is now required is faster economic development to provide opportunities for those people who currently have nothing. The implication is that, without alternative means of making a living, some people may turn to crime or violence more broadly. Similarly, at the Centre for Global Development, US Secretary of State Hillary Clinton declared in January 2010: 'We cannot stop terrorism or defeat the ideologies of violent extremism when hundreds of millions of young people see a future with no jobs, no hope, and no way ever to catch up to the developed world.'

These kinds of arguments have led to what is known as the 'securitisation of development'. Some scholars have argued that securitisation of development and its opposite, the 'developmentalisation' of security, is greatly facilitated by globalisation, the end of the Cold War and the growth of so-called 'new wars'. These wars are discussed in detail below, but briefly the argument is that they have certain characteristics that break down the assumptions of 'old wars', including that wars take place between states, consist of orderly battles and are fought for ideological or political reasons. New wars are intra-state and may involve a range of actors other than the state. They are fought by nebulous groups that are difficult to define, may be motivated by economic reasons such as looting resources like diamonds, and are linked into global criminal networks for arms, drugs and even transnational terrorism.

The process of securitisation developed relatively slowly at first. This was undoubtedly due to a mutual mistrust between militaries and security actors on the one hand and humanitarian aid agencies on the other. Gradually some humanitarian agencies have begun to enlist security actors as a means of delivering aid and protecting aid workers in areas where there may be significant security threats. The risk, however, is that humanitarian aid agencies may begin to lose their reputation for impartiality in situations that could be highly volatile, a process that has effectively culminated in aid workers being targeted by some insurgents, for example in Afghanistan, Sudan and Somalia.

The process was also complemented by other far-reaching processes in the design and delivery of aid. Throughout the 1990s and into the 2000s, private security actors began to assume roles that had traditionally been taken by the state, such as training, guard functions, convoy security and the security of embassies. At the same time, changes in the delivery of overseas aid meant that much aid delivery was outsourced to the non-state sector, including private actors, universities, consultancy companies and non-governmental organisations. The number of actors involved in the process therefore increased rapidly and roles became more flexible and blurred.

There were also rapid changes in role and responsibility in terms of where these actors were working. In the interventions in both Iraq and Afghanistan, development actors were enrolled as a critical element of 'winning hearts and minds'. They have taken up important roles in reconstructing not just the infrastructure within states but also the states themselves, revisiting and developing systems covering security, justice, social support, employment and basic service delivery and even supporting the establishment of specific forms of political settlement predicated on democracy in some shape or form.

It is not just in Afghanistan and Iraq that development and security have become entwined, and, in many ways, these form separate exceptions to the general rule. Africa is the most conflict-ridden continent in the world, and here the security and development agenda has become engrained in a series of policies that have questioned assumptions underlying aid and what it aims to do. In a continent governed by 'new wars', in the sense that there are several conflicts that are unrelated to state wars but involve a variety of actors, among them 'warlords', 'pirates', 'dictators' and 'madmen', security is usually top of most people's agendas on the ground. Add to this an unfortunate history of involvement by security forces in politics across the continent of Africa, as well as in South America, and security becomes essentially a governance problem rather than just a technical military matter. The technical training can teach troops to shoot straight, but it takes good governance to train them when to shoot and whom to shoot at.

As a result, aid agencies have begun to work very closely together with security actors to reconstruct governance more broadly, including security governance. One particular area where this has happened is in the aftermath of war, where disarmament, demobilisation and reintegration (DDR) has become closely associated with more comprehensive development efforts aimed at consolidating peace and then beginning to develop stable political, economic and social systems. DDR itself has become closely related to an influential policy development that is generally labelled security sector reform (SSR), but that takes in a wide range of policy interventions aimed at establishing democratic control over security forces in order to ensure 'human security'.

The core aim of this book is to outline and interrogate the perceived wisdom that 'there is no development without security and no security without development'. It has three key aims:

1   To draw on the best of recent academic theory, field research and policy developments to provide an overview of the connections between security and development, before, during and after conflict.
2   To explore the implications of these connections for the theory and practice of development and the ways in which different actors have sought to manage and resolve conflict in the South.
3   To investigate the challenges that arise for post-conflict reconstruction if we accept that security and development are mutually contingent, and that requirements for each must be fulfilled in order to produce long-term peace and prosperity.

This is clearly a vast subject, and the book is designed as an introductory text for those with no background in the area. In an extremely diverse field the interaction between theory and policy can appear to be extremely confusing and, indeed, can often be fast moving and develop rapidly. As with all academic subject areas, the view of security and development and the way in which they can be described can also be subject to fashion and rapidly changeable terminology. This text aims to provide an overview of the core elements of the subject and a clear explanation of the main issues within it.

One of the key characteristics of our approach is that we are both experienced academics who have worked extensively on the policy of this area. Consequently we try to marry academic teaching and approaches with practical policy experience, highlighting the links between policy and practice.

Outline of the book

The book is divided into eight chapters that are designed to take you through a series of core issue within the subject area. There is no way that any single book could provide a comprehensive picture of everything, so each chapter is designed as a general introduction and provides some key questions and some literature to allow follow-up.

The first chapter looks at the definitions of the terms 'security' and 'development'. These are fundamental issues that are at the heart of this book, but they also stand at the centre of the debate on why people are engaged in conflict and violence. This is *the* core question in many ways: if we can decide why conflict happens, then theoretically we can do something to prevent it happening. This book is in a tradition that holds that security and development are firmly related to each other and there is some form of what policymakers call a 'security–development nexus'. This chapter outlines this idea and some of the implications of taking that approach. Definitions are important in this subject, and you will find that in many areas most definitions are contested both by policymakers and in the academic literature. Fundamentally this chapter introduces you to these concepts and then guides you through the overarching ideas of how 'security' is changing. In particular, it concentrates on the role of the state and the individual in different types of security and the thoughts behind 'human security'. This approach has a number of policy implications and the chapter outlines many of them.

Chapter 2 takes some of these definitions and adds an analysis of what is currently happening in many parts of the developing world. It describes the core areas of conflict and the nature of those conflicts, covering geographical areas as diverse as Iraq and the Congo. It then outlines some academic approaches to these ideas, including the end of the Cold War as a catastrophic event for many states that were reinvented as areas of violent conflict as the central state collapsed. This has led to a situation where many of the world's poorest people live in states that have failed or are failing and where they are subject to repeated cycles of violence. This is where development becomes necessary not only for the well-being of the population but also for conflict prevention – development and security become intertwined.

The third chapter moves on to examine the academic literature on conflict in more detail. There are as many different ways of categorising conflict as there are conflicts. This chapter tries to show how they can be grouped and approached in a logical manner and creates space for the different approaches to overlap. It covers the work of a great many prominent analysts of conflict in order to move beyond simplistic approaches based on single variables such as 'ethnicity' or 'tribalism', which characterises much media coverage of parts of the developing world, and looks at underlying themes: resources, political institutions, social structures and access to resources. In so doing it moves beyond the picture of, say, Africa, as an example of barbarism and into complex social scientific approaches to conflict.

One of the key effects of conflict is dealt with in Chapter 4, which looks at refugees and internally displaced people. Together with Chapter 5, which examines development actors and humanitarian aid in conflict, this analysis takes you through some of the most difficult and yet most covered aspects of conflict. What can you do about large tented settlements of refugees? Where do they come from and what are the effects on those countries or areas that accept them? In addition, what can be done about resettling people who have become displaced, particularly in countries where insurgency has led to rural depopulation and rapid urbanisation and the cities lack the infrastructure to cope with such large populations?

In such environments, how and through whom does the international community act? NGOs are a visible and easily recognised part of humanitarian effort on TV screens, but where do they come from, who are they and how do they receive a mandate to act? In addition, how do they relate to the larger aid flows through multilateral agencies such as the World Bank and the UN and to bilateral flows from country to country? Chapter 5 focuses on the politics of development actors and how people 'doing development' operate in conflict and post-conflict areas, concentrating on non-combat organisations operating in these areas and the process of 'securitisation'. The latter developed relatively slowly at first, and, whilst this was undoubtedly due to a mutual mistrust between militaries and security actors on the one hand and humanitarian aid agencies on the other, humanitarian agencies have increasingly begun to enlist security actors as a means of delivering aid and protecting aid workers in areas where there may be significant security threats. A key risk here is that humanitarian agencies will lose their independence through being incorporated by security institutions and will therefore become legitimate targets in areas where they have traditionally worked.

At the same time, within conflict zones there are other, military international actors in operation, particularly peacekeeping troops. This is a contentious issue and yet a vitally important one, since without peacekeepers much of the development side of the activities covered within this book could not be operationalised. And yet, much peacekeeping is poorly done and can vary in scope and duration. Peacekeepers also bring with them their own politics and political (and economic) impact. As history shows, peacekeeping has had a rather mixed past, with some notable successes but some catastrophic failures that have led to more bloodshed. Chapter 6 outlines this history and then summarises the lessons learned from peacekeeping missions. It also goes on to look at the proposed shift of peacekeeping operations from international to regional actors such as ASEAN and the AU.

One of the main features of contemporary conflict and of contemporary peacebuilding is the large number of private actors involved. Chapter 7 analyses the levels of private security, ranging from individual mercenaries fighting for a particular cause or for payment, through to the private military companies and corporate mercenaries hired by large international organisations or states to provide specific types of military service. We explore debates over whether these companies help or hinder longer-term development and how they affect conflicts.

The last core area within this book is the idea of justice, dealt with in Chapter 8. Frequently a major contributor to wars in the first place, (lack of) justice is a critical area of peacebuilding in terms of rebuilding state legitimacy and providing a visible service to people on the ground. In many countries that have been subject to authoritarian rule or conflict, the justice sector, in keeping with security organs of the state, has frequently acted against the interests of most people, and so creating a viable justice sector that is seen to be fair is a key way in which to restore faith in a state.

The final chapter of the book represents an attempt to provide an overview of the current state of debates on conflict, security and development and the key challenges facing policymakers, institutions and academics within the field. In many ways most development agencies have come to recognise that addressing the issues arising out of conflict requires an understanding of the interrelationships between politics, security and development, resulting in the commonly cited phrase that 'there can be no development without security and no security without development'.

How the chapters are organised

Each chapter provides a clear and concise summary of the main relevant issues within the subject area. All the issues are explained and the links between each section are clearly labelled. The chapters end with five to six summary points. As well as providing a quick reference for the core subject areas and key concerns of a specific subject, these act as a series of issues for students to develop further. They are all issues that have significant literatures in their own right.

The summary points are followed by a short list of key questions to guide student reading. This section is intended to highlight currently 'live' questions – i.e., they are issues that are currently debated within the academic and policy worlds, and there is therefore no generally accepted answer for many of them. The readings are designed to get you started with this. They do not form a comprehensive literature review but rather act as gateways into further exploration of the literature. You can find full references for all the works cited in this book, along with other useful readings, in the bibliography.

1 Are security and development mutually reinforcing?

This chapter investigates what is meant by the terms 'security' and 'development' and the basis for thinking on violence and conflict in the developing world. It interrogates the assumption made in much of the academic literature, and by international policymakers, that 'there is no security without development and no development without security' and begins to unpack and historically situate the notion of a security–development nexus.

We argue that to consider how security issues impact on development, and vice versa, it is important to have an appreciation of the contentious nature of the terms we are using and the understandings which inform them. The chapter provides a historical analysis of how security and development became so closely related and in what ways the concepts are similar or differ from each other. It draws on theoretical literature to provide a clear conceptual approach to the relationship and places policy-relevant approaches within the academic debates about the relationship.

The chapter will explore the shift away from the traditional role of the state in providing security through formal security services, and we analyse the ways in which security services have often come to be associated with oppression within politically failing states as well as how this has affected the development trajectories and the post-conflict politics of many of these states. The close relationship between security and political power leading up to a number of conflicts and the fragmentation of many states where this has taken place allows for a more nuanced and deeper analysis of the post-conflict situation, where the close association of security with particular forms of the state may be problematic.

In terms of international approaches to security and development, this chapter outlines the implications of human security as a way of integrating the development discourse into debates about security, and vice versa, but it also looks at competing ideas of what 'development' might mean in this context. It relates debates around human security back to contemporary theory in international security, questioning the core approach to security analysis, which is based primarily on the state as the key (sole) actor in conflict, outlining the nature of intra-state conflict, the complexity of regional approaches to conflict, and the under-theorisation of much of the security and development discourse. These themes will be developed further in the following chapter, which investigates more fully what conflict looks like in the developing world, and in Chapter 3, which covers some of the different ways conflict has been analysed, interpreted and explained by different schools of thought.

Finally, this chapter moves on to examine the policy implications of the security and development 'nexus'. In practice it may be true that the mixture of security and development approaches has grown out of practice on the ground rather than theory. International Relations (IR) theory in particular has often seemed adrift from this debate, focusing instead

Table 1.1 The widening and deepening of security

Security concept	Widening	Deepening
Traditional security agenda	Formal security services (military, police, intelligence)	Security of the state National security
'New' security agenda	Non-military security (political, economic, environmental, criminal, social, etc.)	Security of the individual Human security

on complex security models based on the behaviour of states – forgetting, perhaps, that some of these states cannot behave in particular ways because of the development challenges they face.

Whose security are we talking about?

Security as a concept and field of academic study has broadened considerably in recent years. Since the end of the Cold War and the collapse of the bipolar world order, it has often been suggested that the number and type of issues that could be labelled security threats has mushroomed. From a relatively narrow focus, particularly in IR theory, on security as an expression of the relative balance of power between the superpowers and their allies, essentially the security of states or networks of states, we see from the early 1990s a growing focus on non-traditional threats, or 'new security' threats, including crime, migration, small arms and insurgencies.

The move from traditional international security to 'new security' has been characterised as a widening and deepening of security that can be summarised as in Table 1.1. From civil war, state 'collapse' and refugee flows to the growth of international networks trafficking in arms and conflict diamonds, threats of environmental disaster and climate change, the range of potential security threats under study and on the agenda of international policymakers has greatly increased in the last two decades. In particular they have become ever more complex and difficult to control, requiring co-ordination of action by a range of actors above and below the level of the nation-state as well as states themselves. But are these 'threats' really new, or are they merely being rediscovered by academics and policymakers who had, until 1990, focused on a security agenda largely captured by Cold War concerns and interests?

Regardless of whether we regard these concerns as new, what cannot be denied is that the range of potential 'threats' to security raises key questions for those interested in the ways security and development are linked in specific contexts. In particular, we can consider understandings of security as revolving broadly around two poles – the traditional 'state-centric' view and the more recent 'human-security' approach. This is a simplistic rendering of a very complex debate which will be unpacked further throughout this book, but to think of the two extremes helps us to locate particular policy interventions and theoretical analyses on a spectrum of approaches to security. Each has significant implications for how we understand the links between security and development. There are specific implications for the types of development which are prioritised if an approach privileges either state security or human security, and, whichever is seen as most important, a wide range of actors, from the state to interstate, sub-state and non-state actors, is charged with particular responsibilities for achieving that development.

A traditional security approach, often associated with the realist or neo-realist branches of IR theory, regards the integrity and security of the state as being critical to creating both security and the conditions for development. In this analysis, the survival, reinforcement and sustainability of the state, its ability to reproduce itself and to act on the international stage, perhaps in concert with others through global governance organisations, is crucial. Such an approach puts an emphasis on the development of institutions and security organisations, necessary for ensuring the state maintains control of its territory through an institutional framework and a monopoly on the legitimate use of force. This is linked to the ideal of the Weberian state, which has not only juridical statehood, internationally recognised and existing in international law, but also empirical statehood, with the ability to extend its reach across its territory and potentially to provide a minimum level of benefits of citizenship in that state, such as public services – especially security – and including welfare provision. This approach attempts to create a *de facto* state measured against formal criteria of what a state is. An example of this is the wide range of indices used to measure 'failed' or 'fragile' states, for example the *Failed States Index* published by the US Fund for Peace.

Fragile states have emerged over the previous decade as a key focus of analysis and as a priority for international intervention. This has resulted from a coming together of several factors, particularly the increasing emphasis on human security, peacebuilding and effective state-building, but also the development of the security–development nexus, whereby security and development are seen as inextricably entwined. The first UK National Security Strategy in 2008 reflected the state of thinking amongst many of the world's policy makers. It states that:

> In the past, most violent conflicts and significant threats to global security came from strong states. Currently, most of the major threats and risks emanate from failed or fragile states … Failed and fragile states increase the risk of instability and conflict, and at the same time have a reduced capacity to deal with it, as we see in parts of Africa. They have the potential to destabilise the surrounding region. Many fragile states lack the capacity and, in some cases, the will adequately to address terrorism and organised crime, in some instances knowingly tolerating or directly sponsoring such activity.
>
> (Cabinet Office 2008)

Similarly, the US National Security Strategy of 2006 argued that:

> The events of September 11, 2001, taught us that weak states, like Afghanistan, can pose as great a danger to our national interests as strong states. Poverty does not make poor people into terrorists and murderers. Yet poverty, weak institutions, and corruption can make weak states vulnerable to terrorist networks and drug cartels within their borders.
>
> (White House 2006)

Around 1 billion people, including some 340 million of the world's poorest people, are estimated to live in a group of between thirty and fifty 'fragile' countries, most of which are in Africa. There is a current international consensus that, without better and more international engagement, these countries will continue to provide insecure environments for their populations. At the same time, most aid agencies have realised that fragile states require co-ordinated and well-thought-out interventions that can contribute both to security and to development more broadly. The key to managing this is the creation of critical effective governance mechanisms in developing countries to provide where possible effective local ownership of development.

In this vision, if the development of the state and the institutions and security apparatus needed to maintain its control and integrity were achieved, the outcome would be stability through the creation of a predictable and stable international order, regulated by international law, and based on sovereign states. This model, where the state is the key arbiter of the relationship between security and development, providing international and domestic security for development to occur, is closely linked in development terms to the state-building approach. This can be seen in practice in the current approach of, for example, the newly created US AFRICOM (see Box 1.1) in providing security support and training for uniformed militaries to reinforce the institutions of the state and its ability to bring about or maintain a monopoly on legitimate use of force in its territory.

Box 1.1 AFRICOM

The US Africa Command was created as a separate entity from other US regional commands in 2008. It is currently headquartered in Germany and co-ordinates US defence and security engagements with African states and institutions.

The US has few troops based in Africa compared with other regions. Its only permanent military presence, a base in Camp Lemonier, Djibouti, was established in 2001 and contains around 2,500 troops.

The National Security Strategies of 2002 and 2006 and statements by US policymakers suggest Africa has increased in strategic importance for the United States. However, given the unwillingness of the United States, following its 1993 engagement in Somalia, to contribute its troops directly to missions in Africa, operations have focused primarily on training, equipping and supporting African militaries to tackle security issues on the continent. This is an approach often defined as supporting 'African Solutions to African Problems'. Among key US-led programmes of this type are:

- bilateral relationships with individual African militaries;
- African contingency and operations training and assistance;
- the Pan-Sahel Initiative;
- trans Sahara Counter-Terrorism Initiative.

Criticisms of AFRICOM, and the US military and security engagement with Africa more broadly, are numerous and include the following:

- The approach is too state-centric, ignoring the complex security environment in Africa wherein states are not the only providers of security and may even be causes of insecurity.
- Reinforcing the military arm of regimes with poor human rights records may lead to a growth in insecurity for some groups and potentially, through generation of popular grievances, to conflict.
- Engagement has focused on US security requirements rather than those of African populations, in particular highlighting terrorism, the need to secure energy resources, and US concern at the rising influence of China in Africa.
- Because of its engagements in the Middle East and elsewhere, the United States has relied on private security companies to deliver its programmes in Africa. Such companies are seen by critics as challenging the accountability and legitimacy of developing states.

In contrast, a human security approach would be significantly different and would clearly focus on the security of the individual within a given society. This would – at least theoretically – provide a far more diverse range of options for development interventions, including a wide variety of local approaches at sub-state level and many at regional level. It also recognises the possibility that a dysfunctional state may be the chief source of insecurity for citizens, through oppression, torture, imprisonment, social exclusion or political persecution. Human security is, however, an even more contested notion than state security. The most widely cited definitions stem from the 1994 *Human Development Report* (see Box 1.2)

Box 1.2   The UNDP *Human Development Report*, 1994

The UNDP *Human Development Report* of 1994 is widely regarded as having signalled a sea-change in thinking about security, encouraging policymakers to shift their focus from nation-states to individuals. Its exposition of the human security term has been the basis for much subsequent debate on what it means to *be* secure and to *feel* secure, and on the interdependence between human security, human development and, latterly, human rights. It suggests that the concept of security must change urgently in two basic ways:

1   From an exclusive stress on territorial security to a much greater stress on people's security.
2   From security through armaments to security through sustainable human development.

The report suggests there are seven main categories that indicate the sources of threats to human security: economic security, food security, health security, environmental security, personal security, community security and political security.

Human security is therefore seen as an integrative concept which relies on the promotion of solidarity. Achieving it requires that organisations and individuals at all levels work towards the attainment of two main freedoms: *freedom from fear* and *freedom from want.*

However, there remains much debate as to what human security is and why it has become such a prominent concept. As a result, supporters of human security have often been accused of not being clear enough about its definition or the policy implications of taking a human security approach. The range of features of conflict in the developing world identified earlier, alongside other less traditional security threats such as climate change, raise questions about the extent to which 'the human', both physically and figuratively, can ever be completely 'secured'. Of particular relevance for war-torn and post-conflict societies, human security is also closely related to notions of peace which go beyond the narrow definition of the absence of war or physical violence. Positive peace, notably espoused by Johan Galtung (1969) in the context of conflict transformation, refers to a situation where individuals are not experiencing violence, the fear of violence, or 'structural violence'. This last pre-dates but clearly resonates with the UNDP notion of human security. Ending structural violence means creating a situation where the life-chances of an individual and their ability to live a full, productive and happy existence are not curtailed by the political, cultural, social and economic structures of the society in which they live. A focus on the human as the referent object of security therefore entails a quite different and much more holistic notion of development.

Achieving human security or positive peace requires development and transformation of structures at the local, national and international level which affect a person's life-chances. Therefore the actors potentially empowered by a human security approach range dramatically from states, interstate bodies, regional organisations and local government to grassroots and community initiatives, charities, churches, schools and all other organisations engaged in aspects of the individual's social life. Furthermore, recognising development as a tool for promoting human security necessitates a system-wide approach, mindful of how the initiatives of these multi-level actors may cause particular types of insecurity for specific groups and also the consequences of their interaction.

As is clear from this brief rendering of the state- and human-centric approaches to security, and their implications for development, the division into two separate approaches is in some ways a false dichotomy. Most contemporary interventions involve elements of both approaches, and there is a clear need for both in a situation where a state may have collapsed and there is widespread humanitarian need, particularly in complex emergencies or post-conflict environments. However, the recognition of a greater or lesser role of the state in both development and security raises the question of whether or not a particular state is legitimate and how to develop that political legitimacy. In mainstream policy narratives, this has led to a focus on good governance and state-building which have at their centre an ideal of the legitimate, representative, responsible and accountable state, commonly conceived of as a liberal state. We will explore this idea further below, but first we need to examine the relationship between development and security.

Development and security: inextricably entwined?

Whilst it is often cited as a truism that development cannot take place without security and security cannot be achieved without development, the apparently broad agreement on this principle hides a multitude of differences in the ways both academics and policymakers understand security and development. There is no one accepted perception of the relationship, largely because these two terms are themselves highly contested. Accounts of this relationship, or the 'security–development nexus', as it has been referred to by Mark Duffield, must always be critically interrogated. To do so, those attempting to appreciate how the nexus manifests in various developing states and societies must attempt to identify the understandings which underpin particular explanations of the relationship. Despite the context-specific nature of the security–development relationship, there have been a few more or less successful attempts to create broad theoretical frameworks which identify how these concepts are linked across different case studies. Notable amongst these, though not without their own shortcomings, are the influential writings of Mark Duffield (2001) and Frances Stewart (2006).

Duffield's work focuses on what he regards as emerging systems of global governance, or political complexes, created to deal with a growing range of threats to the security of the 'North' emanating from the underdeveloped and insecure 'South'. Reflecting on the incorporation of war into development discourse, he argues that the politics of development has become 'radicalised', and that this is characterised by 'the willingness within mainstream policy to contemplate the transformation of societies as a whole'. Furthermore, he asserts that this radicalisation 'derives its urgency from a new security framework that regards the modalities of underdevelopment as dangerous' (Duffield 2001: 22). In this analysis, Northern states and institutions have identified underdevelopment in the South as a threat to global security, particularly as it is regarded as providing a permissive environment for the growth of shadow economies and, importantly in recent years, opportunities for rebels, terrorists and agents of disorder to exist and grow unchecked. As such, the North attempts to fundamentally to transform developing, and especially African, societies to create security and stability, in a policy characterised as 'enlightened self-interest'. The relationship between security and development in this analysis is therefore visible at the international and sub-national level. The security that is most important is that of the North, as a bloc and as individual states, and, to this end, technologies of development are employed to turn developing states into modern liberal states (see below) or to discipline and provide containment and surveillance of potential threats.

This analysis, however, fails to account fully for important aspects of conflict in the developing world. In particular, the focus on global complexes significantly downplays the role of the region in shaping security and development at the state and sub-state level. It is increasingly recognised that aspects of instability and insecurity in a state's immediate region or neighbourhood, as well as local geography, have a significant impact on security within those individual states. Weak states existing in conflict-affected regions are often unable or unwilling to control their borders, constituting essentially *de jure* states which exist in law but are unable to extend their reach across their territory. These failures of governance and state control, or at a minimum the failure of states to control their borders, have a significant impact on how conflict develops in such regions, influencing the means by which combatants sustain themselves, the ability of centralised state military forces to tackle conflict, and the success of strategies for achieving conflict resolution. The importance of regional dynamics is especially clear when looking at two regional conflict complexes in sub-Saharan Africa, the wars in central Africa (1996–2003) which drew in eight surrounding states, and West African conflicts centring on Sierra Leone, Guinea and Liberia.

The inability of these states to enforce their borders effectively means that such regions are fluid, and conflicts and underdevelopment in one state have frequently and significantly affected the others. This is partly a reflection of historical development of the border regions as sites of contested sovereignty or areas which have felt little control and influence from the centralised state. As much as the global and the local, an appreciation of the historical and contemporary dynamics which define the region in which a conflict takes place is therefore crucial in analysing that conflict and its implications for security and development.

Where Duffield adopts what could be considered a critical international political economy approach, Stewart's analysis (2006) approaches security and development from a different perspective. She identifies three possible connections between, broadly defined, security and development:

1   the immediate impact of security/insecurity on well-being and consequently development achievements (or the ways in which security forms part of the *definition* of development) – i.e., security's role as part of our *objectives*;
2   the way that insecurity affects (non-security) elements of development and economic growth, or the *security instrumental* role;
3   the way development affects security, or the *development instrumental* role.

Each of these suggests a different understanding of the relative importance of security and development, though all depict the two as inherently interconnected. In the first, security is clearly subsumed within a holistic understanding of development. In the second and third approaches, development and security are again presented as mutually reinforcing and each as being a prerequisite of the other. This presumption of a circular relationship has resulted in many processes and issues, which are in themselves not new, being relabelled as security threats and, as such, as potential obstacles to security and development requiring action.

The process of defining something in terms of its impact on security leads to the legitimising of particular strategies for tackling that threat. This process, known within IR theory as 'securitisation', is identified with the work of the *Copenhagen School*. This is the process by which, for example, environmental concerns have become prominent items on security agendas. Interstate and intra-state conflicts resulting at least partly from disputes over access to scarce resources are by no means new, but the depletion of natural resources is increasingly viewed through the development–security lens. Economies in both the developed and developing world have been built largely on non-renewable resources, the former through processes of regional and national industrialisation from the eighteenth century onwards, and the latter through the transfer and promotion of extraction-based economic development by colonial powers. The depletion of these resources has been framed increasingly in recent years as an issue of security. The US National Security Strategy (White House 2006), for example, refers to the need for 'energy security', and the focus on energy independence and diversification of sources is a key aspect of US economic freedom and national security. Fears of increased competition over ever scarcer resources have seen climate change discussed as a threat to international peace and security, and, similarly, global health issues such as the spread of HIV/AIDS have been reclassified as security threats with the potential to decimate working-age populations, derailing development at a national level and crippling militaries in developing states. As we will show in this chapter, the wide range of issues that increasingly appear in discussions of security are therefore not new concerns. Rather, they have become securitised as a result of the broadening of conceptions of security and their perceived impacts on the institutions and processes considered necessary for security, not least those concerned with development.

Also bringing into question the notion of a new and mutually reinforcing relationship between security and development, scholars such as David Keen (2008) have pointed out that it is possible for individuals and societies to live in relative security despite levels of development that would be considered low on international indicators. Conversely, even where high levels of development prevail, insecurity often remains a facet of everyday life for marginalised or vulnerable groups within societies. At the international level, the argument that there can be no security without development and no development without security appears to break down even further. As Duffield's analysis shows, it is far from certain that underdevelopment in one country or region affects the ability of individuals and states in others to live in relative security. This is particularly true when comparing whole states and societies. However, as argued earlier in relation to Central and West Africa, developing states are affected significantly by political, security and governance dynamics, as well as licit and illicit economic processes, occurring at the regional level. Whilst it may be difficult to prove that insecurity in Rwanda affects development and security in Colombia or in the United Kingdom, it is difficult not to draw such a relationship between development and security in Rwanda and prospects for development and security in the Great Lakes region more broadly.

Attempts to characterise the links between security and development therefore display both similarities and differences, reflecting the preoccupations and theoretical standpoints of particular authors, but these analyses also suggest differing responses to a range of key questions which this book seeks to unpack: who is security for, what is being secured and how best can security be achieved to facilitate development?; and, on development, what type of development is being promoted, who benefits from it and how might it contribute to improving or diminishing security elsewhere and for particular groups? Despite these differences, in most accounts of the security–development nexus, whether in academia or policymaking, there is a sense of circularity. We see the pursuit of particular forms of development to increase particular types of security as a way of further entrenching particular forms of development and promoting certain types of security. To understand why the relationship is regarded as broadly self-reinforcing, we must therefore look deeper at the historical context of the relationship between security and development, specifically at how the concepts have developed individually over time and in doing so found considerable areas of overlap, but also notable areas of divergence.

How has the relationship developed?

The relationship between security and development is often an expression of the compromised nature of sovereignty in many developing states. Though this trend is not new, and indeed developed states have also seen renegotiations of their sovereignty in an era of increasing globalisation, the nature of relationships between states, between states and societies, and between the myriad other actors involved in creating security and development is always historically defined. For many countries in the developing world, the experience of colonisation has provided a primary historical reference point in the history of the present state.

The demands of 'native administration' and attempts by colonial powers to access the resources of their empires entailed the creation or consolidation of a more or less centralised state apparatus, often, but not always, in regions where no such system had previously existed. This is perhaps best illustrated in the case of sub-Saharan Africa. With decolonisation and international recognition of the resulting states, the political, economic and administrative structures which loosely embodied 'the state' became a prized resource. As William Reno has shown through his studies of Central and West Africa, a state apparatus could be captured by particular groups, often defined by ethnicity, geography or experiences of privilege under colonial administration. Recognising that access to economic and political power was largely synonymous with control of the state, a range of insurgencies sought to gain control of the state through democratic or violent means. This partly reflects the compromised sovereignty of developing states, particularly after independence.

Many theorists have explored the effects of decolonisation on African statehood. They have investigated what kind of states resulted when colonial administrators withdrew from sub-Saharan Africa, the type of international system into which newly independent states were incorporated, and the understandings that underpinned that incorporation. Robert Jackson's work on juridical and empirical statehood, giving rise to the notion of 'quasi-states', was a popular concept within these debates from the mid-1980s and remains a well-used idea. In his analysis, quasi-states possess juridical statehood in that they are internationally recognised and have 'the same external rights and responsibilities as other states'. However, they lack empirical statehood, which requires 'an organised power to protect human rights or provide socio-economic welfare' (Jackson 1990: 21; 1992).

The survival of such apparently weak states is argued by Jackson to be a product of changing norms within the international community. In the post-independence period, these norms precluded colonisation and conquest to subjugate or administrate weak states, and instead led to their being treated in some regards as international protectorates. This portrayal shows African states in particular as weak, their policies reacting primarily to the external influences on them, overwhelmingly dependent for their very survival on the vagaries of international norms and the support of the international community. However, the notion of quasi-states also highlighted the importance of the principles of non-intervention in the internal affairs of other states and respect for sovereignty that formed the basis for African interstate relations. Free from interstate aggression, at least in theory, African regimes focused on countering domestic challenges to their position, sometimes with extreme brutality. This was tolerated, and even supported, by superpower patrons, particularly where such exercises could be portrayed as necessary in the fight against communism or capitalism, depending on whether support came from the United States or the Soviet Union – or sometimes both.

The leaders of developing states in Africa and beyond could therefore frame their domestic disciplining exercises in terms of a broader international ideological contest. Control of the state became, in many cases, an instrument for accessing political and economic power, and accordingly the resources of the state, from the security services to opportunities for development, were deployed in the pursuit of regime security, favouring some groups, excluding or oppressing others, and following a logic of patrimonial rule. This created forms of political authority specific to Africa but with resonance in other heavily aid-dependent states. As Reno observes,

> African societies have their share of tax evasion, barter deals, illicit production, smuggling, and protection rackets … these phenomena have become widespread and integral to building political authority in parts of Africa, which challenges existing assumptions about how political actors calculate their interests.
>
> (Reno 1998: ix)

In this analysis, the ruling elite treats the state as a means to further their own power and wealth and service patronage networks, rather than necessarily as an organisational structure through which to provide security, development and a better quality of life for their citizens. This has also led to a growth in shadow economies, which will be discussed in detail in future chapters.

Is Africa different?

An important body of work, notably analyses such as *The Criminalization of the State in Africa* (Bayart *et al.* 1999) and *Africa Works* (Chabal and Daloz 1999), attempts to show how, despite changing circumstances, African elites continue to pursue the same goal – survival – through a variety of innovative strategies, both licit (aid and international trade) and illicit, including warlord partnerships or involvement in drug trafficking. These processes are not unique to Africa, nor indeed are they associated exclusively with the elites of developing states. The globalised economy offers unparalleled opportunity for national elites to marry their political positions with strategies of economic accumulation, which, although often illegal and therefore risky, offer significant rewards. Many of the activities being engaged in are transnational and international in scale and impact. The trafficking of drugs is a particularly striking example of how criminal activity in developing regions can have significant global political and economic impacts. The use of development aid to attempt to condition societies and prevent, discourage or reverse such criminalisation demonstrates Duffield's earlier identification of a particular understanding of the convergence between development and security.

Continuity, history and globalisation

The relationship between security and development is therefore not new. Studies of the different development opportunities offered to favoured groups by colonial administrators, superpower patrons and their proxies, and denied to others, suggest that the security of the state, regime and individual groups depended on politics of development at international, national and sub-national level. In this vein, Bayart (2000) identifies African elite policies in particular, and the strategies of those they rule, reflecting a sense of continuity from pre-colonial past to the post-colonial present through 'historicity'. Crucially, this analysis implies that the ruling elites and governments of developing states must attempt to satisfy at least two broad constituencies to guarantee their survival. On the one hand, they may court donor states and international institutions that provide much needed diplomatic, military and financial support and resources. On the other, they are responsible to key domestic supporters of the regime, who expect to benefit from the distribution of favours and patronage. Attempting to satisfy both groups is a difficult exercise, and actions which may win favour from one group, such as concerted anti-corruption campaigns, have the potential to alienate the other.

Governments in developing states thus have to make difficult choices to maintain their positions. Representations of such states as 'hollow', 'failing' or 'weak' also have particular implications for how they are perceived and presented in dominant narratives of the development–security nexus. The end of the Cold War has had a strong impact on debates around the nexus. An increase in the proportion of conflict defined as civil war has seen a growth of what have been termed 'complex humanitarian emergencies'. At the same time, the loss of superpower competition as a reference point for international security has refocused the attention of academics and policymakers alike on the relationship between security and development at the national and regional level; it has also encouraged the revisiting of the concept of security by both academics and practitioners in an effort to understand better what now constitutes security and how such a situation can be achieved.

The role of the state can become transformed in situations where there is very little or no economic development providing realistic alternatives for the general population. In particular, the state can be seen as just one economic resource that can be captured by elites. This is manifest in patronage systems that are designed to strip the state of resources and reward followers of the ruling elite. The state may also be viewed as a vehicle that can corruptly award contracts to companies to exploit natural resources, especially large-scale resources such as oil which require significant infrastructure for extraction. Such corruption has also been regarded as a potential negative impact of democratisation. In a context where the state is viewed as an economic resource, democracy imposes limits on access to positions of political power and hence on the time available to use political power to pursue economic goals. This has been seen notably in Kenya's experience of transition to democracy, which has reflected an attitude amongst the country's political elites that political power is synonymous with economic power, and opportunities to enrich oneself and one's supporters must therefore be pursued vigorously in the time available. Kenya's politics reflects the sense among competing groups that, when campaigning around elections, it is not just 'our turn to rule' but 'our turn to eat', something that has become synonymous with Bayart's idea of the 'politics of the belly'. In these situations the state itself ceases to be a politically neutral structure and becomes just another resource, with the corrupted institutions of the state and supporting security services as simply one of many players in the security environment.

Aims of development and the liberal state

Development in mainstream policy discourse has since the 1990s been dominated by attempts to define and find ways of (re)producing liberal states, both in the aftermath of conflict and in more ambiguous contexts of considerable instability and insecurity. This is often identified as being a direct consequence of the end of the Cold War and the presumed triumph of liberal capitalism over Soviet communism or socialism as ideologies around which political and economic life could be organised (Fukuyama 1993). As with the notions of development and security, there remains much debate as to what constitutes a liberal state. However, at its most basic we can consider the liberal state to be an attempt to enshrine, through particular political, economic and social frameworks, the values associated with liberalism, particularly individual freedom.

If we accept that liberal values of individual freedom and equity are the ideological underpinning of the liberal state, the question is then what forms of political and economic organisation are believed to be best suited to incorporate these values. Building on the notion of Wilsonian 'liberal internationalism', the work of Paris (2004) provides perhaps one of the clearest expositions of the features of the liberal state and its place in an international community. In his analysis of international attempts to build peace after civil war, liberalisation – the process of creating a liberal state – is seen to incorporate two key aspects: democratisation and marketisation. Between them these are seen to provide a path to sustainable peace and security, though Paris questions their applicability to such a wide range of contexts and in states with very different experiences of conflict. He goes on to argue:

> Decades from now, historians may look back on the immediate post-Cold War years as a period of remarkable faith in the powers of liberalization to remedy a broad range of social ills, from internal and international violence to poverty, famine, corruption, and even environmental destruction.
>
> (Paris 2004: 35)

An important point to note here is that the liberal state does not exist in isolation; many aspects of its character require integration within a system of similar states in order to flourish. For example, the system of liberal market-based economics is argued to promote peace between members through encouraging interdependence. The state certainly has a role as an actor in this conception of the state and international order, but it is not the only form of political and economic authority. It must give up part of its autonomy, as do citizens to the state, to overarching authorities such as global governance organisations to achieve goals beyond the reach of any individual state and guarantee its own security through a system based on international law and regulation. The sovereignty of the liberal state is therefore not absolute; to enhance its power to act on international issues that affect individual states, such as climate change or international trade policy, it acts through co-operation with other states and specialist international and supranational organisations. This need not, however, be seen as a loss of power; rather, sovereignty is compromised, shared and, to varying degrees, vested in global governance organisations which have authority and a degree of power to act on specific issues on behalf of a collective of states.

In terms of implications for development, the focus on creating liberal states and the systems of global governance in which they can operate effectively has led to the promotion of democracy and the primacy of market economics in developing and post-conflict states. Forms of the liberal state as experienced in many developed countries have certainly provided considerable security and development opportunities for many of their citizens, and it is frequently argued that such states enjoy stable and mutually beneficial relationships. However, there is a growing chorus of concern at the perceived 'one size fits all' approach of Western states to international development, particularly in states considered especially poor or fragile. Scholars such as Pugh (2005) have highlighted the extremely invasive nature of internationally led market liberalisation in post-conflict states, leaving little room for a path to reconstruction which is tailored to local needs and realities. They have also argued that the international community is too quick to declare countries as 'post-conflict' and revert to promotion of development as usual, which may equate to liberal market capitalism. Others such as Collier (2009) have demonstrated through case study-based analyses that democratisation is a dangerous process to embark upon in fragile and often divided post-conflict societies. In countries where both competition for political power and access to the resources of development have recently found expression through violence, can a democratic process that encourages competition for those same resources, through control of the state, occur peacefully?

The virtues of the twin processes which underpin this model of the liberal state, marketisation and democratisation, are therefore highly contested in academic theory, increasingly problematised by policymakers based on lessons of previous experience and subject to resistance on the ground from a range of actors in developing states. A programme of liberal state-building through these two processes may well lead to violence and conflict rather than to improvements in security, and, as we will see throughout this book, when evaluating how appropriate the liberal state is as an aim for development, it is vital to consider the individual country contexts in which such processes take place.

What is a liberal peace?

The liberal ideology outlined above can be reduced to four core themes:

1   individualism (assertion of individuals over social collectivities);
2   egalitarianism (moral equivalence of individuals);
3   universalism (moral unity having primacy over historical association or cultural forms); and
4   meliorism (belief in the ability to improve all political and social institutions).

All of these elements surround the core principle of individual freedom. Thus a liberal peace exists when all of the above constitute normal social relations. For peace to exist, justice and liberty are required, and the liberal political arrangements that make this possible are seen as inherently peaceful. Critically, democracy and capitalism are viewed as the vehicles for peaceful competition underlying liberal structures where even groups that do not hold power can have faith in a system that does not oppress their beliefs.

To these normative foundations of liberalism can be added a belief in universal human rights as being the right to freedom from arbitrary authority, the social rights necessary to protect and promote freedom, and the right to democratic participation to protect the first two.

This has led to a number of important developments in terms of peacebuilding, not least the idea that a post-Westphalian international liberal peace requires non-liberal states to be liberalised in order for that peace to become sustainable. Consequently, the chief aim of peace operations and intervention, as will be discussed, changes from creating negotiated solutions between states to actively contributing to the construction of liberal states, economies and social structures intended to spread liberal democratic political structures. It is this idea that Mark Duffield claims lies behind the merger of security and development policy and the reproblematisation of security as both the result and the precondition of development more broadly.

A further expression of the pacific and international nature of the liberal peace is the idea that human rights are universal and that they should be enforced as such, regardless of the wishes of states. The Rome Statute not only developed this idea further by outlining a consensus on universal human values but also created an international legal mechanism for independent enforcement of those values – the International Criminal Court (ICC).

Does adding security to development just provide an armed wing of the liberal state?

The discussion has so far concentrated mainly on the implications of constructing liberal states for the practice of development. However, there are also significant related implications for the creation of security both within and between states. As has been established, the development of liberal states requires particular prescriptions in the realms of political development (democratisation) and economic development (marketisation). These processes aim to create a state which can take its place in an international system alongside other liberal states. This appears at first glance to lend itself to the state-centric notion of security, with its emphasis on the creation of institutions that can oversee and administer the territory of a given state and reproduce themselves in a sustainable and peaceful way. Such a state requires at the most basic level a monopoly on the use of force within its territory: that the violence produced by the state is legitimate and seen as such by citizens who have consented to be governed. However, in a context of often limited resources, developing states have looked to the organisations of the international community or to particular partner states for funds and technical support to enhance their security forces and achieve this monopoly of force. This also is not a new development.

During the Cold War, the ruling elites in states considered by the superpowers to be of strategic value received military support, training and aid to build up forces to maintain their position, often against ideologically defined insurgent movements. From Mozambique and Angola in Africa to Nicaragua and Costa Rica in Central America, groups sought to define their struggles against incumbent regimes in terms of the ideological East–West confrontation. Similarly, former colonial powers such as France provided military support to elites in what were previously their colonies as part of a larger strategy to retain influence in these territories and to maintain both the prevalence of French culture, language and currency and the investments of French companies. This led to an upsurge in civil conflict in the 1990s, when superpower patrons largely abandoned these groups or scaled back the relationships.

The decline in superpower support both for ruling elites in developing states and for those who sought to challenge them after the Cold War left behind a plethora of armed groups in many developing states. These ranged from state military forces and elite republican or presidential guards associated with the ruling regime to paramilitary groups, insurgent forces, local defence forces, foreign fighters, and ethnically and geographically defined militias. Whether formal or informal, these forces and the individuals that comprise them have become key actors in many developing and post-conflict states, where state provision of security is poor or the state has a history of violence against its people. A key challenge to the creation of liberal states in the developing world has therefore been the complex nature and composition of the security sector, broadly defined.

A functioning, democratically accountable security sector is seen as vital for establishing the political legitimacy of a state and for allowing development, including international investment, to take place in a stable environment. Security sector reform (see Box 1.3, with international aid and assistance, is an increasingly common aspect of the construction of a liberal state, based on the concept of 'liberal peace', whereby it is argued that liberal states are less likely to go to war with each other than are non-liberal states.

Box 1.3 Security sector reform

According to the definition of the UN (UNSG 2008):

> Security sector reform describes a process of assessment, review and implementation as well as monitoring and evaluation led by national authorities that has as its goal the enhancement of effective and accountable security for the state and its peoples without discrimination and with full respect for human rights and the rule of law.

Essentially, SSR consists of a set of principles and a set of activities. The key principles are:

- democracy;
- civilian oversight and control;
- accountability and transparency;
- local ownership;
- professionalism; and
- holistic approaches.

Activities are many and can be summarised as follows:

Overarching activities
e.g., security reviews, threat and needs assessment, SSR and national security strategies

Security and justice institutions	*Civilian management and oversight*	*Post-conflict SSR activities*
• Intelligence reform • Border security reform • Police reform • Criminal justice reform • Defence reform • Prison reform	• Executive management and control • Parliamentary oversight • Judicial review • Oversight by independent bodies • Civil society oversight	• DDR • Small arms and light weapons (SALW) • Transitional justice • Peace agreement issues • Spoilers

Cross-cutting concerns
e.g., gender, child protection, anti-corruption

The dangers of transferring models

However, the historical context of politics in many developing states, outlined earlier, suggests that, even if this model of a democratic, accountable, transparent and capable security sector exists in parts of the West, it cannot simply be exported to developing states. In developing and fragile states the ability of the state to control events within its sovereign space is often lacking, or, as seen earlier, the provision of security and the exercise of force is distorted by political economies based on predation and patrimonialism. Power and violence have frequently been exercised by a ruling elite, elected or otherwise, to maintain their own position and against citizens, either as a whole or as particular groups defined by ethnicity, geography, political affiliation or other markers of identity. Given a historically grounded understanding of power in such developing states, international efforts to support the development of security forces and their capabilities and institutions to regulate and oversee them can therefore be rendered extremely problematic. This raises key questions about whose security is being served by the development of security capabilities within states.

Focusing on enhancing the security apparatus of developing states is a reflection of the securitisation of development, whereby underdevelopment is regarded as a source of threat to the 'developed world'. In this analysis, the use of development aid to train armies or police is aimed not at improving security in developing states but at reinforcing state control over its territory in an attempt to insulate 'the West' from the effects and corollaries of conflict in developing states and regions. Taking this further, it can be, and has been, argued that building up a state's security capacity in a context of limited political oversight and weak state institutions creates conditions which may result in abuse of human rights by security forces and governments or even a higher threat of coup and conflict.

The identification of security, particularly human security, as a goal of development has led donor states and institutions into new partnerships with the militaries and security sectors of fragile states. These can be differentiated from those relationships witnessed during the Cold War by the emphasis on oversight and corollary institutions, though the extent to which such aspects are emphasised varies between locations and donors. The 'global war on terrorism' since 2001 has seen even greater justification for engaging with, building up and seeking to transform security sectors as armed wings of the liberal state to defend not only sovereign states but the international system of liberal states.

International assistance to develop and reform/transform the security sectors of developing states is therefore met with a degree of scepticism, but, given the expansion of the development agenda and the increasing demands placed on donors to justify their spending to sceptical publics, is it so wrong that the West should benefit in this way from its development assistance? Reform of the security sector in Sierra Leone, led by the United Kingdom, and of Liberia, led by the United States, has led to marked improvements in policing and in military professionalism, increasing security in West Africa more broadly and arguably for the international community. Engagement with security forces, though not traditionally a focus of development, is now regarded as crucial for enhancing human security and creating an environment in which development can take place. The question then becomes how the development aspects of security sector reform can be achieved, focusing specifically on accountability, the development of civil society and enhancing democratic/civil control over armed forces. The security sector is envisaged in the model of the liberal state as a series of institutions, alongside others targeted under a programme of state-building, that operate in a transparent and accountable way and can therefore mediate or negate the possible dangers of capture and abuse by political elites. Historical experience, though, has demonstrated the inventive and systematic way in which international assistance has been successfully subverted to the personal agendas of ruling elites, and this suggests that any 'one size fits all' approach to securing the liberal state will remain problematic.

Summary points

1   Security and development have become increasingly linked in both academic and policy terms.
2   This has been partly the result of the widening of the meaning of security away from formal militaries and national security to new issues, including the environment, resources and poverty, and also a deepening of security away from a focus just on the state to one on the security of the individual.
3   This also led to a reassessment of the governance of states and their effects on their citizenry.
4   In policy terms, much development has been linked to the spreading of democracy and liberal values through the liberal state and alongside a concern with liberal peace.
5   The development of security services has been an integral element of this approach but has raised questions about building up security services in politically weak states.

Discussion questions

1   Does security lead to development or development to security?
2   Should the development of security services be for the citizens or the security of the state system as a whole?
3   What alternatives are available to the liberal state, and is the liberal state idea possible in quasi-states?
4   What are the main issues with security sector reform and how might civil control over the military be achieved?

Further reading

Bayart, Jean-François (1993) *The State in Africa: The Politics of the Belly*. London: Longman.
Buzan, Barry, Wæver, Ole, and Wilde, Jaap de (1998) *Security: A New Framework for Analysis*. Boulder, CO: Lynne Rienner.
Clapham, Christopher (1996) *Africa and the International System: The Politics of State Survival*. Cambridge: Cambridge University Press.
Collier, Paul (2009) *War, Guns and Votes: Democracy in Dangerous Places*. New York: HarperCollins.
DFID (Department for International Development) (2005) *Fighting Poverty to Build a Safer World: A Strategy for Security and Development*. London: DFID.
Duffield, Mark (2001) *Global Governance and the New Wars: The Merging of Development and Security*. London: Zed Books.
European Union (2003) *A Secure Europe in a Better World: European Security Strategy*. Brussels, December.
Jackson, Robert H. (1990) *Quasi-States: Sovereignty, International Relations and the Third World*. Cambridge: Cambridge University Press.

2 What does conflict look like in the developing world?

This chapter will analyse the empirical characteristics of conflict and wars in developing states and regions. It explores whether conflict has changed significantly since the end of the Cold War, as frequently asserted by supporters of the 'new wars' thesis (Kaldor, 1999; Duffield, 2001). The chapter therefore considers what conflict looks like in the developing world and the ways in which it has been represented, and identifies some of the key features of contemporary conflict that require incorporation into any debate on post-conflict development. The nature of conflict and war in the developing world has led to important questions being asked about the essence of development, particularly whether the process of development is linked to violent conflict, and about the justifications for and practice of international humanitarian intervention.

The chapter begins with a discussion of whether so-called new wars are in fact new at all, and whether, indeed, the terminology used to describe conflict in the developing world is reliable. Consequently it outlines some of the main evidence about the nature of contemporary war, asking whether war is increasing or decreasing and considering how we attempt to measure conflict. It then moves on to examine questions about the nature of warfare in the developing world, including the movement away from interstate wars and towards intrastate conflict and contested sovereignty.

Are 'new wars' really new?

One of the key debates about contemporary conflict in the developing world centres on whether conflict has changed in recent years, particularly since the end of the Cold War. Narratives on its 'changing nature' often stem from a discussion of how much conflict is taking place, what kinds of conflict are becoming more common, and whether such conflicts are fundamentally or qualitatively different to war and conflict seen in the past. This first section considers the last of these questions: has conflict changed?

In her seminal work *New and Old Wars*, Mary Kaldor used case study evidence from Bosnia (1999), and later in a second edition from Iraq (2006), to argue that a number of shifts had occurred in the nature of war, particularly since the Cold War. She highlighted what she regarded as key differences between so-called old war and new war, recognising that old war as depicted here is a model drawing on experience of conflict up to and during the two World Wars, but acknowledging that in reality no conflict exactly fits all the criteria described:

Old wars:

- occurred between recognised sovereign states;
- were defined largely by direct and often large-scale battles between identifiable, uniformed armed forces distinguishable from civilians;
- had the destruction of these fighting forces as a primary aim, and therefore saw proportionally higher deaths among combatant populations than among civilians;
- had defined beginnings (declaration of war) and ends (ceasefire/peace agreement);
- had the capture, defence or retention of territory as their ultimate goal;
- were underpinned by narratives of nationalism;
- were financed primarily through taxation and a war economy.

New wars:

- occur within and across states, often involving the state as one of many 'sides' in the conflict, rather than simply between states;
- involve a range of fighting forces, including but not limited to state armed forces, ex-combatants, local defence forces and militias, warlords and rebel groups;
- are underpinned by narratives of identity, such as ethnicity, religion or culture, which are used to recruit fighters and inspire loyalty;
- blur the distinctions between civilian and combatant on account of the nature of the fighting forces involved, the identity narratives that permeate combatant and civilian populations, and the adoption of guerrilla tactics;
- may have unclear beginnings and can continue for decades at varying levels of intensity, without a clearly defined end;
- are financed by the engagement of the belligerents, frequently including the state, in a range of economic networks linked into global and regional trades in illicit and licit goods;
- often involve the integration of such war-enabled or war-enhanced economies with criminal enterprises and networks;
- include few direct battles between forces, instead being sites of ethnic cleansing, genocide and guerrilla warfare with considerable violence directed against civilian populations.

Kaldor may be new war's most famous proponent, but she is by no means alone in her assertion that conflict has changed significantly since the end of the Cold War. Münkler (2005) also takes the concept of new war as a starting point for contemporary conflict analysis, arguing that the wars which permeate the developing world have more in common with the Thirty Years' War in Europe than the interstate wars of the twentieth century, thus rather undermining the idea that this particular style of warfare is 'new'. Münkler, however, also echoes Kaldor's contention that old wars were responsible for constructing narratives of state legitimacy and regulating control over territory, allowing the expansion of taxation and the growth of national identity. In short, these old wars are regarded as state-building and state-reinforcing and were closely related to the process of European state-building from the seventeenth to the twentieth century.

In contrast, new wars, with their plethora of combatants and the dominance of identity narratives, encourage citizens to turn away from the state and define themselves by ethnicity, religion or other facets. They are therefore seen as state-'unbuilding', or state-breaking.

This notion of new war as a destructive force has also informed narratives of state failure and state collapse and fed into an assumption that a European-style state is the 'normal' state of being. New wars are therefore a threat to modernity and to the existence of the state itself, drawing as they do on a variety of identities that may be depicted as pre-modern but also are likely to be highly economic in nature.

Mixed pictures and alternative funding

The evidence for a qualitative shift in conflict is, however, extremely mixed. One of the key assertions of new war theory is that the international context in which conflict takes place has changed and, moreover, that this affects how wars are financed. This is one of the more difficult aspects of the new wars thesis to refute; it is undoubtedly true that, during the Cold War, groups challenging the state, from Angola to Chile, incorporated the bipolar world view into their narratives of legitimation. Defining themselves as pro-communism/socialism, as with FRELIMO in Mozambique, or as capitalist or simply anti-communist, such as President Mobutu's regime in Zaire, allowed governments and their challengers alike to draw on financial and military support from Cold War patrons, fuelling a series of rebellions and proxy wars in the developing world. However, these movements were frequently mul-tifaceted and served a multitude of backers. Along the South African border, for example, patterns of support for armed groups may have had more to do with the survival of apartheid than simply being a Cold War battlefront, and so the different organisations involved in conflict reflected anti-South African as well as pro-Soviet feeling.

New war theorists assert that the loss of these external funding streams following the end of the Cold War has led those involved in conflict to exploit domestic opportunities, includ-ing the state, natural resources and a range of criminal and shadow trade networks, to finance their activities. Indeed, it may be true that conflict could have intensified as a result of the state being identified as a source of income, but that source of income declined in absolute value as external support to the state was reduced. This then led to scrabbling over the declining resources available and to an intensification of conflicts over those resources.

The question of how wars are financed deserves greater attention and will be revisited later in the chapter. However, it is important to note here that, whilst the international con-text in which conflict takes place is no longer defined by Cold War politics, other narratives have emerged to take their place. In the context of the global war on terror, for example, since 2001 developing states have been able to draw on support from developed states and international organisations in their fight against 'terrorism'. But there is a lack of agreement on what constitutes a terrorist group. The ease and speed with which governments, particu-larly in sub-Saharan Africa, rebrand their opponents as terrorists rather than rebels suggests that the importance persists of narratives of legitimation and mechanisms for accessing support but the narratives themselves have changed.

Targeting civilians is not new in wars

A second key claim of new war theorists, that contemporary conflicts are defined by the targeting of civilians in ways which old wars were not, is also clearly problematic and potentially misleading. As Newman (2004b: 181) points out, 'Warfare in the 20th century did not move from an ethos of chivalry among uniformed soldiers to one of barbarity among warlords and militias.' Wars of the past, including the nominally quintessential 'old wars' such as the Second World War, involved extremely high civilian casualties and the deliberate targeting of civilian populations, such as the bombings of Dresden in Germany and Coventry in the United Kingdom, not to mention the use of atomic weapons in Japan. Even if we limit our analysis only to so-called civil wars, Kalyvas, a key detractor of the new war thesis, argues that 'the perception that civil wars are particularly cruel predates new civil wars – it is one of the most enduring and consistent observations, stressed by observers and participants alike, ever since Thucydides' depiction of the civil war in Corcyra' (2001: 114). History abounds with examples of state militaries and non-state forces perpetrating massacres and employing torture, including sexual violence and mutilation, against both enemy fighters and civilian populations.

Clearly, the targeting of civilians and the use of such tactics is therefore not new, but it may be possible to claim that in old wars such tactics were subordinated to a broader military strategy, whereas in new war they *are* the strategy, an end in themselves. A widely cited attempt to frame such violence can be found in the work of Robert Kaplan, particularly 'The coming anarchy' (1994). This emphasised what he considered to be the primordial nature of conflict in the developing world, beyond the comprehension and therefore the control, prevention or resolution efforts of outsiders in the West. The article was published at the time when images of the brutality of the Rwandan genocide emerged, and there was considerable interest in this notion of 'new barbarism'. The influence of the new barbarism thesis and its implications are discussed further in the following chapter, but suffice to say that superlative examples of the targeting of civilians or extreme brutality have undoubtedly influenced the ways in which conflict in the developing world is depicted in the popular media and arguably the ways it is understood in Western imagination. However, the new barbarism thesis goes too far in seeking to portray such extreme instances of violence as lacking in logic.

The logic of extreme violence

Far from being an example of unthinking barbarism, the use of extreme violence in many conflicts frequently carries symbolism and political messages to the population as a whole. For example, the work of Jackson (2002) and Vinci (2005) suggests that the Lord's Resistance Army (LRA) in northern Uganda adopt tactics of mutilation and extreme violence for key strategic reasons. Mutilation is a way for a relatively small group (the LRA is estimated to number only a few thousand) to spread fear amongst a larger population and create a lasting reminder within communities of the power they have and of the state's failure to protect its citizens. It may also be an effective way to send clear signals to the population about the consequences of collaboration with government. Richards (1996) similarly highlights the strategic value of widespread torture and mutilation by the Revolutionary United Front in Sierra Leone's civil war, and Ellis (1999) outlines the implications of the potent mixture of quasi-religion, terror and mutilation of the civilian population in the Liberian conflicts of the 1990s.

These analyses, often relying on an ethnographic or grounded theory methodological approach to the study of conflict, suggest deeper contextual meaning to acts of violence. Taylor's study of the Rwandan genocide (1999) draws attention to the importance of ritual and historical, socially embedded meaning in the individual and cumulative acts of violence which constituted the genocide. The new barbarism thesis may be correct in suggesting outsiders cannot understand the social meanings of such violence at first glance, but this lack of understanding and recognition should not be considered proof that the actions are without meaning or are, in some depictions, 'ancient evils'.

The importance of empirical evidence

This points to a wider criticism of the literature on new wars. In particular, several analysts have pointed out that, in the rush to define 'what's new' about war, the analysis of empirical evidence from historical cases of warfare is often neglected. In addition, much work in this area is carried out by political scientists and has no real relationship to the literature on the history of warfare more generally, therefore producing ahistorical and mono-disciplinary theoretical frameworks. Whilst this may not be an issue in some areas, an extrapolation such as Kaldor's that makes a bold historical assertion about the 'newness' of wars, and yet starts the analysis with the highly stylised wars of the eighteenth century, is inevitably limited. In the history of war and human civilisation there is a series of patterns in warfare that are familiar to scholars of contemporary African wars, and a longer timeframe for the analysis of wars, even back to those in Europe in the seventeenth century, provides at least superficial parallels to contemporary modes of warfare. More empirically grounded work suggests that, despite the apparent attractiveness of a superficially neat 'new war' classification, one can infer much about the causes of wars from historical socio-political structures and the spatial aspects of conflict itself.

So what does the new wars thesis tell us?

It is therefore true to say that, whilst it may tell us something about the characteristics of contemporary wars, the new wars thesis tells us very little about the history of conflict. In fact a relatively cursory knowledge of the history of conflict shows that the characteristics of 'old wars' mean that they form a temporary period in the history of warfare intimately related to the rise of the European state. In fact many of the so-called new wars have more in common with the pre-state period and so are in no way 'new'. The thesis does, however, shed light on a number of characteristics that are different, or at least operationalised in different ways, from what happened during the Cold War period – in particular, the breakdown in the relationship between state and war exemplified by the decline in the number of interstate as opposed to intra-state conflicts. 'New' wars are associated far more closely with smaller groups with localised identities which may have been oppressed under a state system that was previously able to control them. The undermining of the state by the ending of Cold War support meant that states such as Ethiopia faced considerable challenges to their legitimacy from local groups with access to external sources of funding, at the same time as central support collapsed.

To explain some of this as being economic in nature is, of course, accurate. Much of the warfare we see today relates to economic and political exclusion or control over economic resources. However, this has always been the case and this is certainly not new. What is different is that states face challenges to their legitimacy in pursuing these goals as well as becoming an economic objective in themselves.

How do we measure wars?

Apart from the qualitative evidence presented by supporters and opponents of the new wars thesis, to ascertain whether conflict really has changed since the beginning of the twentieth century, or even since the end of the Cold War, it is important to consider the ways in which we define and measure conflict. It is often suggested that conflict in the form of civil war is becoming more frequent, and that the world is therefore becoming somehow more dangerous. However, the measures used to define a period of violence as 'civil war', or indeed 'war' more generally, are varied. Some of these measures even indicate that, contrary to popular narratives of global danger and rising civilian death tolls in intra-state war, the intensity of civil wars and their direct impacts on developing states – in terms of national mortality rates in conflict-affected states – is actually decreasing (HSRP, 2009). This section will begin to explore some of these inconsistencies and demonstrate that the way we measure war and define an episode of violence as conflict has significant implications for our understandings of what war is and how much of it is happening.

There are a range of ways to measure and try to categorise conflict, one of the most common being the counting of 'battlefield deaths'. Recognising the assertion of new war theorists that civilians are often targets of excessive violence in contemporary civil war, some go beyond the battlefield and attempt to count the number of deaths attributed to a conflict which may not result from actual fighting. Each of these approaches is potentially problematic and may mislead us in attempting to assess how much conflict is actually occurring at any given time and whether the overall trend, particularly for civil war, is rising or falling.

Formal databases and measurement

The work of Cramer (2006) provides a useful critical interrogation of the ways in which conflict is measured and explores how conflicts are classified and categorised for analysis in three well-known databases on armed conflict. These databases have been used to plot both how much war is occurring and the intensity of war, based largely on battle deaths. Indeed, one of the most popular models for explaining and analysing civil wars is the 'greed or grievance' model produced by Collier and Hoeffler (2002). We will return to a discussion of this econometric model, used to attempt to predict the likelihood of civil war occurring in a country during a five-year period, in the following chapter. However, it is useful to note here that Collier and Hoeffler base their definition of 'large-scale civil war' on that adopted by the Correlates of War project, which requires '1,000 combat-related deaths' within the five-year period being surveyed. Cramer's review covers this frequently used database of the Correlates of War project, the University of Uppsala Conflict Data Project and the German Arbeitsgemeinschaft Kriegsursachenforschung based at the University of Hamburg. A key mechanism which such datasets use for classifying wars is the threshold criteria – how many battle deaths make a particular episode of violence officially a conflict or war? For Correlates of War the figure is 1,000 in a single year, but for Uppsala twenty-five battle deaths is considered politically significant and therefore sufficient enough to count as conflict. As Cramer points out, this means that the violence in Northern Ireland is not registered at all on the Correlates of War database but, because it included over twenty-five deaths per year with a cumulative total of over 1,000 (though never more than 1,000 in any single year), is classed by Uppsala as an intermediate conflict. The threshold, and related criteria such as whether the deaths occur in one year or over a number of years, therefore affects the level of severity ascribed to instances of violence, and indeed whether they are recorded as conflicts at all.

Issues with formal measurement and civilian casualties

Cramer has also pointed out that, by defining conflict using an absolute and quite arbitrary number of deaths rather than relating this to the proportion of population, larger countries are more likely than smaller countries to be classed as experiencing conflict (2006: 60). The use of a threshold may also hide the fact that deaths may fluctuate quite dramatically during a conflict, with periods of intense fighting at some intervals and lulls at others. However, going beyond the question of thresholds and how the numbers of battle deaths are counted, it is possible to deconstruct the typology even further and ask whether *conflict-related* deaths would be a more accurate measure of the impact of war. Crucially, are 'civilian' casualties included in the counting of conflict-related deaths and, if so, how can these accurately measured? The ongoing debate between the International Rescue Committee (IRC), an international relief and development NGO, and the team behind the Human Security Report Project, based at Simon Fraser University in Vancouver, over the number of deaths attributed to the war in the Democratic Republic of the Congo (DRC) is a powerful recent illustration of this problem.

The conflicts in the DRC are believed by the IRC to have caused over 5.4 million *excess*[1] deaths between 1998 and 2007 (IRC 2007). However, the IRC attributes only 0.4 per cent of the deaths in the period of the most recent survey (2006–7) to violence. The majority of deaths are instead attributed to 'infectious diseases, malnutrition and neonatal- and pregnancy-related conditions' (ibid.: iii). The figures therefore incorporate not only casualties incurred by the fighting forces, which could be considered 'battle deaths', but also deaths among the civilian population resulting not from actual fighting but, according to the IRC, still as a direct result of the presence of conflict. This includes deaths which they believe would have been avoided in a non-conflict zone, such as those resulting from diseases and injuries that would not necessary have been life threatening but which become fatal when insecurity prevents people from accessing medical assistance.

The *Human Security Report*, however, argues that estimating excess war deaths based on an estimate of what peacetime mortality would have looked like is a task 'so fraught with challenges that it can rarely succeed' (HSRP 2009: 1). It challenges the methodology of the IRC in a range of areas, notably its reliance on sampling in areas in the east of the DRC, which experienced the most intense conflict, its failure to sample across the country in every period for which it gathered data, and its calculation of a baseline-expected mortality rate which was too low. Taken together, these criticisms suggest that the number of excess deaths has been grossly overestimated. When the *Human Security Report* team made adjustments to the calculations based on their criticisms of the methodology, the number of excess deaths fell by around 60 per cent, both for the period of the first survey and for the period of the final three surveys. The IRC for its part has since recognised and acknowledged the difficulties in gathering reliable data and in ensuring a representative sample in a conflict-affected state, admitting that 5.4 million is the current best estimate based on established methodology and conservative assumptions, but the real figure could be as low as 3 million or as high as 7.6 million. The range here demonstrates that counting the number of deaths from conflict is therefore an extremely difficult task, and, as in the example above, it is virtually impossible to work out the number of deaths which, though not a result of direct fighting, could have been avoided if the conflict were not taking place.

Calculating battle deaths

Even if this contentious issue of civilian deaths is left to one side, just counting the number of casualties amongst the fighting forces in contemporary conflict is difficult. As interstate conflict is recognised to be declining, outright battles between clearly defined and recognisable military forces are becoming less common and lines between civilian and combatant are increasingly blurred, how do we define a battle or a battle death? This difficulty reflects

---

[1]The IRC establishes a baseline-expected mortality rate for the country, drawing on data from the average mortality rate in sub-Saharan Africa. The excess is therefore the number of deaths which occur above the average that might be expected if the country were not suffering from ongoing conflict.

the reality that in contemporary conflict it is more and more difficult to separate combatants from civilians, and indeed to distinguish between categories of combatants, such as soldiers and rebels, as individuals may perform roles identified with more than one of these categories. Individuals in conflict zones may straddle multiple identities, as soldiers by day but rebels by night (Reno 1998), or as self-defined and self-organised militias, often without uniforms and fixed command structures. As with other aspects of the new war thesis discussed above, this is by no means a new phenomenon. The multiplicity of roles played by individuals – as saboteurs, collaborators, rebels or soldiers – is witnessed in historical conflicts, from the Spanish civil war and the French resistance forces under Nazi occupation to the Viet Cong in South Vietnam. The difficulty arises when, for purposes of counting deaths and classifying conflicts, we try to determine if these are battle deaths, civilian deaths, or both. When categories are so poorly delineated such tasks becomes replete with complications. These are further exacerbated by the myriad challenges in gathering reliable statistical data in conflict-affected areas particularly and many developing states more generally.

The measures used to define a particular period of violence as conflict, and as a specific type of conflict, are therefore extremely important. These questions of definition become vital when we attempt to assess the reliability of claims being made about 'how much' war is actually occurring and the types of conflict seen to be declining or increasing, and then to discern trends in warfare globally or in the developing world. We can now turn to this question of the global trends in conflict. If we cannot say for certain how war and sub-types of war should be classified and measured, is it possible to discern any reliable trends in conflict?

How many wars?

Since the end of the Cold War, it has generally been accepted that the instance of interstate conflict has declined whilst intra-state wars have displayed a more complex pattern. Drawing on data from the Correlates of War project discussed earlier, Fearon and Laitin's analysis (2003) suggests there was a sharp rise in the number of civil wars in the first half of the 1990s followed by a steep decline. It implies, bearing in mind the high threshold applied within this database in identifying an episode of violence as war, that the number of wars in which over 1,000 battle deaths occurred declined significantly in the latter half of the 1990s. This does not, however, allow us to draw even tentative conclusions as to the prevalence of smaller-scale civil wars, such as those captured by the Uppsala database.

Gleditsch and his colleagues (2002) apply the lower threshold of battle deaths, also suggesting that recorded conflicts increased significantly in the early 1990s before starting to decline, though not in a consistent and linear fashion. Both analyses intimate that recorded conflicts peaked before the end of the Cold War and argue that since then, perhaps despite popular perceptions of conflict, the instance of civil war has declined. Given this decrease in interstate war, based on two different measures, it is therefore important to ask what kinds of conflict we are left with, particularly in the developing world.

Fearon and Laitin say that 'there is no significant trend up or down' in terms of the rate at which new civil wars are starting, which remains at around 2.1 per year. However, they also note that civil wars have ended at a rate of only about 1.85 per year, which means that there has been a steady, almost linear accumulation of unresolved conflicts since 1945. This suggests that long-term chronic conflicts create conditions that make it difficult for conflict to be ended in a definitive way. This further implies that, once a country has experienced conflict, it is very likely to experience it again. This certainly fits with the view that conflicts in general increased during the 1990s after the end of the Cold War. This was then followed by a period of consolidation and the ending of some conflicts. However, there is a significant group of conflicts that have continued, as the state is not in a position either to end the fighting or to come to an acceptable peace. The example of the DRC is telling in this context, with a relatively stable core surrounding the western area of the country, but with large areas of the periphery not controlled by the central state at all. This failure of the state to project security and power up to its formal borders is a feature of the 2000s in some parts of the world, notably in those areas affected by powerful non-state actors, among them warlords, secessionist movements and criminal networks. This core group of states in a perpetual state of semi-collapse is where there are continuing areas of chronic conflict.

The primacy of long-term chronic wars has a number of implications for external intervention. In particular, it raises questions about what sort of state can be realistically supported by the international community in this type of context. The idea of a liberal state being transplanted to the DRC, to Nepal or to Laos is problematic for a number of reasons, not least because of the lack of political infrastructure and the institutions needed to support functioning democratic rule based on an effective state.

However, the earlier set of questions here may be even more crucial, particularly whether or not the international community can actually intervene successfully or if its range of options is too constrained. An interesting test case here is that of Sri Lanka. Following a chronic conflict during which the international community tried to broker peace and then supported both sides in humanitarian terms, the civil war has recently been decisively ended by the victory of one side – the government – with the critical support of China, which chose a side, backed it and supported it sufficiently to win a comprehensive victory. There is now no war in northern Sri Lanka, although the country faces a number of significant long-term security and development challenges. The key question here is whether it is acceptable for an external agent to intervene in this way to help one side win a war.

Zones of conflict

The data used by Gleditsch *et al.* (2002) also identify some key trends in terms of the locations of conflicts and the nature of the actors involved in them. They note that there are three distinct zones of conflict: 'from Central America and the Caribbean and into South America, another from East Central Europe through the Balkans and the Middle East and India to Indonesia'. The third zone they identify is Africa, spanning 'almost the entire continent' (2002: 624). This suggests that incidence of conflict maps broadly onto areas of the developing rather than the developed world, and indeed that such conflicts are clustered into particular regions rather than being bound strictly within individual states.

Gleditsch *et al.* also confirm a declining overall trend in wars between states and that internal conflict has been overall the dominant form since the mid-twentieth century (2002: 623). This does not, however, mean that states are not involved in these conflicts. As indicated in the previous chapter, states have fought against insurgent movements and rebellions, and also assisted rebel groups in their fights against other states. At the same time, the state may in fact become just one faction within a conflict, or even the end target of a conflict, since the state can still command or attract considerable external resources.

The continuing importance of the state

The state remains a crucial actor to consider when analysing conflict for a number of reasons, even though it is often just one of the competing sides in a multidimensional conflict system which may involve a range of non-state, or extra-state, fighting forces. States can command considerable external resources that may make them powerful players in any conflict. They tend to have access to significant external resources that may mean that a particular faction can remain powerful even if support for war on the ground is thinning. An example is Zimbabwe, where the resources of the state can be used to control political resources and therefore a security infrastructure that may be used as a security actor in neighbouring states. The use of Zimbabwean troops to secure access to diamond mines inside the DRC is an illustration of how states can become personalised or at least used for the benefit of an isolated elite.

States also remain central to conflict in the developing world as a potential prize of war sought by challengers and as a source of revenue to fund conflict. In fact it was one of the key elements in the strategy of Charles Taylor in Liberia to become head of state and thereby to gain not only legitimacy but also the potentially lucrative external funding stream that comes with the international community and investment opportunities. The Liberian example is an interesting one, since Taylor had managed to construct impressive external trading networks, and quite why he needed the state as another source of power is shrouded in mystery. However, it is clear that control of a state means moving up in terms of trading networks, providing the ability to raise external finance and also to charge legitimate (as opposed to black-market) prices for goods and services. An important element is that states as entities exist independently in law from the individuals that run them. A state may therefore be run by one elite and then be succeeded by a different elite, however many changes they may make. This makes states valuable pieces of infrastructure that can be populated by loyal political networks.

State power, in terms of both its extent and the ways in which it is exercised, is crucial in understanding why conflicts start, how they are able to continue and the difficulties in ending them. The inability of some developing states to exercise even basic control over their internationally recognised territory has, in extreme cases, led to the emergence of local polities and alternative forms and structures of power and authority. Like states, these form just one complex and splintered group within the range of actors in contemporary conflict which must be considered in analysing the conflict and in any plans for post-conflict reconstruction and development.

Conflict actors

This section identifies some of the key actors engaged in conflict, beginning with a brief discussion of the role of the state. As argued above, states are central both to the study of conflict in the developing world and to strategies for development during and after conflict. This is certainly true of empirically 'strong' states, whose elites may maintain a high degree of control over their territory and even direct violence against their population or parts thereof to maintain their position. For example, the state in Rwanda before 1990 was empirically relatively strong, with the Hutu elite maintaining a high degree of control over the territory and population. The onset of civil war after the invasion of the Tutsi-dominated Rwandan Patriotic Front challenged this dominance, and the ensuing genocide could not have been executed so efficiently were it not for the strength and penetration of the Rwandan state in society. However, though empirically or militarily strong states can play a relatively obvious role as perpetrators of violence, it is just as important to consider the part played in conflict by weak states. States with limited control and influence over their territory and citizens may actively, or by default, facilitate the growth of alternative centres of power and authority such as warlords, insurgent leaders or 'terrorist groups'. Such actors challenge the state monopoly of power through their engagement with the local populations in both positive and negative ways. These processes have specific implications for development and the construction of the liberal state discussed in the previous chapter.

Warlords and insurgent leaders

There is considerable debate over the defining characteristics of warlords, and there is also frequently an unhelpful conflation of the terms 'warlord', 'rebel leader' and 'bandit'. This is partly a reflection of the ways in which such individuals, and the fighters they nominally control, finance and support their activities. Warlords exist in popular imagination as individuals who prey on citizens bereft of the protection of the state, often looting and seizing what they need or desire with impunity. However, the reality of the strategies of warlords for financing their operations and establishing control over a territory or group of citizens is much more complex.

Essentially the distinction relies on the difference between a bandit, who roves across territory without an interest in developing that territory, and a warlord, who is concerned to exercise control over a geographical area or group of people and an interest in extracting tax. Whereas bandits essentially operate a 'hit and run' system, warlords levy taxes, maintain some sort of order (even if it is based on terror) and administer governance. Reinforcing and maintaining control of a defined territory may serve to cement a warlord's dominance of the local economy, providing continued access to the resources needed to pay followers and discipline or dissuade challengers. This may appear reminiscent of some of the strategies employed by the national elites of developing states, discussed in the previous chapter, and these methods have been as vital to the maintenance and consolidation of power of national elites as to warlords. Building a presence in a particular region also allows warlords to tap into local narratives of identity, and potentially grievance against the state, in order to recruit followers and establish a power base.

Warlords, then, may act as an alternative form of governance from the state. They often display five key characteristics:

1   emerging in the context of a collapse of centralised power;
2   using violence to reassert power locally;
3   possibly replacing formal social and military structures with gang mentality;
4   evolving some governance structures (performing 'state' functions such as tax collection in the absence of centralised authority); and
5   frequently having links to international trade.

Warlords are important within the context of state collapse or degrees of state failure. They are found mostly where there is no legal enforcement of market mechanisms and where the application of economic contracts and the acquisition of resources involves a resort to violence. For banditry to occur, the state must be failing in its duty to protect citizens, but for the more complex forms of warlordism to develop requires more fundamental failings by the state. The capacity of warlords to establish a degree of control over the population and local economy is partly a function of their ability to instil fear and discipline local actors using violence.

Warlords may also draw on local narratives of grievance, including exclusion from or abandonment by the state. The inability of the state to control its territory and provide public goods associated with citizenship, such as basic social services, thus provides the opportunity for warlords both to occupy public space and to claim they are acting in the interests of the local population. Beswick's account (2009) of the rise of Laurent Nkunda's rebel movement, in the east of the DRC illustrates this phenomenon. Nkunda was able to consolidate power in the region by highlighting and demonstrating the failures of the Congolese government, in this case to provide security for the country's Tutsi population. He also maintained connections to international economic networks through his ties to Rwanda's military and political elite. However, as is often the case with such rebel groups, his authority relied largely on creating fear rather than on acceptance by the majority of the local population.

Child soldiers and youth in violence

The NGO War Child estimated that 300,000 children were involved in conflict in 2009 across the world, most of these in sub-Saharan Africa. Child soldiering is a contentious and emotive issue eliciting considerable media coverage, and it is a site of intersection between the processes associated with conflict and those which comprise development. However, there are important questions around the phenomenon of youth in conflict which need to be explored, such as how 'children' are defined in this context, whether their involvement in conflict is a new phenomenon, or indeed one limited to the developing world, and the nature of the role played more broadly by youth in conflict and post-conflict reconstruction.

The forced recruitment and use of child soldiers by states and non-state actors is prohibited in a range of international agreements, notably the Geneva Conventions (Protocol 1, 1949) and the 1989 UN Convention on the Rights of the Child (CRC). Such legislation sets out the minimum age at which children can be compulsorily recruited and the age at which volunteers can be accepted into fighting forces. For the Geneva Conventions, the minimum ages are eighteen and fifteen respectively. The CRC set the age for both at fifteen, but subsequent additions (Protocol to the CRC on the Involvement of Children in Armed Conflicts, 2000) have revised this to eighteen for forced recruitment and sixteen for volunteers. However, the use of children in fighting forces, whether in a war-fighting capacity or in supporting roles, has a long history and is not limited to developing states. From ancient Rome to the drummer boys and 'boy soldiers' of the two world wars and the UK and US deployment of soldiers under eighteen to combat roles in recent conflicts in Iraq, youth have played a varied and controversial role in conflict.

Whilst child soldiering may be a historically grounded phenomenon, it is frequently asserted that it has become more common, particularly in the context of civil wars. It is necessary therefore to consider what makes young people join fighting forces, whether state, paramilitary or rebel, and also what factors make them susceptible to forced recruitment, most often via abduction. Zack Williams (2001) sees development as a process bound up with the creation of child soldiers. His study of Sierra Leone argues that development processes in this extremely poor country have led to a breakdown in traditional social networks such as the family and community. These networks had previously provided some stability and socialisation for orphans and other children within the community who were disadvantaged. The loss of these networks and structures has led, in his analysis, to an increase in the number of street children, a key recruitment pool for child soldiers (2001: 77) (see Box 2.1).

Box 2.1 Street children to child soldiers

- Family breakdown as a result of impoverishment leads to children living on the street for all or most of their time (the former known as children *of* the street, the latter as children *on* the street). Some follow a more circuitous path to the street, being fostered out to more affluent families, where they often face abuse and exploitation and have limited access to education compared with the biological children of the foster family.
- On the streets the children are incorporated into informal networks: the *agba* (big man) leads the group, *bras* (big brothers) exist below him, providing a measure of protection in return for the children's loyalty and payment from informal work, whilst *alagbas* below them act as gang leaders.
- The system runs on loyalty, to a particular network and the individual's immediate senior, and patronage, the process whereby protection is offered in return for payment.

(Adapted from Williams 2001: 75–8)

Box 2.1 explains how children can become integrated into networks on the street which are then replicated within rebel groups and armed forces, easing their recruitment. In the case of West African urban centres in particular, aspects of youth culture are incorporated to attract children and youth, using the culture-industry setting of rap or reggae and corresponding promises of consumption and status to draw in and motivate future fighters. This also corresponds with earlier views on the adoption of 'gang mentality' by warlords. The parallels between life on the street and life as a soldier may make these children an attractive source of recruitment for rebels and government forces alike, but not all are forcibly recruited, and the question remains as to why some children and youth 'choose' to fight.

Returning to the debate on age and agency, it has been argued that children, some no more than teenagers, are able to make the decision to fight from the subjective appraisal of their options and safety. Youth 'volunteering' to fight against the government is extremely contentious. De Berry's (2001) well-known study of volunteering in Teso, Uganda, emphasises the subjective rationality of this decision. Frequent cattle raiding, which the state failed to prevent, left young men in Teso with limited prospects of marriage in a society where status is inextricably linked to cattle ownership and where cattle numbers had dwindled from 1 million to 10,000. Anger and frustration, as well as the need for protection from government forces attempting to quell the rebellion, were frequently cited as grounds for joining the fighting forces.

Of course, not all, and perhaps not even most, child soldiers are even nominally 'volunteers'. The LRA in northern Uganda is believed to have kidnapped or forcibly recruited tens of thousands of children in the region since 1987. The FARC in Colombia relies on the recruitment or kidnap of children and young people. Likewise, according to UNICEF, the Liberation Tigers of Tamil Eelam in Sri Lanka, commonly known as the Tamil Tigers, conscripted children as young as twelve to lay mines and take direct part in fighting against government forces. The range of tasks performed by children in conflict is vast, including roles as fighters, porters, scouts, intelligence gatherers, and layers and clearers of land mines. Roles may also vary according to gender, with girls who are recruited, conscripted or abducted at high risk of sexual violence. Such girls are frequently forced to act as 'wives' to their male counterparts or seniors in return for protection and to avoid further violence. Such activities carry attendant risks of infection with HIV/AIDS, pregnancy and the dangers of giving birth in unsanitary conditions.

Youth are therefore a key group to consider in analysing conflict. Preventing their recruitment, forced or otherwise, and facilitating their reintegration into society after conflict remains one of the key challenges for post-conflict societies and the international community. Development can, however, play a part in facilitating or derailing this process.

War economies

The political economy of conflict is a key theme running through this chapter, and indeed a key area for analysts of conflict and development to consider. It is therefore important to explore briefly the kinds of economies which develop in and around zones of conflict and those which make use of areas beyond the control of the rule of law to facilitate their activities. Of particular concern here are shadow economies, their links to criminal activities such as drugs and arms trafficking, and the connections between grey trades, private actors and the funding of conflict which exacerbates state weakness. In such a context, key individuals, insurgent groups and even governments may have more to gain from instability and conflict than from peace and stability. Tackling these perverse incentives is a key challenge for development during and after conflict.

The term 'shadow' is often used to describe political and economic activities and processes that are informal, transborder, illicit, illegal, or any combination of these. The shadow metaphor emphasises the nature of these strategies and forms of rule and accumulation: they often parallel or cross over into formal state structures, taking advantage of informal, illicit and transboundary networks ill-policed by established regimes of global governance. Duffield also points to another common use of the shadow metaphor, arguing that:

> [the] South has effectively reintegrated itself into the liberal world system through spread and deepening of all types of parallel and shadow transborder activity. This represents the site of new expansive forms of local–global networking and innovative patterns of extra-legal and non-formal North–South integration
>
> (Duffield 2001: 5)

Though the term 'shadow' by its strict dictionary definition may therefore seem to suggest an ephemeral quality to the phenomena it describes, shadow trades and networks have shown remarkable resilience and adaptability.

Africa is perhaps unusual in that the informal shadow economy is believed to be larger than the formal. However, the shadow networks that operate through and around formal markets and supply chains, particularly in conflict zones where state control of territory is patchy or limited, do not traffic only illegal goods. Informal networks are crucial in distributing everyday goods such as foodstuffs, fuel and even aid. However, the informal, ubiquitous and transborder character of these networks, operating outside the formal regulatory and disciplining mechanisms of the state, make them a natural conduit for illicit and illegal goods. There is evidence that those involved in controlling and facilitating such networks, and therefore potentially in the movement of people, aid, arms, drugs and resources, can help sustain conflict and fighting groups. Concern has therefore grown internationally about the global reach of these networks and their value to organised crime, terrorists and 'entrepreneurs' of war.

Ungoverned spaces and security threats

Illicit economic activity, particularly the trafficking of drugs, weapons and natural resources, is depicted in the policy documents of Northern states as threatening – a potential source of terrorist funds and providing opportunities for money laundering. The trafficking of drugs is an obvious example of how criminal activity in developing regions can have significant global political and economic impacts. There are also recognised synergies between organised transnational crime, conflict and 'terrorist groups', actors in which may use the same routes and providers of services, such as violent enforcement, money laundering and international banking.

The presence of such networks has informed images of some developing states as failing or weak, a potential danger to themselves and others. The existence of interconnected shadow economic and political networks is seen as proof that developing and conflict-affected states harbour dangerous 'ungoverned spaces'. A worldwide threat briefing by the Central Intelligence Agency in 2003 identified such areas as 'lawless zones' and 'no-man's lands'. Yet, paradoxically, recognition that such networks exist points explicitly to the fact that such spaces are subject to some degree of control and governance, though not necessarily from the state. This reflects the earlier discussion of conditions which facilitate the emergence of warlords, reliant on governance failings of the state but also on their ability to raise funds through connection to the global economy. The merging of violence with economic accumulation at the local level and the creation of economies which depend on conflict and a permissive titular 'ungoverned space' therefore create incentives for the continuation of conflict. The links between violence, accumulation, conflict, crime and instability are therefore a key feature of contemporary conflict, giving rise to particular challenges for development actors and those in conflict-affected societies who seek peace.

Summary points

1   New war is not new, but the shift in emphasis to different factors provides a useful way of analysing conflicts.
2   Conflict does not leave developing states in a situation of anarchy.
3   Social relations and structures are reordered by conflict in ways which must be considered when designing development interventions and strategies for reconstruction.
4   Features associated with new war have direct development impacts on, for example, war economies, the targeting of civilians, displacement, environmental damage and resource stripping.
5   There are challenges in measuring conflicts and very little agreement exists as to what actually constitutes a conflict or a 'battle death'.
6   Alternative governance systems form where states collapse completely, meaning there are challengers to the monopoly of force that states are conventionally able to exercise.

Discussion questions

1   What are the core debates in terms of measuring conflicts and does it matter that there is no overall agreement?
2   What are the main features of new wars and how are they similar or different to old ones?
3   Are new wars new?
4   What does conflict look like in the developing world?
5   What are the core implications of the nature of conflict for development more broadly?

Further reading

Cramer, Christopher (2006) *Civil War Is Not a Stupid Thing: Accounting for Violence in Developing Countries*. London: Hurst.

Duffield, Mark (2001) *Global Governance and the New Wars: The Merging of Development and Security*. London: Zed Books (see Introduction and chapter 1).

Fearon, J. and Laitin, D. (2003) 'Ethnicity, insurgency and civil war', *American Political Science Review*, 97(1): 75–90.

Gleditsch, Nils Petter, *et al.*, (2002) 'Armed conflict 1946–2001: a new dataset', *Journal of Peace Research*, 39(5): 615–37.

Kaldor, Mary (1999) *New and Old Wars: Organized Violence in a Global Era*. Cambridge: Polity; 2nd ed., 2006.

Kaplan, Robert (1994) 'The coming anarchy: how scarcity, crime, overpopulation, tribalism, and disease are rapidly destroying the social fabric of our planet', *Atlantic Monthly*, February; www.theatlantic.com/magazine/archive/1994/02/the-coming-anarchy/4670/ (accessed 25 February 2011).

Newman, Edward (2004) 'A normatively attractive but analytically weak concept', *Security Dialogue*, 35(3): 358–9.

Richards, Paul (1996) *Fighting for the Rain Forest: War, Youth & Resources in Sierra Leone*. Oxford: James Currey.

3   How do people analyse conflict?

This chapter will identify the main narratives which have been used to explain conflict in the developing world. In order to look at how actors have attempted to tackle development challenges during and after conflict, it is useful to have an understanding of the different ways in which these conflicts have been characterised. The aim of the chapter is to outline a number of different ways in which analysts have looked at conflict, but clearly it cannot be entirely comprehensive. It is based on the work of a great number of researchers, including Paul Collier and Anke Hoeffler, Mats Berdal and David Malone, Jeffrey Herbst, Stephen Ellis, David Keen, Thomas Homer-Dixon and Stathis Kalyvas. Whilst it cannot cover all of their ideas, they should form the core of any further reading. The chapter will examine differing explanations for conflict and look at the underpinnings of some of the labels applied to violence in the developing world, such as ethnic conflict, irrational violence and resource war.

There are as many theories on conflict as there are conflicts. Rather than giving a comprehensive survey of all the different conflict theories, what we will try to do is to provide a brief overview of different approaches to conflict that may interact with each other.

Greed and grievance — *Collier - Hoeffler*

As discussed in the previous chapter, though the number of conflicts occurring at any given time and the number of deaths resulting directly from conflict may be in irregular decline, civil wars and chronic conflicts in developing countries account for a large share of the conflict that remains. Chapter 2 described how realist views of the international system, focusing on the state as primary actor working to maximise its advantage in an anarchic system, developed to explain conflict between states. Conflicts within states, however, do not fit into such a neat state-centric analysis, and those seeking to explore the causes of civil wars have therefore sought other explanations. Popular amongst these is the *greed and grievance, or greed versus grievance,* hypothesis.

Analyses which emerged during the Cold War often drew on anthropological perspectives, or frameworks dominated by colonial perceptions of developing countries as backward and pre-modern/traditional, in explaining the civil wars and rebellion that occurred after decolonisation. These placed a heavy emphasis on the role of grievance and the nature of post-colonial states, and this will be discussed further here through explorations of tribalism, ethnicity, post-colonial statehood and structural violence as lenses through which to analyse conflict. However, these explanations tended to be extremely context specific, in the case of anthropological approaches, or to suggest that the roots of conflict lay in the nature of developing societies and their populations (*new barbarism/tribalism*). Each in its own way highlights largely endogenous processes as the cause of conflict, though these may intersect with international economic and political networks and process, and implies a relatively limited role for international actors in preventing and resolving conflict. In 2000, World Bank economist Paul Collier and Anke Hoeffler, an Oxford University researcher, created a relatively basic statistical model to determine whether greed- or grievance-based motives caused the outbreak civil war between 1960 and 1999 in 161 states surveyed. It also sought to determine whether a 'feedback effect' led to countries which had experienced conflict, motivated by either greed or grievance, being more prone to future outbreaks of conflict. The model has become extremely influential, generating debate amongst academics, researchers and policymakers alike, and it is necessary to consider the assumptions on which it is based.

How does the model work?

The Collier–Hoeffler model compares the relative importance of greed and grievance as motives for conflict, using proxy measures to represent each concept. For greed these are:

- dependence on primary commodity exports, measured by ratio of these exports to GDP;
- the proportion of young males in the population; and
- the average years of schooling undertaken.

In societies which depend significantly on primary exports, the model suggests that, if there is a high proportion of young men in a society who have few opportunities for employment (proxied by lack of education), and where there are opportunities for instant gratification through looting, greed may be an important motive for violence and therefore an important variable in analysing conflict. For grievance the proxy measures adopted are:

- low economic growth;
- inequality (measured using the Gini coefficient);
- political repression (measured using indicators of levels of civil rights);
- ethnic grievances; and
- the 'utility of rebellion', a composite indicator which includes the probability of victory, the level of defence spending, the windfall gains from accessing resources, the expected duration of conflict and the co-ordination costs of rebellion.

Based on these proxy variables Collier and Hoeffler conclude that grievance-based models are less powerful in explaining conflict than those based on greed. The degree of dependence on natural resources, through primary commodity exports, is the largest risk factor. The statistical incidence of civil war was highest in those countries where opportunities for greed-based rebellion were high – i.e., where the opportunity cost of war was very low. At the same time, grievances are real, but never strong enough to mount a successful rebellion; only greed is capable of doing that.

Given this, the poor are no more prone to conflict than anyone else, but are more likely to choose it because they have a comparative advantage in violence, suggesting it is cheaper for them to do this because they forego little else in the way of alternatives. Often forgotten in this analysis is that one thing that may be foregone in conflict is life; thus the assumption made is that poverty is so bad that the risk to one's life is worth it. The other side of the equation is the incentive for violence provided by economic gain through engaging in looting rather than in the production of public goods such as 'security'. The assumption here is that competition for survival produces a form of rivalry where those with little to lose can make gains through risking what little they have.

The model remains an attractive one, particularly for those development actors seeking ways to prevent or reduce the longevity of civil wars. It claimed to provide a way of predicting which countries were at high risk of civil war through an analysis of key variables which could be directly affected through international intervention seeking to reduce conflict. Its most attractive feature, however, was the statistical analysis and social science methodology, which had the effect of simplifying the conflicts confronting policymakers. It concentrated the analysis on how rebellions are funded and how they sustain themselves, through economic opportunities and mobilising populations around grievance, especially highlighting the role of resources and diasporas. Policymakers therefore were presented with a clear entry point for conflict prevention and management. If they could disrupt these economic processes, then the risk and longevity of conflict could theoretically be reduced. The policy interventions suggested by the model were simple: reducing both the absolute and relative attraction of primary commodity predation and the ability of diasporas to fund rebel movements.

Common criticisms

The model is based largely on abstractions and bundles of variables, and critics question the appropriateness, measurability and categorisation of the proxies. The authors themselves admit that limited opportunities for education and employment could be an indicator of grievance as well as a factor in greed-based explanations. For example, the original model takes lack of access to education as an indicator for greed rather than as a legitimate grievance. However, Collier and Hoeffler conclude that political and social variables that are most obviously related to grievance have little explanatory power. By contrast, economic variables, which could proxy some grievances but are perhaps more obviously related to the viability of rebellion, provide considerably more explanatory power.

A key question here is whether accurate figures, such as on primary commodity exports, can be gathered to provide the necessary data for the model. It can be extremely risky to rely on data obtained within developing countries because of, for example, concerns about coverage, completeness and accuracy. All of these problems are multiplied when the data refer to countries experiencing conflict, where it may not be possible to gather accurate figures at all, or at least coverage may be biased towards those areas that are not subject to conflict. Basing policy decisions on statistical models may therefore be misleading.

It is also problematic to attribute individual variables, even if these can be accurately measured, either to greed or to grievance. Emphasis must be placed on the specific ways in which economic (greed-) and political (grievance-based) agendas interact to produce particular types of rebellion. This requires an understanding of the differences between specific resources and economic opportunities (including opportunities generated by capture of the state and state power) and the contexts in which conflicts occur. Whilst the proxies suggested may contribute to a bigger picture of conflict, civil wars cannot be reduced to a simple 'greed or grievance' discussion.

A related issue is whether similar dynamics can be applied to very different conflicts. The motivations of guerrillas in the Lords' Resistance Army in Uganda are likely to be different from those in the Maoist movement in Nepal or the FARC in Colombia. Providing a relatively simple equation to explain all of these diverse contexts is problematic, even if there is an overlap between them. At the same time there may be differences in motivation within groups themselves. A leader or warlord may have a different set of objectives to the rank and file of combatants.

In short, the model turns on a sharp distinction between greed and grievance, whereas in reality they are intertwined and cannot be separated so simplistically. The model itself is also extremely selective in its approach. The results are very sensitive to the countries chosen for the dataset and also the separate variables used. This is acknowledged by Collier and Hoeffler themselves but, even given this sensitivity and the selectivity of the sample, the original paper shows that, retrospectively, the claims to be able to predict where civil war would break out apply to only around half of the sample countries chosen – about the same result as tossing a coin. This also implies, of course, that, even given the selective use of data and definitions, nearly half of the cases do not show that greed is a more important variable than grievance.

Later work by Collier and Hoeffler (with Dominic Rohner, 2009) has suggested that both greed and grievance, and qualitative as well as quantitative studies, are important in exploring why conflict starts and how it is continued. However, they maintain that economic factors are more important than political ones, and that the two can be usefully separated for purpose of analysis, hypothesising that it is the economic factors that determine the feasibility of rebellion and thus remain more critical than grievances. Such quantitative explanations of conflict present a rather static, culturally blind and extremely ahistorical picture of civil wars and so could never provide a comprehensive explanation of conflicts driven by a complex bundle of factors.

Though the quantitative models presented here have many shortcomings, the original greed and grievance model raised important questions about how wars are prolonged and highlighted the importance of shadow economies in funding conflict. They encouraged a renewed focus on the global economic context in which conflicts occur and the role of international actors in what can be erroneously depicted as localised or purely national conflicts. They also led to greater exploration of the role natural resources play in conflict, a re-evaluation of such notions as 'resource wars', and a proliferation of qualitative studies seeking to paint a more complex picture of the motives for rebellion and the relationships between political and economic explanations. Berdal and Malone's important edited collection (2000) provided particularly useful examples of the broadening of the debates around greed and grievance and the need for country contexts to be taken into account.

The analysis also pointed to a series of questions that could not be answered by using the national datasets themselves. Most conflicts in the developing world are not contained by formal state boundaries. Thus, whilst they can provide insight into the dynamics of rebellion, the greed versus grievance set of ideas cannot tell the whole story based on data gathered and collated at national level. For example, the diamond fields of the Mano region river basin in West Africa are present in Sierra Leone, Guinea and Liberia, but may play slightly different roles in each conflict. At the same time, many conflicts happen, or at least start off, in border regions which may be inaccessible or far away from state control; hence the rebels are able to cross such areas with the minimum of interference.

Overall, therefore, the theory is just that – a theory. It can provide insights and ask relevant questions about the nature and dynamics of conflict. In particular, it raises issues of economic motivations for combatants and starts to explain why people pick up arms and risk their lives in sometimes extremely dangerous conflicts.

Resource wars and environmental explanations

The notion of a resource wars has become increasingly popular since the 1990s, and it belongs within a wider discussion of what are frequently known as 'environmental conflicts'. Reflecting the work of Thomas Malthus in the eighteenth century, theorists have argued that the world has a limited 'carrying capacity', or a threshold number of people which existing resources can sustainably accommodate. Specifically, Malthus argued that, although food production increases at an arithmetic rate, population increases geometrically, with a resulting higher population who must live on, if distributed equally, a smaller amount of food and other resources per head. This, in Malthusian analysis, is not sustainable, and he posited that famine, disease and death, especially through war, were amongst the key correcting mechanisms that stabilised the relationship between population and resources. The global population is estimated to have grown from 1.6 billion to 5.3 billion between 1890 and 1990, much of this having taken place in developing countries, leading some analysts to conclude that the world will increasingly face crises and conflicts generated by fast-growing populations competing for declining resources, along with associated issues of urbanisation, migration and reduced government capacity.

Resources here are defined more broadly than food and the agricultural land and freshwater needed to produce it, but this raises key questions: What is a resource? What makes a natural product – an ore, a mineral or a plant – valuable? Resource value is a relative concept. Diamonds and oil are frequently discussed as playing a role in causing or financing conflict, but they have no intrinsic value; they become valuable because of human processes. Fashion and industrial applications have led to a demand for the former, and the ways in which industrialised economies have developed, including their energy sources and transport systems, have increased demand for the latter. Resources are not all alike, and different characteristics have different implications for how they are used to finance, or how they can motivate, conflict. They can be categorised in various ways, as shown in Box 3.1.

Aside from the question of defining resources and accounting for their value, there is much critique of Malthusian theory as being too environmentally deterministic. Notable criticism emerged from what are known as 'technological optimists', who point out that, if a carrying capacity for the earth exists, then it is elastic rather than fixed and immutable, and thus is able to accommodate a growing population. Food production from the same geographical area of land can be increased exponentially through emerging agricultural technologies such as high yield seed varieties, as seen in the 'green revolutions' in countries as diverse as Mexico, India and Mauritius. Population growth is not, however, the only mechanism or process which advocates of the environmental conflict thesis believe will put pressure on the earth and lead to conflict.

Environmental conflict theory

The most well-known strand of the environmental conflict theory stems from the work of Thomas Homer-Dixon (1994). His argument starts from the premise that the world's renewable resources are becoming scarcer through three main processes: human activity reduces the amount or quality of a resource faster than that resource is renewed; population growth reduces the amount of resource available per person, as highlighted by Malthus; and, finally, changes in the ways resources are distributed in a given society can reinforce unequal access to available resources between groups.

Scarcity, like value, is a relative concept, and, whilst enough of a resource may exist in a given system, whether a society or the world, its distribution can create localised or even widespread scarcity for some and a sufficiency or relative surfeit for others. The processes Homer-Dixon identifies are all intrinsically bound up with the processes of development. Development strategies, which are recommended by donors and international financial institutions in return for aid to developing states, require the construction of particular types of economies. These strategies have led to increased demand for some resources, such as oil, which has in turn caused greater use of non-renewable resources, depleting total reserves. They have also encouraged developing states to import crops such as wheat or rice, having reduced production of indigenous food crops in order to produce cash crops for export. It seems from these strategies that economic growth requires changes in the balance between population and resources. Through processes such as intensive use of agricultural land, the burning of fossil fuels, and overfishing, resources are used and their quality depleted faster than they can be renewed by natural processes, causing scarcity.

Homer-Dixon further suggests that this scarcity has previously caused and will continue in the future to cause three types of intergroup conflicts:

- *scarcity conflicts*, where groups clash over access to resources that are vital to survival, such as land or water;
- *group identity conflicts*, linked to notions of 'tribal' or 'ethnic' conflict, whereby populations displaced by resource scarcity, and those with whom they come into contact, will have heightened awareness of their group identity and clash with other groups over who has rights to access resources; and
- *deprivation conflicts*, resulting from the widening gap between the haves and the have-nots; as the resources available diminish, those in power will use their influence to maintain their standard of living at the expense of others.

He uses examples ranging from Bangladesh to the Philippines to demonstrate how scarcities have caused disputes and violent conflict. However, conflict cannot be reduced to a simple resource–population model, despite the increasing interest in the arguments of Malthus and Homer-Dixon. As the latter freely admits, to understand why scarcities lead to conflict in some contexts but not in others requires an understanding of the ways in which resources are managed and distributed. The 'resource curse' thesis is an attempt to bring issues of environment and governance together in explaining the risk of violent conflict in a society with significant mineral wealth. It presents a 'double curse' of poor governance allied to irresponsible economic behaviour, closely related to corruption surrounding high value resources such as oil.

Based on the work of Richard Auty (1993), the resource curse also referred to an apparent paradox: those countries which had relatively high reserves of valuable mineral resources, and therefore economic means to develop, experienced lower levels of economic growth and less development, broadly defined. This initial observation has been supplemented over the last two decades with statistical modelling and databases attempting to explain the link between resource abundance and conflict (Collier and Bannon 2003: 3; Lujala *et al.*, 2005). There are also many country or region case studies, exploring links between resource abundance and conflict in countries such as Angola (Le Billon 2001; Frynas and Wood 2001) and Nigeria. Many of these case studies take the debates further, situating resources in political and social context. Le Billon's 'political ecology' approach (2001) is a key contribution, examining how resources are socially constructed and identifying what particular characteristics may lead a resource to support more easily a secessionist movement, a warlord enterprise, or a military coup. Whilst environmental factors such as resource abundance or scarcity may affect conflicts, they therefore do so in a contingent rather than a deterministic way, altering incentive structures for elites and citizens alike. As with other lenses for analysing conflict, environmental approaches thus require a consideration of other analytical perspectives, from intergroup dynamics to ethnographic approaches and resource construction, if they are to improve our understanding of why conflict occurs and how it is shaped.

Box 3.1 Some notable resource typologies

Renewable resources are those which are constantly being produced, specifically at a rate which is higher than that at which they are being used. Renewable resources can therefore replenish themselves as long as they are being utlised at a sustainable rate. Examples are fish stocks, timber and arable land. All can be exploited by humans at a rate which allows them to self-replenish.

Non-renewable resources are those which are not naturally replenished as rapidly as they are used up. This includes resources which are created over a long period of time, such as oil, natural gas and the ozone layer. As they are consumed faster than they are created, the total amount of these resources is depleted over time.

Point resources are those which are concentrated in a relatively small geographical area, often represented on a map as a point. Concentration in a small area can make such resources easier to capture and defend, for national governments or those opposing them, with a smaller number of fighters than those spread out over a large area. The most commonly cited example is kimberlite diamonds, but columbium tantalite (coltan) and gold are also highly valuable point resources which can be sourced with limited technology and transported with relative ease compared with resources such as offshore oil, which requires significant investment in infrastructure.

Diffuse resources are those spread out over a larger geographical area. To secure a diffuse resource takes more manpower than securing a point resource, and their extraction or exploitation may require more people and possibly more equipment. Examples are water resources and forests.

'New barbarism' and 'tribalism'

As discussed in the previous chapter, 'new barbarism' is most commonly associated with the work of Robert Kaplan (1994), but its assumptions are reflected in the work of other analysts. Samuel Huntington's important work *The Clash of Civilizations* (1996) contains echoes of Kaplan's argument and the premises upon which is it based. Strains of new barbarism thinking are also frequently observable in Northern media representations of conflict, particularly in sub-Saharan Africa. It is an approach which emphasises the importance of divisions within society, most often on tribal or ethnic lines, in understanding conflict. Developing societies are depicted as pre-modern, or traditional, and prone to violence in general and internecine violence in particular. Two particular quotes from Kaplan's 'The coming anarchy' (1994) illustrate this approach:

> In places where the Western Enlightenment has not penetrated and where there has always been mass poverty, people find liberation in violence.

Sierra Leone is a microcosm of what is occurring, albeit in a more tempered and gradual manner, throughout West Africa and much of the underdeveloped world: the withering away of central governments, the rise of tribal and regional domains, the unchecked spread of disease, and the growing pervasiveness of war. West Africa is reverting to the Africa of the Victorian atlas.

Kaplan argues that the new barbarism presents the international community with an uncomfortable realisation: Western civilisation will increasingly be confronted with conflicts that it cannot hope to prevent or even to understand. Furthermore, the dynamics associated with such conflicts present a direct challenge to the West, through processes such as the breakdown of weak states into numerous autonomous sub-regions governed by warlords, and the flow of refugees and economic migrants away from regions of deteriorating state control and limited security towards developed regions. Kaplan draws on the work of Malthus, as well as on environmental determinism, to argue that 'scarcity, crime, overpopulation, tribalism, and disease are rapidly destroying the social fabric of our planet'. This reflects the arguments of Homer-Dixon, discussed earlier, and the assumption that unemployed young men in particular represent a valuable pool for recruitment into rebel movements, criminal enterprise and shadow economies (see *Greed and grievance* above).

Underemployment and identity

Underdevelopment, and particularly underemployment, is therefore seen as a cause of conflict, but this raises a key question: what determines whether these conditions lead to rebellion and violent conflict? For Kaplan, an important factor is the development of exclusionary identities rooted in what are perhaps subjective but nevertheless longstanding differences between groups, especially tribes or ethnic groups (for the latter, see following section). The focus on tribalism as a driver of conflict and insecurity has been interpreted by Duffield, amongst others, as indicating that new barbarism implies a form of racism, or bio-cultural determinism. It suggests, perhaps implicitly, that civilisations or races found primarily in developing societies are characterised by primordial, innate and irrational cultural and ethnic identity.

The discussion of civil war in the previous chapter highlighted the innate and socially grounded logic which exists within even the most seemingly senseless violence, demonstrating that externally produced concepts of rationality/irrationality are not particularly useful in telling us about why conflict starts and explaining the forms that violence takes. Ethnographic approaches instead offer a way of situating violence in a social context and understanding why it may take forms which draw on cultural – including tribal – traditions and frames of reference. Similarly, political economy analysis of conflict draws attention to the need to understand opportunity and incentive structures within society as a way of framing what is labelled as 'tribal violence' and exploring how tribal identity is constructed in ways which reflect those opportunities and contexts.

Identities may be powerful, but they are not necessarily fixed. The composition of an individual's identity may reflect many sub-identities which are foregrounded or backgrounded in different social settings and circumstances. Similarly, identities such as tribe, ethnicity, race or gender can change over time. What it means to be a Hutu in Rwanda is very different in 2010, with a Tutsi-dominated party in power, than in the 1960s, when an explicitly Hutu movement won political power at independence. The implications of a particular identity and the emotions and characteristics associated with it can be considered its 'content' – what it means to be identified as, for example, a woman in Iran, a Tamil in Sri Lanka or a Christian in Iraq. Facets of identity can certainly affect an individual's chances of fulfilling their potential and to what extent they are excluded from or given access to opportunities for social, political and economic advancement. However, the term 'facets of' identity here is crucial; identities are multifaceted, and individuals can hold many identities at once without necessarily being in conflict with those holding other identities. Ethnicity is perhaps the form of identity in developing states which is most commonly articulated or explored as an explanation for conflict. It therefore deserves further attention.

Ethnicity

Much of the literature which attempted to identify and categorise different ethnic groups up to the twentieth century was based on ideas about physiognomy, suggesting that ethnic groups were physically different from each other and also that innate characteristics associated with particular groups could be identified. Since decolonisation, there has been a shift in focus away from what is now considered 'scientific racism', associated with the ideas above, which saw the development of hierarchies of race based on qualities such as an individual's physiognomy or skin colour. Race and ethnicity are now more commonly viewed as complex social constructs resulting from pressures within and outside social groups, rather than as the result of innate or essential physical and biological characteristics. This is not to say that ethnicity is any less powerful a form of identity, rather that it is label given to a set of beliefs, practices and characteristics which as a bundle create a specific cultural, racial or ethnic identity.

In developing states, ethnic identities were often highly politicised by colonial administrations which followed a policy of 'divide and rule', whereby some groups were favoured and given access to positions of greater political and economic power than others. The British, for example, tended to characterise different groups according to racial characteristics, treating some (the Hausa in West Africa, the Acholi in East Africa) as 'martial races', whereas others were considered as being naturally good at other sorts of activity. The favoured groups, such as the Buganda in Uganda, typically had greater access to opportunities in education and positions in the colonial administration, whilst the martial races were treated as sources of recruits for the military – a dichotomy that has continued well into the post-colonial period. In some cases the efforts of colonial administrations to count, register and categorise their populations led to the reification of ethnic identities, as people were encouraged or even forced to self-identify in terms of their ethnic group. Attitudes to race and ethnicity meant that these facets of identity had social and political implications. Rwanda provides a particularly stark illustration of this, with the manipulation and hardening of ethnic divisions by colonial powers playing a crucial role in enabling the 1994 genocide.

Ethnicity and conflict in Rwanda

Demographically, the Rwandan population comprises the majority Hutu, the Tutsi (18 per cent), and around 1 per cent Twa. Following the approach outlined above, Rwanda's Belgian colonial rulers identified Tutsi as racially superior to both the Hutu and the Twa. Tutsi were regarded as being stereotypically more 'Nilotic' in appearance and purportedly more intelligent. It was therefore under Belgian rule, via a Tutsi monarchy, that primarily socio-economic divisions between the three groups acquired greater political significance and became more entrenched. During this period a system of obligatory identity cards was introduced for all Rwandans, stating an individual's ethnic identity based on racial stereotyping and socio-economic status. Colonial rule also entrenched the idea of Hutu and Tutsi identities as monolithic and defined chiefly in relation (or opposition) to each other.

Tutsi were considered to be significantly superior to Hutu, based on physiology and intellect, receiving preferential access to employment and education. In contrast, Hutu were regarded as inferior and, to some degree, naturally subservient. The Twa were also marginalised as a 'pygmy group', defined as having less social status than Hutu. These identities were presented as inherently oppositional and homogeneous categories, and such representations informed propaganda by the immediate post-independence government. As independence from colonial rule became more imminent, these identities were further politicised and instrumentalised by Rwandan politicians seeking to enhance their own legitimacy as potential rulers. It became logical for Hutu politicians to promote an idea of 'Hutuness' which would enable them to challenge established Tutsi elites, whereas Tutsi politicians happily adopted colonial ideologies which identified them as inherently superior. Since 1994, acknowledging that narratives of 'essential difference' between Hutu and Tutsi made the genocide possible, many scholars and the current Rwandan government have rejected notions of Hutu and Tutsi as oppositional.

In thinking about the relationship between ethnicity and violence, there are perhaps two main poles to the debate, though many shades exist in between. The first argues that ethnicity is primordial, maybe even genetic, and therefore fundamental and persistent and stronger than loyalties to larger social units such as the state. The second suggests that ethnic identities are no more salient than any other kind of identity and become significant only when they are invoked by entrepreneurial political leaders and are linked to material gain for that group.

From the first perspective, ethnic violence can be considered natural or inevitable. This perspective sees ethnicity as a fixed and essentialised part of individual and group identity. It also considers ethnic identity to be defined in opposition to at least one specific 'other' group. Proponents of this view have argued that ethnic differences had been held in check during the Cold War, but that political liberalisation and pressures for democratisation since the late 1980s have caused an upsurge in conflict between groups over power and left ethnic groups seeking to protect their members from those who would try to dominate, destroy or disenfranchise them. The opposite approach sees ethnicity as a social category which is constructed by individuals and the structures and processes in which they engage. It depicts ethnicity as a label whose content – i.e., what it means to be of a particular ethnicity – can be altered. This allows difference to be viewed as a force for peace rather than as a cause of conflict. If the political, social and economic implications of being of a particular ethnicity can be changed, then that identity can be defined other than in terms of comparison with other ethnicities.

Both poles of the debate presented above suggest that what makes ethnicity an axis of identification for groups involved in conflict is the associations connected with an ethnic identity. This reflects the importance of horizontal inequalities in explaining and analysing conflict.

Structural and political violence

The data are extremely confusing in terms of providing a clear picture of the relationship between ethnicity and conflict. The structural violence thesis provides an explanation for this, based on seeing ethnicity as one factor within a broader set of issues that are part of social, economic and political structures. In this view, the mobilisation of Hutu along ethnic lines can also be seen as the culmination of a long-term structural issue whereby one particular sub-set of the population were systematically excluded from political and economic networks. The majority of these people were Hutu, and the violence at independence, whilst clearly ethnic, could also be interpreted as a rebellion of the disenfranchised against a ruling elite.

An even clearer example of this type of structural violence is provided by Sierra Leone and Liberia. Within this West African conflict, there were echoes of a class war based on the 'have-nots' rebelling against the 'haves'. The majority of those taking up arms were rural youth, usually male but also female, who had found themselves excluded from political and economic networks in terms of both isolation from urban areas and opportunities for work, education and opportunities to migrate, as well as being subject to the whims of a rural elite of chiefs who maintained a rule of old men against the young. A clear example of this was in the tradition of the chief controlling land and resources at a local level and thereby people's ability to get married. Should a young man wish to marry traditionally, he should obtain permission from the chief and also be able to provide land, but the only way of gaining land was through the chief. If the man had no means to pay, then the chief could extract payment through forced labour; as the periods of this labour grew ever longer, so the young became set against the traditional ruling elite. This was exacerbated by the diamond trade, as the chiefs also controlled access to diamond mines.

The structural nature of the war was shown by the pattern of the violence during the conflict. Once the rebels took over an urban centre, the first victim was invariably the paramount chief, followed by the district officer and all related signs of governance. In fact, the paramount chief was not usually killed immediately but, rather, humiliated. All government buildings and all government records were destroyed across the country. This paints a very clear picture of structural violence directed at those in power by those who felt excluded and who were very clearly rebelling against authority.

Structural and political violence as an approach to analysing conflict therefore requires us to consider the power relations between groups and any social patterns in inequality. This relates to the ideas of horizontal inequality. If members of a particular group, defined by a specific quality such as ethnicity, geographical location, religion or caste, are less able to fulfil their life potential than those of another, then structural violence may be a lens which can be usefully applied to understanding why violence occurs. Adding to this an ethnographic approach allows us to probe further and explore what kinds of violence are occurring, as well as what form it takes and what the characteristics of the victims tell us about the reasons for it.

Structural violence is not always as easy to identify as direct physical violence. This raises a key question: how can we identify if structural violence is occurring? Galtung (1969) suggests that one possible way would be to compare the average life expectancy of different groups, juxtaposing the 'real world' with a 'potential world'.

Samuel Huntington and structural violence

The structural violence idea, coupled with social and cultural factors, saw its zenith with the theories of international relations produced by Samuel Huntington. His seminal book *The Clash of Civilizations* (1996) aimed to try to understand the changes in international power that came after the Cold War. Kaplan had taken the view that his new barbarism thesis reflected the processes unleashed by the ending of the Cold War. The superpower balance of nuclear terror had kept the lid on most social conflicts, but once the Cold War ended endemic hostilities and 'ancient hatreds' reasserted themselves, particularly in Africa and the Balkans. It implied a non-interventionist stance at the international level. If wars are the result of ancient hatreds, then international intervention cannot stop them.

The question therefore becomes how to understand these patterns and how the international community could attempt to deal with unacceptable levels of conflict. It implies that culture is important, and that ethnic mobilisation involves cultural approaches to international relations but provides no real answers.

Huntington provides a partial answer to this issue by taking cultures or 'civilisations' as the key building block of international relations. He developed the idea of 'cultural blocs' based on a variety of factors, including ethnicity, but primarily religion. Although his book focuses on several different civilisations, it is clear that Huntington's main concern was the purported clash between Christianity and Islam. He divided the world into a number of separate civilisations:

1   Western Christianity (Europe, the United States, Australia, New Zealand);
2   Islamic (Middle East, North Africa, South East Asia);
3   Orthodox (Russian and Greek);
4   Latin America (Catholicism and corporatism);
5   Sinic/Confucian (China, Vietnam, Korea);
6   Japanese;
7   Hindu;
8   Buddhist (Sri Lanka, Burma, Thailand, Laos, Cambodia);
9   Sub-Saharan Africa.

For Huntington, 'civilisation' is culture writ large: 'It is defined both by common objective elements, such as language, history, religion, customs, institutions, and by the self-identification of people' (1996: 41). Culture matters in that cultural values in contemporary society are path dependent on history. Of the main cultural factors involved, religion is the central defining element, although Huntington does distinguish between religious sub-regions, particularly Catholicism in Europe and Latin America. At the same time, there is a sharp cultural difference between core political values in countries sharing a Christian heritage and the rest – particularly Islam. In addition, some of the sub-divisions are somewhat false, given that three of the main ones are all Christian. However, in the West, the relationships between religion and secular authority have implications for other relationships, including those between the rule of law, social pluralism and democracy. Whilst the West does not have a monopoly in each of these areas, it is the linkages between them that create a particular 'way of doing things'. The core of Huntington's claim remains a conflict between Western representative democracy and its rival in Islam. He argues that these important and longstanding differences will lead to an ethnoreligious conflict between states.

The solution to this issue, according to Huntington, is not direct action or intervention. In essence, he proposes a new 'Cold War', with Islamic countries as the opposition. The way to counteract this cultural conflict is for the West to develop Cold War-style intelligence networks and militaries to address the Islamic threat. Huntington effectively proposes an 'us versus them' solution, whereby a Western, Christian order is maintained and works to develop disorder within Islamic rivals.

There are a number of issues with Huntington's thesis that mean that some of the conclusions should be treated with caution. First, the real situation on the ground has not developed as predicted. In particular, capital has not retreated into the Christian West and continues to expand globally. Whilst there may be clashes between Islam and Christianity, much of this has been perpetrated for particular political reasons and is not widespread in either sphere of influence.

Huntington and Kaplan's main contribution was to bring culture into the study of conflict, but they have underestimated the interaction between culture and capital – modernisation and class, for example. As countries modernise and become richer, culture changes, and what might be a logical stance in poverty is rarely the same when one is in employment. As Islamic countries have modernised, the development of pro-Western middle classes has meant that there is no clear political clash between states, even if there remains a group of actors who would deliberately encourage conflict between Islam and Christianity.

Huntington also makes the erroneous assumption that all Islamic countries are the same and can therefore be treated as a homogeneous bloc for political purposes. However, the diversity between, say, Iraq, Iran, Pakistan, Indonesia and the Sudan is marked. Not all Islamic 'civilisations' are the same. Huntington also fails adequately to discuss the relevance or importance of the Eastern grouping of religions – Confucianism, Buddhism, (presumably) Shinto and Hinduism. In terms of security this may be important, given the colonial history of India, for example, as a Hindu state, but one that exhibits many of the features of the British colonial tradition. This means it has more in common with some of the Christian countries, including antipathy towards Pakistan as an Islamic country.

In the end Huntington also ignores the continent that has the highest incidence of conflict in the world – Africa – and he doesn't really clarify if he thinks there is a distinct African civilisation, even if he implies it. The net result of this is that he manages to lump thousands of ancient cultures, ranging from those of Egypt to Lagos, Nairobi and Cape Town, into one undefined group.

Summary points

1   Greed versus grievance theory is an economic approach to conflict, in which individual actors and groups are motivated by trying to gain economically, usually by looting.
2   Looting and corruption rely on the availability of resources to plunder, and the resource curse thesis argues that competition over scarce resources generates conflict.
3   Structural violence is a useful approach to understanding power structures in societies that experience conflict. It can be applied to other sub-theories such as ethnicity or class.
4   The 'new barbarism' idea suggests that, once the Cold War ended, much of the world outside the liberal West was engulfed by 'ancient hatreds', leading to extremely violent conflict.
5   A link between barbarism, the Cold War and structural violence is provided by Samuel Huntington through his 'clash of civilisations' theory.

Discussion questions

1   What is the main contribution to the understanding of conflict of the greed versus grievance approach?
2   How far do natural resources play a role in starting or continuing conflicts?

3 What is structural violence and in what ways can political structures create the opportunity and motivation for violence?
4 In what ways does ethnicity play a role in violent conflict?
5 What are the implications for international intervention of the 'new barbarism' thesis?
6 What does the potential clash between a liberal, Christian West and the Islamic world mean for international approaches to conflict?

Further reading

Collier, Paul, and Hoeffler, Anke (2004) 'Greed and grievance in civil war', *Oxford Economic Papers*, 56(4): 563–95.

Goldstone, Jack (2002) 'Population and security: how demographic change can lead to violent conflict', *Journal of International Affairs*, 56(1): 3–21.

Homer-Dixon, Thomas F. (1994) 'Environmental scarcities and violent conflict: evidence from cases', *International Security*, 19(1): 5–40.

Huntington, Samuel P. (1996) *The Clash of Civilizations and the Remaking of World Order*. New York: Simon & Schuster.

Nathan, Laurie (2005) *'The Frightful Inadequacy of Most of the Statistics': A Critique of Collier and Hoeffler on Causes of Civil War*, Discussion paper no. 11. London School of Economics, Crisis States Research Centre.

Peluso, Nancy Lee, and Watts, Michael (eds) (2001) *Violent Environments*. New York: Cornell University Press.

Ross, Michael L. (2004) 'What do we know about natural resources and civil war?', *Journal of Peace Research*, 41(3): 337–56.

4 Refugees and internal displacement

This chapter considers the work of aid agencies and other actors with displaced populations, both internally within states and as refugees across borders. Using case studies from Central and West Africa and the Middle East, we will examine the reasons why people become displaced, demonstrating that refugees are a crucial aspect of conflict in the South, with particular implications for development strategies and local and regional security. Despite a frequently asserted 'neutrality', through their work with refugees and in conflict situations – discussed in the following chapter – humanitarian actors affect strategies of militias, peacekeepers and civilian authorities, and these links and effects will be further explored using case study evidence. The issues surrounding refugees and internally displaced persons (IDPs), and how to cope with them, are amongst the key challenges for development actors and those working in conflict-affected states. However, the factors that lead to individuals and/or whole communities becoming refugees, or to their displacement within their own state, are many and varied. To appreciate the complexity of the problems caused by refugee flows and displacement, and their impacts on conflict dynamics and processes of development and security, it is useful to explore some of the main causes of such phenomena and to identify where refugee and IDP populations are currently located.

Terminology: differences between refugees and IDPs

Refugees and IDPs differ in important ways, with implications for the responsibilities of the states and the international community under international law. A refugee is defined, under the UN Convention on the Status of Refugees (1951), as an individual who:

> owing to a well-founded fear of being persecuted for reasons of race, religion, nationality, membership of a particular social group or political opinion, is outside the country of his nationality, and is unable to, or owing to such fear, is unwilling to avail himself of the protection of that country.

This definition suggests some possible reasons for individuals becoming refugees, which will be examined further in the following section, but also highlights the defining features of refugees compared with IDPs. Refugees are recognised as those who have crossed an international border and are no longer under the legal protection of their home country. By crossing a border for one of the reasons outlined above, refugees are automatically covered by particular international treaties and are entitled to protection by agencies such as the Office of the UN High Commissioner for Refugees, UNHCR. Once they leave their home country and arrive in a host state, these displaced individuals can apply for asylum. Asylum is a process under which a determination is made of an individual's situation to decide whether they are classed as refugees under the terms of international law, with the rights and protections such a designation entails. However, in practice, given that refugee movements may be large scale and relatively rapid, such as the estimated 1 million Rwandans who fled into Zaire immediately following the 1994 genocide, an approach based on establishing individual circumstances is not always practical. In such cases, refugees are granted *prima facie* status, meaning that they are assumed to be eligible for the protection and assistance that comes with refugee status because they are part of a (usually large-scale) flow of refugees resulting from an identifiable crisis or set of circumstances (UNHCR 2001). Most designations of individuals as refugees by UNHCR is on this prima facie basis.

By contrast, IDPs are those who have fled from their homes but remain within their country of origin. The introduction to the *Guiding Principles on Internal Displacement* (UN OCHA 1998) define them as those:

> who have been forced or obliged to flee or to leave their homes or places of habitual residence, in particular as a result of or in order to avoid the effects of armed conflict, situations of generalized violence, violations of human rights or natural or human-made disasters, and who have not crossed an internationally recognized State border.

They are therefore considered legally under the protection of their home state, and national authorities are responsible for their protection and humanitarian assistance (ibid.: Principle 3.1). In practice, however, these populations are often fleeing from a state which is responsible, directly or through failures to provide protection, for their insecurity. The main IDP populations identified by UNHCR during 2008 were in Iraq, Sudan, the DRC, Somalia and Colombia (UNHCR 2008). IDPs are not granted refugee status as they have not crossed an international border; however, some of the approaches which have been developed to care for them, and the agencies involved in doing so, are similar to those available for refugees. The degree to which approaches are similar, such as the use of camps to house and provide services for displaced populations, depends largely on the geographical spread of the IDPs. Where they flee a particular disaster or outbreak of violence they may remain clustered in specific locations. However, it is also common for IDPs to become scattered across their home countries and to disappear into urban areas, where they can become difficult to monitor, to reach and to reintegrate into their home communities. This makes it all but impossible to know whether IDPs have integrated into new communities, and difficult to gather useful data on the composition of IDP groups (Internal Displacement Monitoring Centre 2009).

What are the causes of refugee flows and displacement?

There are many factors that result in people leaving their homes and their countries on a short- or long-term basis. These can be proximate or more long term, voluntary or forced. There are also push factors which mean people leave an area and pull factors that attract them to another place. There are, however, a few broad categories of triggers of displacement – conflict, natural disaster and persecution – which have particular implications for development and impacts on conflict dynamics.

Whilst the 1951 UN Convention does not explicitly mention fleeing from conflict as grounds for refugee status, the most cursory review of worldwide refugee populations suggests that conflict and insecurity are key factors in precipitating refugee flows. The UN *Guiding Principles* refer specifically to conflict as a push factor in internal displacement. As will be discussed below, the largest current refugee populations are from Iraq and Afghanistan, reflecting military interventions in 2003 and 2001 respectively and subsequent insecurity in those states. Large IDP populations in countries such as Sudan and the DRC likewise reflect ongoing insecurity in parts of those countries. Conflict can, however, be both a cause and a consequence of displacement. In some cases, such as that of Colombia (Muggah 2000), displacement can be used as a tactic by military forces and rebels to access resources, in this case land and coca-growing areas. Displacement can therefore play a role in the political economy of conflict, making the process difficult to prevent and beneficial for some of the actors involved.

Hurricanes, earthquakes, volcanic eruptions, tsunamis, drought and floods are amongst the natural phenomena[1] which can cause extreme devastation. Such devastation can occur in a very short period or over a longer timeframe, and the speed of change can determine whether people are able to adapt and move or whether they are forced to move at short notice. This timing and the nature of a natural disaster affect how prepared people are to move, the level and type of assistance they require from international and national agencies, and the possibility of return to their original locations. Any one of the processes listed above may lead to high levels of casualties, disruption to livelihoods and local coping mechanisms, and large-scale displacement within states and across borders. There may also be links between such natural disasters, displacement and the onset of civil war. Disasters can lead to a reduction in available national and natural resources, potentially causing competition between groups in society, and there is ample evidence of, usually short-term, breakdown in the rule of law in post-disaster environments (see Nel and Righarts 2008). The agencies which provide support and protection for large groups of refugees are often also called upon to help those displaced by such disasters, given their experience in rapid response and in the provision of shelter and immediate humanitarian aid to affected populations.

Refugees may also flee an area or country due to persecution on religious, racial, or ethnic grounds, or on the basis of political opinion.

Development may incorporate processes which can work to help the displaced, but it should also be remembered that development can be a cause of displacement. In particular, indigenous populations and poor communities who lack official ownership of their land, or whose use of it is not deemed productive, can be forcibly displaced by governments wishing to develop that land. Projects which cause displacement include the creation of national parks, development of infrastructure, and a desire to reorganise land tenure and use. For indigenous groups and the poor, difficulties in advocacy, along with social stigma and the perception of their being 'backward' or 'pre-modern', devalue their way of life and limit their potential for advocacy, resettlement and integration into new ways of life and areas. Frequently, where displacement in the

---

[1]There is a considerable debate as to whether some of these phenomena are caused simply by nature, or whether they are caused or exacerbated by human actions. These include the more abstract actions, such as the effects of industrialisation on climate and global warming which affects weather patterns, as well as more direct actions, such as the settlement of people on flood plains or in drought belts. The latter may result from individual location to these sites out of choice or necessity or from forcible resettlement and displacement.

name of development does take place, the compensation and resettlement schemes offered are inadequate and can lead to further impoverishment for those who have been displaced.

How many refugees and IDPs are there, and where are they?

The 2009 *World Refugee Survey* (USCRI 2009) estimated that, at the end of 2008, over 13.5 million individuals were refugees or seeking asylum outside their country of origin. Of that total almost half, around 6.3 million, were to be found in the Middle East and North Africa. Of these, around 1 million refugees were in Iran (primarily from Afghanistan) and the Gaza strip, and the largest single refugee population, of 1.7 million, was found in Syria. Over half of the refugees and asylum seekers in Syria were from Iraq, whilst another 450,000 Iraqi refugees were identified in Jordan. Other notable large refugee populations are over 3 million people from former Palestinian territories scattered across the Middle East and North Africa and 1.7 million Afghans in Pakistan. In Africa, the consequences of conflict and insecurity are clear in the presence of over a quarter of a million Somalis in Kenya, a similar number of Sudanese refugees in Chad, and 100,000 Zimbabweans in South Africa.

Internal displacement affects even more individuals, with the Internal Displacement Monitoring Centre (2009) estimating there were approximately 26 million IDPs worldwide in 2008. However, these numbers are extremely contested and it is difficult to get an accurate estimate. IDPs, as suggested above, may leave communities for short periods in response to specific triggers or localised insecurity and return relatively quickly once that threat has passed. Others may be displaced to and settle, for a fixed period or sometimes indefinitely, in neighbouring communities where they have extended family or ethnic kin. Ibeanu's analysis of internal displacement in Nigeria (1998) noted a range of factors that hamper attempts to get an accurate picture of internal displacement. First, governments may have an interest in downplaying the numbers of displaced. This may reflect an attempt to avoid international scrutiny of the causes of displacement and to prevent the state from appearing ineffective at dealing with its 'internal' affairs. Second, displaced populations may, as mentioned earlier, be absorbed into family or wider community networks. Local community-based organisations can also provide a level of material and social support for integration and in doing so encourage resettlement in new locations. Frequently lacking a focal point such as a refugee camp, and the levels of international attention and assistance which refugee crises typically generate, IDPs are, quite literally, a 'moving target' (1998: 93). They also often lack their own representative organisations and therefore the ability to act collectively to raise awareness of their displacement, their needs, and their strategies for return and reintegration, either at home or elsewhere. In the case of Colombia, Muggah (2000) also notes the lack of a universally accepted methodology for measuring displacement and the dynamism of displaced populations.

How have states and other agencies dealt with refugees?

Having established a range of causes of refugee flows and displacement, it is necessary to explore in more detail the systems and processes which have been set up to deal with these phenomena. In framing these responses it is also necessary to consider the legal and normative frameworks within which humanitarian actors working with displaced populations operate. These frameworks have developed considerably over time, and individual agencies have adopted their own approaches and codes of conduct. Some of the most well-known and widely adopted frameworks, principles and legislation are listed below.

Refugees and the stateless

The UN Convention on the Status of Refugees and Stateless Persons[2] was originally intended to address the issue of displacement resulting from the Second World War, but it has come to form the bedrock on which subsequent law and frameworks have been built. It was adopted in July 1951 and set out minimum standards for the treatment of refugees. In particular it details rights and recommendations in a range of areas: travel and movement of refugees; the need to maintain the integrity of families; meeting the welfare needs of refugees; and the need for international co-operation to fulfil obligations to refugees in terms of resettlement and asylum. It also established the right of refugees to work, form associations, access education and basic services, and practise their religion. Importantly, it provided a definition of who would be considered a refugee – someone whose reasons for displacement occurred before 1951 and who:

> owing to wellfounded fear of being persecuted for reasons of race, religion, nationality, membership of a particular social group or political opinion, is outside the country of his nationality and is unable or, owing to such fear, is unwilling to avail himself of the protection of that country; or who, not having a nationality and being outside the country of his former habitual residence as a result of such events, is unable or, owing to such fear, is unwilling to return to it.

The Convention would not, however, apply to those who had committed a war crime, a crime against humanity or a 'serious non-political' crime outside their country of refuge. Nor does it apply to serving soldiers. Illegal entry to a country was not considered a reason to discount an application for refugee status or asylum. Finally, the Convention sets out Article 33, the principle known as non-refoulement, under which 'No Contracting State shall expel or return ['*refouler*'] a refugee in any manner whatsoever to the frontiers of territories where his life or freedom would be threatened on account of his race, religion, nationality, membership of a particular social group or political opinion.' This enshrines a duty on states which are party to the Convention to provide the rights and assistance set out in its articles. The Convention on the Status of Refugees and Stateless Persons was limited by its focus only on pre-1951 refugees. As new situations causing refugee populations continued to occur after this date, an additional protocol was adopted by the UN in 1967, the Protocol relating to the Status of Refugees. This removed the date restriction and also the focus on refugees resulting primarily from events in Europe, giving a broader geographical and temporal scope to the international legal framework. By 2008, 147 states were party to the Convention, the Protocol, or both.

 The Convention and its Protocol provide a foundation for refugee protection, but alone form general guidelines rather than advancing practical recommendations for how states should deal with displacement. Recognising that displacement is an enduring feature of the international system, and that it is possible to identify guiding principles and best practice

---

[2]This is sometimes referred to as the Geneva Convention, reflecting where it was signed, though this is to be distinguished from the Geneva Conventions which deal with conduct of armed conflict.

based on prior experience, the Office of the UN High Commission for Refugees in 2000 organised global consultations on international protection, resulting in 2001 in the production of the *Agenda for Protection*. This included a declaration reaffirming the importance of both the Convention and the Protocol and committed signatories to a Plan of Action covering six areas:

> strengthening implementation of the *1951 Convention* and its *1967 Protocol*; protecting refugees within broader migration movements; sharing burdens and responsibilities more equitably and building capacities to receive and protect refugees; addressing security-related concerns more effectively; redoubling the search for durable solutions for refugees; and meeting the protection needs of refugee women and children.
>
> (UNHCR 2003a: 11)

This document represents an attempt to find ways forward on some of the key challenges that face states, international organisations and non-governmental agencies in dealing with refugees and providing for the protection of their rights and welfare. It acknowledges that refugees do not move as a coherent block separate from other forms of migrants, and that there are significant challenges in developing effective and economically sustainable systems for answering such key questions as

- who is a refugee;
- who is an economic migrant; and
- who is entitled to asylum (see *Displacement and security* below).

This is made more difficult by the overlaps between routes used and intermediaries involved in human trafficking and those used by refugees seeking protection or asylum outside their home country. The focus on security issues is also of particular interest for those concerned with the links between displacement, vulnerability, crime and insecurity, which cross borders and even continents.

Finally, given the primary focus on refugees in the documents above, it is worth mentioning again the *Guiding Principles on Internal Displacement*, established by the UN Office for the Coordination of Humanitarian Affairs (UN OCHA) in 1998. The growth in numbers during the 1990s of those recognised as internally displaced, who were not afforded the international protection, rights or legal status of refugees because they had not crossed a border, raised concerns about the lack of established guidelines for dealing with such populations. The principles created in response to this concern are similar in some ways to the frameworks governing rights and treatment of refugees. Among the thirty principles, however, is a reaffirmation of the responsibility of the national government to provide protection and humanitarian assistance to IDPs. There is also a recommendation that steps be taken to prevent arbitrary displacement, including that caused by armed conflict, attempts at ethnic or religious segregation, natural disasters and large-scale development projects. The *Guiding Principles* do, however, recognise that displacement in these circumstances may sometimes be necessary for reasons of protection, security or national development. They are essentially an attempt to ensure that those who are displaced have their basic rights protected and their essential needs provided for, whilst advocating against actions and policies which cause displacement. They further highlight the need to protect IDPs before they are displaced, during the displacement process, and in the process of return, reintegration or resettlement, as appropriate.

Institutionalising protection

The use of refugee and IDP camps

Once populations have become displaced, whether within or across international borders, it becomes necessary for the actors involved to develop systems for dealing with them which recognise at least the minimum rights and responsibilities laid out in the above documents. Temporary camps, particularly in dealing with refugees, have been regarded as amongst the most effective ways of administering displaced populations. This may be in the case of short-term emergencies, where existing host country facilities for refugees may be overwhelmed, or in longer-term protracted situations, where refugees are unable to return home and, for a variety of reasons, are unable or unwilling to settle in their host state or resettle in a third country (see *Solutions to displacement* below).

Refugee camps are usually set up by an international agency such as UNHCR or by NGOs in response to movement of a population across a border. They provide a focal point for gathering refugees, ideally allowing them to be counted and assessed on arrival. They also provide a central location for delivery and distribution of humanitarian aid and, depending on the length of time of displacement, for the establishment of basic services such as clinics, employment programmes and schools. Camps represent a pragmatic response to the needs of both refugees and host countries, which often lack the resources and capacity to deal with large influxes of people. UNHCR estimates that 80 per cent of the world's refugees are living in developing countries, by definition those who will face particular difficulties in establishing systems to deal with them on a long- or short-term basis. For example, tens of thousands of new refugees continue to arrive in Chad every year fleeing conflict and insecurity elsewhere in Africa. Chad is ranked 175th on the UNDP *Human Development Index* and is currently host to the sixth largest refugee population globally, with 330,000 refugees out of a total population of around 10 million.

Given the difficulties faced by host countries in meeting their obligations to refugees, international agencies have developed systems to respond rapidly to crises, and camps are an important part of this approach. One particular concern, as set out in the Convention, the Protocol and other guidance on displaced populations, is security. Security is ostensibly the responsibility of the host state in which the camp is established, but again the resources and type of armed forces required to secure a camp are considerable. Refugee camps may provide a way to target assistance to refugees, but they also provide a ready target for those seeking recruits for militias and rebel groups, and the resources they attract are similarly sought after (see *Displacement and Security* below). Disease is also a pressing concern, particularly in the early stages of establishing camps, when those displaced may have had to travel difficult journeys to reach them, often having fled with limited possessions and provisions. Once they reach the camps, emergency relief, potable water and sanitation may not yet be available or adequate for the numbers arriving. One study of the public health implications of refugee situations (Toole and Waldman 1997) estimated that up to 9 per cent of Rwandan refugees who fled into Zaire during the 1994 genocide died within a month of arrival. It also highlights the particular vulnerability of young children in camps for the internally displaced, as well as those who cross borders, citing the deaths of 75 per cent of all displaced Somali children under the age of five at one camp in the space of six months (1997: 289). Similarly, the cholera outbreak in refugee camps in Goma, eastern Zaire, in 1994 is an frequently cited example of the considerable number of deaths which can be caused by a water-borne disease present in a camp that is densely populated with undernourished and vulnerable refugees.

The issue of who pays for the camps, emergency relief and longer-term assistance is also contentious. UNHCR receives some funding from the UN but relies on donor states and private sources for its recurrent expenditure, along with regular public appeals for emergencies. In 2008, the top twenty countries contributing to UNHCR and UNRWA, measured in the total amount donated, were the United States, the European Commission, Sweden, Japan, the Netherlands, Norway, the United Kingdom, Denmark, Canada, Germany, Italy, Spain, Australia, Switzerland, France, Finland, Ireland, Belgium, Luxembourg and Austria.[3]

Camps have been criticised as a form of 'warehousing' of refugees, especially in cases where host countries have been unable or unwilling to guarantee some of the rights enshrined in international law. For example, where refugees are unable to work and, sometimes because of security concerns, unable to freely travel to and from camps, the camp population can become dependent on humanitarian aid and assistance. This chimes with the UN definition of protracted refugee situations:

> A protracted refugee situation is one where, over time, there have been considerable changes in refugees' needs, which neither UNHCR nor the host country have been able to address in a meaningful manner, thus leaving refugees in a state of material dependency and often without adequate access to basic rights (e.g. employment, freedom of movement and education) even after many years spent in the host country.[4]

The capacity of refugee populations to work, move freely, access credit, and own or lease property may be difficult for host states to provide, particularly where their governance structures and resources to facilitate these processes for their own citizens are limited. However, they are crucial in ensuring refugees do not lose their livelihoods and the means to support themselves and their families. As one report from UNHCR attests, 'If it is true that camps save lives in the emergency phase, it is also true that, as the years go by, they progressively waste these same lives' (2004: 3).

Urban refugees

UNHCR reported in 2009 that over half of the refugees covered by its mandate now live in cities rather than in refugee camps. This reflects a larger process of urbanisation, especially in the developing world. Whilst delivering the rights and protection ascribed to refugees under international law in the context of a city may be more difficult, it is still the legal responsibility of host countries and agencies such as UNHCR. Cities may be seen as relatively attractive options by those who have been displaced, whether within or across borders, as they present potential opportunities for work and avoid the isolation of refugee camps, which are frequently located in inhospitable border regions and away from urban centres. However, displaced individuals may lack the permissions needed to engage in formal employment and end up in the informal sector, working for relatively low pay and vulnerable to exploitation. Where the geographical spread of refugees and displaced people in cities is considerable, it is difficult for agencies to identify and support them effectively.

[3]Top 20 contributors 2008: www.refugees.org/FTP/WRS09PDFS/Contributions.pdf.
[4]UNHCR Global Consultations on International Protection, 4th meeting, 'Local integration,' EC/GC/02/6, 25 April 2002 (Global Consultations 2002), p. 1, n. 2; cited in Smith (2004).

Those who are not registered as refugees may also fear deportation, further reinforcing their unwillingness to identify themselves to agencies working with the displaced.

Where displaced groups cluster together in neighbourhoods defined by ethnicity, nation or religion, as for example have Iraqi refugees in Syrian and Jordanian cities, this can cause friction with local populations (see *Displacement and security* below). To encourage greater focus on the specific problems of the displaced in urban settings, in 2009 UNHCR issued a Policy on Refugee Protection and Solutions in Urban Areas. This acknowledged that, whereas urban refugees historically were primarily young men, adopting particular survival strategies, the rising proportion of women, young children and the elderly changes this dynamic and reaffirms the need for assistance to target displaced populations in urban settings. Regardless of age and gender, these groups are vulnerable to harassment and detention by state security forces, to criminal violence, and to exploitation or deportation on account of their illegal or unclear status. Whilst some of these threats are undoubtedly also a feature of life in refugee camps, in an urban context the element of protection is often sorely lacking.

Solutions to displacement

There are three recognised 'durable solutions' to displacement of people across borders (UNHCR 2003b). The first, often argued as most desirable, is voluntary repatriation to the country of origin. Repatriation can be spontaneous, when refugees decide themselves to return, or be through organised programmes, encouraged and incentivised by home countries, NGOs and international agencies. These will also be required to provide some degree of support for reintegration and the resolution of barriers to return, such as disputes over property which has been damaged or occupied since refugees left. The second, local integration, is the process by which a refugee is integrated into the host country, eventually acquiring citizenship and therefore no longer being a refugee. This is a difficult end to achieve because of the relative poverty of many countries in which refugee camps are located, the size of some of the refugee groups concerned, and particularly in cases of conflict-induced displacement. In practice, some refugee populations may self-settle without acquiring the status of citizens, especially where the host community is one with which the refugees have historical or ethnic ties. Bakewell's study of Angolan refugees in Zambia (2000) demonstrates the need to view refugee flows in historical context, showing that self-settlement need not disrupt host communities and can, in particular circumstances, be welcomed.

The final option, resettlement, allows for refugees to be relocated to a third country, neither their home country nor the host to which they fled. The resettlement programme is intended in part to facilitate burden sharing, assuring that the country of first asylum, which is often the poor neighbouring country of a similarly poor state, is not expected to shoulder the burden of protection and support alone. The ten countries currently accepting the highest numbers of refugees through the resettlement programme are the United States, Australia, Canada, Sweden, Norway, New Zealand, Finland, Denmark, the Netherlands and the United Kingdom. However, this accounts for a relatively small proportion of the total refugee population worldwide.

As acknowledged earlier, some situations are now classed as protracted, meaning that individuals are living outside their country of origin as refugees, often in camps, for over five years. In such a context: 'Their lives may not be at risk, but their basic rights and essential economic, social and psychological needs remain unfulfilled after years in exile. A refugee in this situation is often unable to break free from enforced reliance on external assistance' (UNHCR 2004). Some of the refugees in these situations may be relatively integrated into their host state – not citizens but not entirely reliant on international support either. However, of thirty-eight protracted situations at the end of 2003, UNHCR estimated that in only six was there sufficient integration for refugees not to require economic assistance. The most frequently cited case is that of the Palestinian population, a group of 4.7 million refugees scattered across the Middle East with its own dedicated UN agency – the UN Relief and Works Agency for Palestine Refugees in the Near East (UNRWA). For UNRWA's purposes, their mandate covers anyone whose

> normal place of residence was Palestine during the period 1 June 1946 to 15 May 1948 and who lost both home and means of livelihood as a result of the 1948 conflict' ... 'Palestine refugees are persons who fulfil the above definition and descendants of fathers fulfilling the definition.
>
> (UNRWA 2010)

Given this definition, it is possible for children to be born and to live out their lives as refugees, with little prospect of the kinds of durable solution outlined above.

Bearing in mind the discussion in this chapter of what causes displacement, the strategies adopted for dealing with displaced populations and the challenges to finding durable solutions, particularly in protracted situations, we turn now to address specifically the security challenges posed by displacement. Refugees, IDPs and diasporas arguably pose security threats in their home and host countries and potentially beyond. They also face significant security threats, whether in camps or cities or after resettlement. The following sections will explore some of these dynamics to elaborate the security dimensions of displacement, and the chapter will conclude by drawing together implications for development.

Displacement and security

The difficulties described above in registering, administering and policing refugee and displaced populations, whether in camps or otherwise, make them vulnerable to a variety of threats to their physical security, health and well-being. They are also sometimes regarded, either through their actions or as a result of the kinds of systems which develop to facilitate their displaced existence, as a potential source of insecurity for home states, for host states and, more broadly, on a regional and international level. The following sections outline some of the main threats to the security of the displaced, the ways displacement can be argued to cause insecurity more generally, and some of the responses that have been adopted by a range of actors to deal with these concerns.

Threats to security of displaced people

Many of the threats to be discussed in this section are exacerbated by the particular characteristics of the displaced, which deserve brief consideration. By the very fact of their displacement, whether the process has occurred rapidly or over decades, these populations are inherently vulnerable. They may have limited resources, be travelling only with what they can carry, and often involve large proportions of the very old, the very young, women and indigenous groups.

Muggah's work on displacement in Colombia (2000) supports this contention, highlighting the relatively high proportion of women and youth amongst displaced populations. In 1999, he estimated that 70 per cent of those displaced in Colombia were under nineteen years of age and over 58 per cent of all the displaced were women. Though there are inevitable concerns about the validity of these statistics, given the difficulties in monitoring and registering displaced populations discussed earlier, the prevalence of young people and women broadly reflects findings from agencies working in refugee camps, where a concentrated population allows for more reliable statistics.

Displacement also affects women and men in different ways and children again potentially differently. Meertens's work on Colombia (2010) suggests that the more restricted social worlds in which women often operate – focused on local area, community and family networks – particularly in developing countries, make displacement especially disruptive to their social bonds and their sense of identity. The security threats to the displaced mentioned below therefore act as a guide, but it is important to remember that they can impact differently on different groups.

Displaced populations often find it difficult or impossible to access adequate medical facilities, as those in the area to which they are displaced may be designed to cater for a much smaller population and be subsequently understaffed, underfunded and overwhelmed. Disease and conditions such as malnutrition can become commonplace in such conditions and spread quickly in overcrowded camps with limited sanitation. As discussed in the examples of Zaire and Somalia above, poor health and disease can affect the very young and old disproportionately in such circumstances.

Refugee camps are often poorly policed, leaving women and young girls in particular vulnerable to sexual and gender-based violence. UNHCR Guidelines on the prevention of sexual and gender based violence drawn up in 1995 identify some of the main causes, and suggest that:

> Perpetrators of sexual violence are often motivated by a desire for power and domination. Given these motivating forces, rape is common in situations of armed conflict and internal strife. An act of forced sexual behaviour can be life-threatening. Like other forms of torture, it is often meant to hurt, control and humiliate, violating a person's innermost physical and mental integrity.
>
> (UNHCR 1995: 4)

They also highlight the escalation of domestic violence and abuse committed within families as a result of the pressures associated with displacement such as living in closed camps. Refugees are vulnerable during their displacement and continue to be so after arriving in their new location. There are documented cases of women and girls forced to grant sexual services to other refugees, individuals in positions of authority in camps or the host area, and even UN peacekeepers to attempt to ensure their safety and to access food and other basic necessities (UNDP 2005).

A lack of security and inadequate policing, whether in refugee camps or in large urban areas, also leaves displaced populations vulnerable. Crimes may be committed against them by other displaced persons, including robbery, physical assault and sexual violence as outlined above. The limited amount of possessions which people are able to bring with them also means that being a victim of such crimes has a disproportionate impact on their means of survival and their ability to earn a living or to pay for lodgings and basic necessities. Being a victim of crime can lead to further impoverishment for individuals and families with already limited resources and enhance their dependency on charity and aid.

Displacement can lead to a breakdown in family life and community support structures. Oucho (1997) argues that it also has demographic implications, potentially resulting in separation of families and disruption of reproductive cycles. Forced displacement can, when targeting a specific group defined by race, ethnicity, clan or other identity group, be regarded as an act of ethnic cleansing. The separation of families and communities between and within camps disrupts existing coping mechanisms and support structures, leaving groups such as the elderly, orphans and the infirm especially vulnerable.

Where displacement is a result of conflict, armed factions will often try to infiltrate movements of refugees or IDPs, and the camps or areas in which they settle, to recruit new members to their forces. This recruitment may be forced, through kidnapping or other forms of coercion, by government and non-state forces. It may also be voluntary, though the question of how voluntary is debatable, given the often squalid conditions existing in refugee camps, the limited opportunities to earn a living and feed one's family, and the prevailing insecurity. Children are particularly vulnerable to forced recruitment, especially when separated from parents and family members during displacement. Analysing two periods of civil war in Liberia (1989–96 and 1999–2003), Achvarina and Reich (2006) demonstrate convincingly that the level of protection for IDPs was a significant factor in determining how many child soldiers were recruited. In the first civil war IDPs had the option of seeking protection in the capital, under some degree of control by West African peacekeeping forces (ECOMOG), or leaving the country. By contrast, during the second conflict, closed borders and a lack of protection from international forces left camps vulnerable. According to Achvarina and Reich, it is the ease of supply of child soldiers caused by poorly guarded camps which differentiates the levels of recruitment in the two conflicts.

Denial of rights to work/move

For the displaced, the state may also act as a crucial conduit through which assistance is distributed. If the displacement of a particular group results from the actions of the state, perhaps through neglect, underinvestment or failure to provide for the security of the uprooted population, the state's incentive to support this group in returning or reintegrating is potentially limited. Furthermore, as Ibeanu (1998: 96) argues in the case of Nigeria during the 1990s, a government may use its control over the distribution of humanitarian assistance to 'enhance its capacity to seek obedience from the populace, especially where those concerned have been displaced as a result of demands for the restructuring of the state'. Such threats to the security and well-being of displaced people are exacerbated by the challenges they face in making their voices heard and ensuring their rights are upheld. Displaced people may find it difficult to press host governments (or home governments in the case of IDPs) to ensure their rights under the relevant conventions and international guidelines. This is compounded by difficulties in organising to advocate for their rights, particularly in urban areas, where they may be relatively dispersed, lack focal points for coordinating their efforts, or fear identifying themselves to the local authorities.

Threats to the home state

Depending on factors such as the size of the group and the reasons for displacement, refugee populations in exile can pose a significant security threat to their home state. Perhaps the most infamous example is that of the Rwandan Hutu refugee camps in Zaire, which between 1994 and 1996 were heavily infiltrated by individuals who had taken part in the 1994 genocide against Tutsi and those Hutu who favoured power sharing between the groups. In one example from the Middle East, Palestinian refugees displaced following the 1948 war became trapped in refugee camps with little chance of return after the creation of Israel. Sarah Kenyon Lischer (2003) describes how it was from these refugee groups that organisations such as Fatah and the Palestinian Liberation Organisation emerged during the 1950s and 1960s, directing attacks against Israel and fuelling regional insecurity. These provide useful case studies of what are sometimes referred to as refugee warriors or refugee armies in exile (Zolberg *et al.*, 1986). For insurgent groups in particular, as Lischer argues: 'a displaced (and concentrated) population provides international legitimacy, a shield against attack, a pool of recruits, and valuable sources of food and medicine. In essence, refugee camps can function as rear bases for rebels who attack across the border' (2008: 99). A fuller explanation of the refugee crisis in Zaire serves to demonstrate how humanitarian operations during and after displacement exacerbated the security threat posed by the refugees and precipitated the subsequent wars in Central Africa.

The international community and the humanitarian organisations on the ground in Zaire proved unable and unwilling to separate refugees from militia. In their attempts to provide for the needs of the refugees within the camps, humanitarian organisations found themselves feeding and supporting an army in exile (Lischer 2003). Expressly against the UNHCR requirement that refugees must be civilian in character, the camps contained individuals who had organised and perpetrated the genocide in Rwanda. Many of these would face arrest and punishment if they returned to their homes, and the more radical amongst them were determined to return to Rwanda to finish the genocide. This Hutu opposition in exile objected fiercely to what they felt was a Tutsi-dominated post-genocide government. On arriving in the camps, political and militia leaders established structures which allowed them to dominate the camps and essentially hold the refugees as hostages. These individuals acted as conduits for humanitarian aid and its distribution, using their control over resources to militarise the refugees, supporting those who accepted their goals and neglecting those who did not.

The threat posed by the refugees to the new Rwandan state was clearly exacerbated by the aid provided by agencies and donors supporting the refugees. However, international operations intended to support and protect refugees had already sown the seeds of future confrontation through the actions of the UN-mandated and French-led Operation Turquoise. This was intended to establish a safe haven in the west of Rwanda, to protect refugees fleeing from those carrying out genocide or from revenge attacks by those trying to end the genocide. The failure to separate refugees from perpetrators and organisers of genocide during this operation allowed thousands such individuals to escape into Zaire and ultimately to take control of the refugee camps (see also Chapter 5, Humanitarian aid and conflict). In 1996, Rwanda invaded Zaire to repatriate those in the refugee camps by force. This allowed them to pursue and arrest or kill those who threatened Rwandan security and free refugees trapped in the camps, but it also resulted in a hard core of the militarised refugees retreating deeper into Zaire. Over a decade later, this group continues to cause insecurity within Zaire, now the DRC (see *Threats to the host state* below) and to present a threat in exile to Rwanda.

A second category of displaced people which has the potential to cause or fuel insecurity in their home state is diaspora groups. There is little agreement on a definition of diaspora, which may include refugees, exiles and their descendants, but, as Smith and Stares (2007) argue, they share one particular characteristic – a broad connection to a specific homeland. Diaspora groups have been identified in quantitative analyses of conflict as a statistically significant factor in predicting the outbreak of civil war (Collier and Hoeffler 2000). Refugees who have left their homeland as a result of conflict or persecution, or because of perceived injustices such as forced removal from their homes and land, can become a powerful force in influencing events in their original home state. The role of the ethnic Tamil Sri Lankan diaspora in financing the operations of the Liberation Tigers of Tamil Eelam (the so-called Tamil Tigers) is well documented (Wayland 2004). Similarly, the Palestinian diaspora has played an important role in sustaining both political and armed movements in Israel and the occupied territories (Sheffer 2007; Brynen 1990).

Threats to the host state

Thomas argues that people generally respond positively to refugees in initial stages, given their humanitarian plight. However, he continues:

> If there is not an immediate out-movement of refugees, signs of resistance begin among the indigenous. While these feelings may be stirred by the difference in cultural characteristics or fear of competition for jobs, the main question arises: who is going to maintain these people?
>
> (Thomas 1981: 22)

Refugees and IDPs can place considerable strain on local resources and services, including medical and educational services. This can be especially acute on account of the relatively high proportion of youth and elderly amongst displaced populations and the poor state of their health before, during and following displacement. The limitations of capacity and resources in many host states make international assistance vital in caring for refugees, but providing longer-term support in protracted crises inevitably creates a burden on local and national economies.

An influx of displaced people to a new area, within or across borders, can also result in the exacerbation of local intergroup tensions. The Rwandan refugee crisis discussed above, which took place primarily between 1994 and 1996, had long-term consequences for security and intergroup relations in the eastern DRC. Defining themselves by their opposition to Rwanda's Tutsi-led government, Hutu militia who left during the 1994 genocide and refugees who became militarised during their time in the camps have launched attacks on Congolese Tutsi. Local self-defence forces and warlord groups have subsequently been established, gaining support and allegedly even patronage from Rwanda in response to this threat. These warlords, notably Laurent Nkunda up to 2009, pose challenges to the DRC government by highlighting its inability to provide security for the Tutsi population. Where refugees share characteristics such as ethnicity, religion or other form of kinship with a local population in a host state, or where they define themselves in opposition to a locally relevant identity, their influx can therefore challenge existing intergroup dynamics and cause considerable physical insecurity.

Indeed, whether displaced across borders or within a state, groups which experience a lack of access to basic services or minimal physical security may turn to local warlords and militias. These can be defined by aspects of identity such as ethnicity or religion and may offer a degree of security, or even provide some of the services one might expect of a state – such as sanitation and delivery of humanitarian aid. In the case of Iraq, as Lischer (2008: 106) argues, supporters of Moqtada al-Sadr (Sadrists) follow 'the pattern set by Hezbollah in Lebanon and Hamas in Gaza ... [offering] social services and humanitarian aid to Shiite residents, as well as protection by militia members'. Such activities can allow the displaced to meet their basic needs but may also serve a strategic purpose for the provider. It can help to establish support for the group among the displaced, working as a recruitment tool for the groups providing the services. It can also provide groups who are distributing aid – whether provided by themselves or by humanitarian organisations – with a measure of legitimacy and raise their perceived status as power-brokers controlling access to the displaced and to resources.

Where displaced populations exist in urban settings, groups seeking a feeling of greater security and links to others from their homeland may set up their own communities or concentrate within particular areas or neighbourhoods. This may in turn reinforce divisions between the displaced and the 'indigenous' population, or between different groups within the indigenous population. In some cases it can lead to segregation of neighbourhoods. Reinforcing the ethnic or other identity-based character of a particular neighbourhood or area can be both a cause and a consequence of displacement. Again taking the example of Iraq, Lischer (2008) highlights the use of displacement as a tactic by militias attempting ethnic cleansing of the areas they control. This allows for the creation of greater group consciousness and militarisation, heightening fear and encouraging groups to think of themselves as requiring (self-)defence against 'others'. By encouraging refugees to think of themselves as a vulnerable target group, a perception often lent validity by inadequate international and national response to their situation, those seeking to use them for strategic purposes can also seek to exploit them as a reserve pool of potential recruits.

The difficulties of securing refugee camps from infiltration and forced recruitment have been discussed above, but it is also worth considering the opportunities for armed forces to recruit 'volunteers' from within camps and among IDP populations. These groups offer a potential avenue for refugees to support themselves through association with a fighting force. For male refugees this may entail fighting or taking an active part in operations; for women the roles could involve acting as a support mechanism for the fighter – cleaning, providing care, cooking, raising children or, in some circumstances, co-option into acting as a bush-wife to one or more fighters. Joining an armed group also offers refugees who are fleeing conflict a way of fighting against those whom they blame for displacement. On a more basic level, it may simply represent sa way of escaping the dependent existence within a refugee or IDP camp. As a UNHCR report attests: 'the frustration of being a refugee – of living in squalor and obscurity, and of feeling that injustice continues in one's homeland – can lead persons to commit dramatic actions that draw attention to a cause' (2004: 3).

Refugees and IDPs attract resources from states, NGOs and international agencies. Reflecting much of the analysis above, Lischer (2003: 82) identifies four main ways in which humanitarian aid in refugee crises can contribute to the emergence or exacerbation of conflict: 'refugee relief can feed militants; sustain and protect the militants supporters; contribute to the war economy; and provide legitimacy to the combatants.' The dangers of 'feeding a refugee army' have been discussed above in connection with Zaire, but other cases are also apparent, including alleged instances of civilian support for the Lord's Resistance Army in Uganda and the role of international agencies in supporting conflict in the Sudan.

Finally, on a regional and international scale, refugees are often moved using the same networks and agents involved in human trafficking, the smuggling of economic migrants, and the trafficking of illicit resources such as arms, drugs and conflict resources. These systems and processes benefit transnational criminal networks, considered a threat to states who may be neither exporters nor recipients of refugees.

Implications of displacement for development

The discussions above of the security challenges which often face displaced people begin to suggest some of the potential implications of displacement for development. Many of the challenges facing such people stem from their lack of certainty as to whether and for how long they will be staying in the same place. Families who consider themselves to be only temporarily displaced will find it difficult to invest in the areas they occupy. Whether through lack of resources or an unwillingness to commit to a new location in case they are again displaced, or are able to return home, there is limited possibility of, for example, building more permanent housing or planting crops. This means that many displaced people continue to live in inadequate housing long after their initial displacement, whether in temporary camps or in urban areas.

A lack of resources with which to improve their situation also has implications for the ability of refugees to pursue livelihoods in their new locations. Camps are often established in relatively harsh environments and away from population centres, a measure favoured by many host governments in order better to secure and control movements of the displaced and to avoid conflict between them and the host population. This, however, also has the effect of isolating some communities of displaced people, limiting both their access to basic services and their ability to find employment. A combination of the difficulty in ensuring their rights to work, and often facing discrimination and the impossibility of proving their qualifications and skills, many refugees end up in comparatively poorly paid, casual or temporary work. This again reduces their ability to invest in improving their lives and those of their families.

Displaced populations, particularly in the case of the urban internally displaced, are by their very nature mobile, and organisations which attempt to support them may find them difficult to reach. When the displaced are situated in camps it is somewhat easier to establish their needs and to attract funding and assistance for them. They may also face challenges in establishing new livelihoods, particularly if they have limited resources and, for the reasons outlined above, find it difficult to access loans or micro-finance schemes.

Summary points

1   One of the greatest costs of conflict is the enforced migration of the civilian population.
2   This is seen in international migration across borders, but also in internal displace-ment away from conflict-affected areas to areas regarded as safe – usually urban areas.
3   Forced migration of vulnerable people imposes huge costs on the receiving community, in basic service provision and emergency relief but also in social costs such as crime or disease.
4   The costs of migration are disproportionately felt by the most vulnerable, particularly women and children, who may be subject to domestic or systemic violence within camps.
5   There are significant costs in maintaining migratory populations, and international aid may support conflict actors, who might receive logistical support through migratory camps.

Discussion questions

1   What are the main definitions of migration caused by war? Why do they matter?
2   What are the main costs of migration to the communities forced to flee?
3   What kind of threats may then be faced by the population that takes up residence within an IDP camp?
4   In what ways does the international community intervene to support the population in these camps?
5   What are the main issues for the displaced population in relocating back to those areas they originally vacated?
6   In what ways has the international community tried to overcome these obstacles?

References and further reading

Achvarina, V., and Reich, S. (2006) 'No place to hide: refugees, displaced persons, and the recruitment of child soldiers', *International Security*, 31(1): 127–64.

Lischer, Sarah Kenyon (2003) 'Collateral damage', *International Security*, 28(1): 79–109.

Muggah, Robert (2000) 'Conflict-induced displacement and involuntary resettlement in Colombia: putting Cernea's IRLR model to the test', *Disasters*, 24(3): 198–216.

Oucho, John (1997) 'The ethnic factor in the internal displacement of populations in sub-Saharan Africa', *African Journal of Political Science*, 2(2): 104–17.

Smith, Merrill (ed.) (2004) *Warehousing Refugees: A Denial of Rights, a Waste of Humanity*. Arlington, VA: US Committee for Refugees and Immigrants.

Wayland, Sarah (2004) 'Ethnonationalist networks and transnational opportunities: the Sri Lankan Tamil diaspora', *Review of International Studies*, 30(3): 405–26.

Zolberg, Aristide, Suhrke, Astri, and Aguayo, Sergio (1986) 'International factors in the formation of refugee movements', *International Migration Review*, 20(2): 151–69.

5   Conflict and the role of development actors

This chapter looks at how development actors have attempted to adapt and redefine their roles in regions of conflict and insecurity in the developing world. It interrogates the 'do no harm' principle and looks at the role played by aid workers, NGOs, bilateral donors and international organisations in such regions. The chapter will draw on the work of scholars and practitioners. It will also consider the argument that development has become 'securitised', sketching out the process by which this has occurred and its consequences for development activities and policymaking. We will also recap the role external agencies play with IDPs, introduced in the preceding chapter, and how they affect conflict dynamics. This chapter focuses on the politics of development actors and how people 'doing development' operate in conflict and post-conflict areas. The following chapter deals with international peacekeeping, specifically, but this chapter looks primarily at those non-combat organisations operating in such areas.

What is development?

Development is a highly contested concept. Considering how often the term is used, there is surprisingly little agreement amongst theorists and practitioners as to what development is, how it can be measured, and how actors nominally outside developing states can help to make it happen. One way to explore the some of these questions is first to run through the origins of development aid. Following this, we will outline briefly some of the key paradigms or understandings that have been dominant since the Second World War of what development is and how it can be achieved. This section will form a background to the later discussions of how development actors, and to some extent humanitarian agencies, who often rely heavily on donor states for funding, operate in conflict-affected environments.

Development as we tend to think of it has its roots in the reconstruction of countries such as Germany and Japan after the Second World War. The US-led Marshall Plan envisioned reconstructing Europe and strengthening the region against communism by promoting stronger economic ties between states. This use of aid and technical assistance to alter countries' economies is seen as a forerunner of the development programmes that were later rolled out to countries leaving colonial rule, though with far fewer resources being transferred. Many such former colonies had received a measure of development assistance, often through the reorientation of their economies to produce materials required by the colonial power. A range of theories and approaches have been put forward to explain how countries are believed to develop. These prescribe particular changes in a developing state's economy, politics and society in order to create economic growth. As ideas about what development is and how it can be achieved underpin the actions of aid agencies working in conflict-affected and insecure environments, it is useful to consider briefly some of the key theories and approaches to understanding development.

Modernisation theory is closely associated with the work of Walt William Rostow and formed the most influential school of thought in development during the immediate post-war period. Based on the paths to development taken by already-developed states, particularly the United Kingdom, developing states were prescribed a series of reforms and expected to pass through stages similar to those experienced by the industrialised powers. It was believed that for countries to develop they needed to pass through particular stages in a linear fashion:

- *traditional society*, in which productivity is limited mainly to subsistence agriculture;
- *preconditions for take-off*, including an industrial revolution;
- *take-off*, incorporating investment in infrastructure;
- *the drive to maturity*, incorporating greater technology in production, the growth of new industries and consistent investment and, finally,
- *the age of high mass consumption*, regarded as the current status of the developed West or North.

The theory reflects the political context in which it was developed, designed to show how values associated with capitalism rather than socialism or communism were key to economic development. It also assumes that states which are to follow this path will be able to access the primary resources needed for industrial revolution. For states such as the United Kingdom, this stage was enabled by drawing on the resources of the empire, an option which is not open to today's developing countries. Modernisation theory has been criticised for its limited ability to take account of an increasingly globalised and interlinked world economy. Rigid linearity, the devaluing of 'traditional' aspects of culture, and the emphasis on capitalism and entrepreneurialism means it is no longer as fashionable as a theory. However, the notion endures that countries must develop through stages based on social, economic and political change and experience a shift in culture and values. Aspects of Rostow's vision continue to underpin some contemporary thinking about development.

A key counter-proposal to modernisation was dependency theory, often associated with the work of Dos Santos, which evolved partly out of a need to explain more clearly how the economic relationship between states affects their economic development. Dependency theory argued that the development of some states was being limited in order to allow others to develop. This was later further expanded and augmented by thinkers such as Immanuel Wallerstein in World-Systems Theory. Drawing on Marxist approaches, this suggested that the less developed states were effectively locked into a system which benefited rich states to the detriment of poorer ones. The natural resources of poorer countries in particular were viewed as key to the development enjoyed in rich states. Crucially, dependency theory and its associated concepts claimed that, contrary to the arguments of modernisation theory, the growing power and wealth of a small group of core states would not necessarily result in the enrichment and economic growth of those with which they had economic ties.

The failure of many developing countries to make significant progress, whether measured by economic growth, human development or the numbers of people living below the poverty line, encouraged a debate in the 1980s and early 1990s about how to improve and tailor development to meet individual countries' needs. Through reports such as *Sub-Saharan Africa:From Crisis to Sustainable Growth* (World Bank 1989), it became clear, however, that the limited development success in countries in Africa in particular was not considered to lie with the development policies and prescriptions of donors and international financial institutions. Instead policy failure was regarded as a consequence of the environments in which these policies were being implemented. If developing states had similar political systems and ways of practising political and economic power to those of developed states – especially those in Europe and North America – development aid would be more effective.

This has led to a greater focus on good governance and ways of exercising power which are based on the neo-liberal models favoured in many developed states. In particular, donor states and international financial institutions have emphasised the need for predictable, enforced and transparent rule of law to govern economic and other forms of activity in developing states. This helps to reassure private investors that the capital and funds they invest in developing states, for example in building up infrastructure or extractive industries, will not be seized by governments or local strongmen. It also allows outside investors, whether public donors or those in the private sector, to assess more easily risks to the success of their development interventions. Theoretically, in a society based on established and well-known rules and procedures there is less chance of projects being derailed by unforeseen events such as political unrest, a coup or financial collapse. The reality is much more uncertain, and even states regarded as highly economically developed can experience shocks and events: consider Japan during the 1990s or the dramatic collapse of the Argentine economy.

Notwithstanding such contrary examples, development has increasingly come to be regarded as a more holistic process than during the period following the Second World War and up to the 1980s. For economic development to take place, it is argued there must be political and social development. Again, this is not necessarily an accurate picture, and it depends very much what you understand by the term 'development'. The Asian Tiger economies have recorded impressive levels of growth, whilst their political systems have remained relatively undemocratic or stagnant. The rapid growth of China, certainly not a model of neo-liberalism in either its political or its economic development, also suggests there are alternatives to the so-called post-Washington Consensus, emphasising free markets, small government and privatisation. However, for those states relying on aid from Western developed states and international financial institutions, there has been an expectation that they will follow a trajectory which incorporates the values and systems loosely associated with liberalism – especially free markets and multiparty democracy, both underpinned by the rule of law.

This promotion of neo-liberalism as the basis for reform, development and good governance can be considered an overarching or 'macro' narrative of development. Within this there is discussion about how far countries should be able to interpret the idea of good governance more flexibly to suit their own histories, experiences and current conditions. There are also questions about how emergency and humanitarian aid to fragile and conflict-affected states can or should be incorporated into longer-term development objectives (see below). What is clear, however, is that the debate on how to 'do' development better and, in recent years particularly, how to ensure 'poverty reduction' is dynamic.

Since the turn of the millennium a number of new buzzwords have surfaced, among them 'partnership', 'ownership' and 'accountability', and these have particular resonance in situations where states may be weak and find the requirements for broadly neo-liberal reforms unsuitable, difficult or even impossible to meet. At a more micro-level, development activity has been shaped by an emphasis on co-ordination and harmonisation – trying to ensure donors work together (or at least not to duplicate or hamper each other's efforts). One broad attempt to encourage the prioritisation among donors of particular development goals, and encourage benchmarking through which states could demonstrate progress, is the Millennium

Development Goals (MDGs; see Box 5.1). Adopted in 2000, and intended to be completed by 2015, these tackle specific aspects of what can be considered social and human development, in line with the UNDP view of human development. This is closely related to ideas of human security and positive peace which, as discussed previously, emphasise an individual's ability to fulfil their potential and enjoy life without fear of violence of any kind. There is also an emphasis on human dignity and basic needs.

Box 5.1 The Millennium Development Goals

1   Eradicate extreme poverty and hunger
2   Achieve universal primary education
3   Promote gender equality and empower women
4   Reduce child mortality
5   Improve maternal health
6   Combat HIV/AIDS, malaria and other diseases
7   Ensure environmental sustainability
8   Develop a Global Partnership for Development

These goals are broken down into targets which can be measured by particular indicators. UNDP releases regular reports on the progress of developing countries towards these goals.

Development is therefore a multifaceted process, and the strategies adopted for achieving it have varied considerably over the past sixty years. The emphasis has, however, consistently been on economic change, with a more recent and growing focus on the political and socio-cultural environment in which such change occurs. This is particularly true of donors that form part of OECD's Development Assistance Committee (DAC), though it should be noted that other countries – notably China and to a lesser extent India – are becoming key donors and that their understandings of how development occurs, and the role they see their aid playing in this process, are less well understood.

Types of aid

Aid involves a range of different kinds of assistance offered to a developing country by another state or international organisation. Bilateral aid refers to aid given by one country to another, whilst multilateral aid is provided by an institution or organisation, such as the UN or World Bank, on behalf of a group of states. Aid can be in the form of cash, which may be used to fund a developing state's general budget in the same way as taxes. Depending on the donor and its relationship with the recipient, cash transfers may or may not be tied to a particular project or sector such as education or health. The general term 'aid' also covers technical assistance and debt relief, as reduction in a country's debt frees up funds it would have used in liabilities and interest payments to pay for other items. Aid comes in many forms and can be broken down in the ways above or, alternatively, into two different but closely related types: development aid and humanitarian aid.

The fact that aid is so often discussed in a general way, with little differentiation between humanitarian and development assistance, partly reflects the growing number of contexts in which humanitarian and development actors operate in the same space, even in the same sectors and working together. However, there are some differences between the idealised models of the two in terms of who provides the aid, for what purposes, through what systems, and with what conditions. There are also overlaps and similarities in terms of underlying assumptions about the relationship between aid and development, as will be discussed later in the chapter.

Humanitarian aid

Humanitarian aid is closely associated with complex emergencies. It is aid offered to alleviate the suffering of populations which have been displaced or otherwise affected by conflict or natural disaster such as drought or tsunami. It can be considered aid which is intended to prevent and alleviate human suffering (Hilhorst 2002). Whilst it is usually intended to be a short-term measure, in reality it can continue for decades, particularly in the case of protracted refugee situations, where those displaced may rely on aid to meet their basic needs – food, potable water, shelter and medical assistance.

The political impact of humanitarian aid has also changed. Barnett and Duvall (2005) argue that, historically, humanitarian action referred simply to impartial provision of relief to victims of man-made or natural disasters, but that it now encompasses much more. Where agencies must negotiate access to insecure spaces to provide relief, and where aid and relief have become bound up in the language of human rights, humanitarian aid is seen as part of a continuum from relief to development. The latter is intended to create states able to avoid or ameliorate the effects of disaster and conflict, though, as discussed in earlier chapters, the role of the state in conflict makes this assumption problematic.

The liberal underpinnings of changes in humanitarian aid and the perceived relationship between relief, development and the creation of liberal states and societies will be discussed further later in this chapter. It should also be acknowledged that humanitarian aid has been used by states for strategic purposes – Keen (2008) points to the example of provision of humanitarian aid to North Korea by the United States. This can be seen in altruistic terms but also forms part of broader United States policy to discourage North Korea's nuclear ambitions and to urge peaceful relations between North and South Korea.

Development aid

Development aid more commonly refers to assistance, financial or technical, that is given to encourage longer-term development. It is differentiated from short-term relief or humanitarian assistance, though in practice the organisations which give and administer both humanitarian and development aid may be closely linked, or indeed the same, and may operate in the same contexts. A full analysis of development aid is beyond the scope of this book, but a basic difference between humanitarian and development aid would be that the former would provide food aid in the immediate aftermath of a conflict whilst the latter would be involved in rebuilding the institutions that might prevent conflict happening again – a more long-term project.

Development aid is underpinned by particular understandings and assumptions about what development is and the kinds of economic changes, structures and political systems needed to make it happen. Some of these approaches are identified earlier in the chapter, and, when considering how different actors operate in conflict-affected environments, it is important to bear in mind the assumptions which underpin the aims and strategies of states and development agencies.

We will start with a focus on humanitarian aid because such actors have operated in conflict-affected and insecure environments longer than donors, and many of the approaches donors use are built on the principles (at least some) and lessons learned from humanitarian operations.

Developments in humanitarian aid

Humanitarian aid has become an extremely diverse field. Organisations of different sizes and with varying specialisms and capabilities are operating in increasingly insecure environments. They are also adopting different approaches to dilemmas such as whether and how to work with state-based military forces and non-state actors, such as warlords and militias. Some look to the military for protection, whilst others may be willing to negotiate with local militias for access to areas affected by conflict. They also vary in their approach to fundraising, with some relying on individuals and the private sector and others depending to a significant extent on government funding. This has potential implications for the level of independence an organisation can exercise in decision-making. Approaches to these key issues – of funding, access to affected populations and the organisation's own security – have therefore become possible axes of differentiation between organisations.

Dunantist and Wilsonian humanitarian agencies

Humanitarian organisations can roughly be split into following two particular paths, though some are not easily identifiable as belonging to one or the other. The first type of organisation can be broadly described as 'Dunantist'. Dunantist organisations are 'committed to neutrality, impartiality and independence', often refusing to accept funds from donor states for fear of compromising these principles or being seen as politically influenced (Stein 2005: 741). The name is taken from Henry Dunant, a Swiss activist whose experiences organising care for those wounded in battle led him to advocate for a neutral organisation to care for all those injured during conflict. He was a founding member, in 1863, of the International Committee of the Red Cross (ICRC). The principles of impartial assistance and the freedom of the agency or organisation from political interference in decision-making set Dunantist organisations apart from others. Examples often cited are the ICRC and Médecins Sans Frontières.

In contrast, Barnett and Duvall label a range of other large humanitarian agencies with which most of us will be familiar, including Oxfam, World Vision and Save the Children, as 'Wilsonian' organisations, identifying with US President Woodrow Wilson's vision of the possible transformation of 'political, cultural and economic structures so that they liberated individuals and produced peace and progress' (2005: 728). These organisations are often more closely engaged with politics, undertaking advocacy and campaigning particularly on issues of structural inequality and violence which leave individuals and communities at risk. They may, and often do, accept funding from states but act according to principles of neutrality in the sense that they argue the values they promote are universal – in line with human rights and development goals such as the MDGs.

The ability to be neutral in the provision of humanitarian aid relies on clear distinctions between combatants and non-combatants, military actors and civilians. These distinctions, as we saw in the earlier discussion of the features of conflict, are extremely blurred, with individuals moving in and out of ostensibly neat, often externally defined and politically loaded categories. At the same time, humanitarian organisations have a need to ensure their own survival and their ability to fulfil their particular goals. This requires access to affected populations and also funding. Accepting large amounts of funding from one particular donor can affect an organisation's perceived or actual neutrality. Furthermore, the fact that humanitarian organisations are working in the same spaces as donor states and military forces can lead to populations identifying them as affiliated with those who fund them and therefore part of a broader agenda. Barnett and Duvall (2005) recount the 2003 statement of a USAID administrator in Iraq, who told humanitarian NGOs that if they accepted US funds they must fly the US flag. This poses a dilemma for aid agencies and creates confusion for recipients of aid and other actors operating in the affected area, including those engaged in insurgency and fighting. Representatives from Médicins Sans Frontières, a staunchly Dunantist organisation which eschews government funding, have consistently argued that such branding of aid, and identification of NGOs as part of broader international military action, puts all aid workers at risk by blurring lines and bringing neutrality and the moral authority of NGOs into question.

Professionalisation of the humanitarian sector

The professionalisation of the humanitarian sector is a process which began in the 1980s. Over the past three decades, donors have increasingly sought evidence from aid agencies and recipient governments that their money is being well spent. They demand evidence of effectiveness and to be shown that their aid is used as it was intended – i.e., that it is not being wasted or diverted. Recipients of aid, whether governments, NGOs or humanitarian organisations, have therefore been obliged to develop procedures to allow donors to assess and evaluate their programmes, the way in which funds are used, and their effectiveness. This produces a requirement for transparency and also for ever more efficient aid distribution practices. As these processes have become a part of daily life for recipient governments and organisations, training has been developed to allow individuals to fulfil these requirements, and new specialisms have emerged within the humanitarian sector. Willingness and availability alone are no longer sufficient qualifications to work in the sector: increasing competition for roles and the rise of training and qualifications designed to produce specialists have made the humanitarian sector an industry in its own right. This is further reinforced by the development of codes of practice and standards which agencies adopt or sign up to in order to demonstrate their commitment to working effectively and, increasingly, in a way which at least does not worsen conflict and at best works to address its underlying causes (see *Humanitarian actors and conflict dynamics* below).

The professionalisation of the sector can be seen on the one hand as a welcome development, forcing agencies to ensure that they can give donors value for money, that they can justify their operations, and that they can demonstrate real impact. It also encourages agencies to adopt specialisms, emphasising their competitive advantage in particular sectors, such as education, food distribution or water provision, in order to compete with other agencies for available funding. The requirements placed by donors upon small agencies and organisations can prove costly in time and manpower, especially where they rely on local volunteers in relatively less developed countries. It can also lead to donors favouring larger agencies with established systems for writing funding requests, administering donations and fulfilling reporting requirements. Considering the growing sentiment that development should be recipient led, community based and flexible, especially in conflict-affected areas, as will be discussed in this chapter, the dominance of large professionalised humanitarian agencies can be regarded as something of a dilemma.

Humanitarian actors and conflict dynamics

Humanitarian aid is part of the context of conflict, and where it is given it will inevitably become a part of the political economy of conflict. It influences the decision-making of key actors in conflict and in post-conflict reconstruction, especially elite actors, who often direct or control economic resources and political power and may have a localised monopoly on the use of violence. These may be politicians, local militias, warlord-led groups, insurgencies, rebel movements or military forces whose command, control, organisation and discipline has broken down or been restructured in the context of conflict. Keen (2008) describes how some powerful actors in affected societies, often but not always reinforcing this power through violence or the threat of violence, pursue three sets of agendas in their diversion and manipulation of aid.

- The first set of agendas pursued by locally powerful groups reflects a desire to demonstrate a bond between these influential actors and a particular constituency and is manifest by an emphasis on the need to protect and prioritise resources for an 'indigenous' population. This requires the identification of a deserving population, for whom the group will ostensibly work to secure resources and which they will portray as being in competition with outsiders, often refugees or displaced groups.
- The second set of agendas is primarily economic. Examples abound of local politicians and powerful non-state actors confining populations to particular areas to which they control access and aid distribution – allowing them to appropriate some of the aid for their own purposes, often to sell or to support their armed factions and core followers.
- The third set highlights the salience of military agendas of locally powerful groups. These may be difficult to distinguish from the other two agendas, since defining a constituency may allow for higher levels of recruitment to military forces, and diverting aid to sell or manipulate local prices can fund war coffers.

Control over the distribution of aid also serves military objectives. If governments can prevent aid from reaching rebel populations or supporters of opposition movements, this can effectively work to starve them out, reducing war-fighting capability and sapping morale. As we saw in the previous chapter, by both controlling whether aid reaches refugee and displacement camps and then managing aid within the camps, groups can arm fighters and supporters, potentially perpetuating or facilitating conflict. The example of Rwandan refugees in Zaire is the most stark and frequently cited, but Afghan refugees in camps in Pakistan during the 1980s and since 2001 have also been similarly militarised.

Resource transfers

Looking at aid and conflict dynamics from another perspective, Mary Anderson (2001) identifies two broad ways in which aid affects conflict: resource transfers and implicit ethical messages. These overlap to some extent with those agendas outlined by Keen, above, but Anderson's discussion takes the perspective of an aid agency or worker on the ground trying to ascertain the many ways in which their actions can reinforce or worsen conflict dynamics. The two broad mechanisms are therefore a useful way of categorising aid's impact on conflict and potentially for conceptualising and designing strategies to minimise harmful impacts (see *Do no harm* below).

The political economy of conflict incorporates a range of possible sources of income and support for societies and those involved in directing or committing acts of violence. Aid is one aspect of this political economy, alongside natural resources, for example, and its importance varies from one conflict to another. However, the expectation that humanitarian crises will be tackled by the international community means that aid inevitably finds its way into the broad political economy of conflict. Anderson (2001) identifies five ways that aid can affect conflict.

1   Aid can be appropriated by fighters and used to support their activities. This is more likely where affected populations are concentrated in defined areas, perhaps in camps or by military operations or the physical terrain. This concentration does not, however, preclude mobility, as Keen (2008) suggests a fighting force can move a civilian population with it to act as a magnet for humanitarian aid, which can then be appropriated.

2   A second way resource transfers affect conflict is through the impact aid has on markets. As conflicts become protracted, the economy which had prevailed during peacetime breaks down and, for many, life becomes geared towards avoiding war-affected areas or finding some degree of paid employment in one of the sectors which continue to operate. The distortion of economies by war also encourages inflated prices for essential goods, and this can undermine local prices and damage livelihoods where agencies import goods.

3   A third impact is created by the distributional effects of aid. As discussed when we reviewed causes of violent conflict, inequalities between groups, perceived or actual, can be a powerful driver of conflict. Where aid agencies prioritise distribution to specific groups – such as those considered to be most in need or those in a particular geographical location –divisions and animosity between groups may be strengthened. Anderson (2001) refers to this as reinforcing intergroup dividers.

4   The fourth effect, substitution, refers to an issue of moral hazard: where agencies take responsibility for providing essential goods and services, responsibility is removed from powerful local actors, including governments, politicians and non-state actors such as warlords. At its extreme, this allows such actors to define their role and responsibility purely in terms of physical security. With aid agencies accountable for maintaining civilians, war-fighters are free to concentrate their resources purely on their own survival and objectives. Related to this, Duffield cites the example that providing transport and shelter for ethnically cleansed populations, forcibly displaced from their homes, facilitates and may even encourage the process of ethnic cleansing (2001: 90–91).

5   Finally, Anderson (2001) identifies legitimisation as a key effect of aid. The fact that aid agencies need access to affected populations means that they must negotiate with local political actors and strongmen. The very act of negotiating, recognising them as power-brokers in that arena, affords a measure of legitimacy to those actors and the opportunity to bargain. The latter can impose taxes and tariffs on aid in return for allowing access or dictate schedules on agencies for delivery, reinforcing and emphasising their power over affected populations. This effect of resource transfer is closely related to the second group of effects, implicit ethical messages.

Implicit ethical messages

The implicit messages Anderson (2001) identifies go to the heart of aid agency dilemmas of how to reach populations in need, how to protect themselves and their resources, and how to conduct themselves in insecure environments. Of these, the use of armed guards in protecting agency staff and resources is seen as particularly damaging, suggesting that militarisation is acceptable. The evacuation of international staff during times of crisis, when local staff are often left behind, also sends out a signal that some lives are more important and worth saving than others. When aid workers are observed using agency resources such as vehicles to facilitate their own rest and relaxation, however necessary such respite may be, there is an impression of advantage-taking which mirrors that of those involved in the conflict.

Anderson (2001) lists other messages, but the overall point to take from this is that the ways aid agencies and aid workers act can seem to have parallels with the attitudes of those perpetuating the crisis. There is a need, therefore, to consider not only what may be the most obvious strategies for the aid agency and workers in, for example, securing themselves and dealing with local power-brokers and strongmen but also the impact their approach may have in the wider context of the conflict.

It is, however, possible for humanitarian actors to minimise the chances for local actors to misappropriate, divert or abuse aid. Keen (2008) lists a range of possibilities, such as distributing cooked rather than dried food, which is easily stolen, and that ensuring supplies are not stored for too long in warehouses, where they are vulnerable to looting. Anderson (2001) suggests that, to minimise the impact of aid on local markets, agencies should seek to source local goods and produce where possible and attempt to peg prices at peacetime rates to stop profiteering, which prices many out of the markets and forces dependency on aid. There are many examples of flexible and tailored strategies adopted by specific NGOs in particular contexts to minimise the risk that their operations will reinforce conflict dynamics. One well-known approach to systematically analysing the extent to which an intervention may affect conflict dynamics is the 'do no harm' approach, closely associated with Anderson's work.

Do no harm

'Do no harm' is an approach developed by a group of NGOs working in the Local Capacities for Peace Project during the 1990s. It aimed to provide a better understanding of the ways in which the activities of NGOs can affect and have affected conflict dynamics. Drawing on the field experience of agencies in a range of contexts, and looking for patterns and best practice, the discussions led to a framework which can be used by those working both in conflict-affected environments and more generally. The approach recommended by the project involves several steps.

1   First, it is important to understand the possible axis of conflict within a society. What are the salient identity groups which may be in conflict with each other, and what interests held by particular groups could clash with those of other groups?

2   Conflict, or potential conflict, exists within any society, but 'do no harm' is concerned primarily with violent conflict, so the second step is to identify which of these divisions has the potential to lead to violence. This is referred to as 'identifying dividers and tensions'. Knowing what is likely to divide a society makes the task of assessing how aid fits into existing dynamics more possible.

3 The third step also requires a focus on potentially competing or conflicting identities and groups, but instead of looking for causes of tension it seeks to identify the links and relationships which connect them. Family networks, market relationships and shared history, culture or religion could all be potential ways of appealing to connections between groups and individuals. This step requires identification of 'connectors' and also local capacities for peace: what systems and individuals, such as local police, NGOs, schools and religious figures, could prove to be a resource in preventing violent conflict? These, as in the case of religious leaders or community elders, may have a particular ability to use the ties between groups to encourage peaceful relations.

4 Step 4 requires agencies to review their programme and ask a range of questions about it to identify possible implications. Among such questions are: Which groups will the programme target? Will staff be local or international or both? How are staff to be recruited? What resources will the project supply? Who decides who has access?

5 Having identified these key aspects of the context in which aid is being used, the agency must then look at all the aspects of their planned programme and consider how their actions take account of, and may affect, the context, dividers and connectors. Step 5 requires a consideration of the two means, discussed above, through which aid can affect conflict: What resource transfers are taking place and what implicit ethical messages does the programme send? It also necessitates understanding which groups may benefit from the programme and which may be excluded. If these categories overlap with the potential axis of conflict identified earlier, then aid is likely to impact intergroup tensions. Similarly, whether the programme undermines or supports connectors and local capacities for peace may also affect conflict dynamics.

6 In step 6, we look at the information generated by step 5. If it suggests that the programme will affect conflict dynamics negatively, then it is necessary to review the programme, considering the range of aspects under step 4, in order to try and remove these negative effects or to maximise positive impacts.

7 The final step takes the new programme back through steps 4 to 6, to be unpacked, checked again for its impact on context, dividers and connectors, and amended as necessary.

The approach is relatively straightforward, and aspects of it have been widely used by NGOs and donors. There are rich case studies made available by NGOs through the Local Capacities for Peace project website (www.donoharm.info/), showing the challenges they have faced in different countries and how they have used 'do no harm' to assess and amend their programmes. However, commentators such as Duffield have argued that 'do no harm' remains a relatively minimalist approach, aimed primarily at making sure the actions of NGOs don't make conflict dynamics worse. A more maximalist approach would instead place greater emphasis on the need for aid to tackle the underlying reasons for the conflict. This would link aid more specifically to peacebuilding, focusing not only on the local capacities for peace but also on longer-term development objectives – whether economic, political or social. This places NGOs and humanitarian aid within the context of broader approaches to development. As discussed earlier in the chapter, development has become intertwined with a particular set of understandings about what is necessary to create economic growth, reduce poverty and ensure peace within and between states. It is useful at this point to consider how development and humanitarianism have become bound up with the creation of liberal peace, as discussed back in Chapter 2.

Humanitarianism, development and furthering the 'liberal peace'

As Duffield argues development in general has become transformative, so Barnett and Duvall (2005) also argue that humanitarianism has become transformative. It is not concerned solely with relief but also with effecting changes to avoid future humanitarian crises, conflicts and emergencies. They state that 'towards that end, aid agencies desire to spread development, democracy and human rights, and to join a peace-building agenda that aspires to create stable, effective and legitimate states' (2005: 733). This sees humanitarian organisations as part of, and potentially subordinated to, the overarching agenda of transforming states, societies and interstate relations through the spread of values and systems built on broadly liberal principles – free markets and multiparty democracy (Paris 2004). This reflects in some ways the Wilsonian approach to humanitarianism outlined earlier in the chapter. Many of those working in development, whether for NGOs, multilaterals or bilateral donor agencies, think of it in a way that privileges values and rights they consider 'universal'. It is of course difficult to argue with the UNDP focus on human development and the aims of the Millennium Development Goals. Who would not want reductions in infant mortality, or to work towards universal primary education?

However, it is possible to make a case that some of these dominant principles and values can hamper the achievement of long-term development objectives or even of sustained peace. For example, the leverage which international donors can have in discussions with governments such as that of Sudan over the crisis in Darfur or that of Sri Lanka during the offensive to destroy the Tamil Tigers is arguably lessened by the preoccupation with gaining humanitarian access. The prioritising of relief may reflect a humanitarian imperative and a desire to uphold universal human rights and prevent immediate suffering, but tackling the root causes of these conflicts requires political engagement. This in turn requires leverage for negotiation between international actors and powerful local actors, including governments. The expectation that a humanitarian crisis will not be allowed to continue unabated, and that governments should pressure key actors to allow access for relief, affords those denying access to affected populations a measure of power and reinforces their position as key to resolving the crisis.

The preoccupation of donors with quickly instituting democracy is also potentially incompatible with ensuring stability and legitimate, accountable government. In the interim period after conflict, donors may be dealing with unelected parties, warlords or rebel groups, and elections are frequently seen as a way of choosing a legitimate government which will then have the mandate to govern and negotiate on behalf of the state. Elections may also form one of the conditions in a negotiated peace process. The experiences of many post-conflict states, such as Angola in the 1990s and Iraq and Afghanistan more recently, show that elections can become flashpoints for violence. This is true even of states not experiencing large-scale civil conflict, such as Kenya in 2007–8, but in conflict-affected states the dangers can be exacerbated. Elections and democratisation, in its donor-preferred liberal form, encourage competition between political parties and their supporters. They transfer conflict from violence to politics, but in a highly militarised society, where groups may fear for their own safety – or their position, if they are not adequately represented in government – elections become an existential matter. There is no guarantee that groups who are defeated at the ballot box will accept the results, a danger which is magnified when demilitarisation has been only partial.

There is also a strong emphasis on a staged approach to assisting conflict-affected states. The balance of aid provided is expected to shift from emergency humanitarian and relief aid in the short term to longer-term development assistance. The timescales for this vary, and, in the case of countries which have recently experienced conflict, the shift in aid profile can be linked to the negotiation and implementation of a peace process and other markers of reconstruction. It is usual for this transition period to involve in addition the deployment, or continuation, of a peacekeeping mission by the UN or other organisation (see Chapter 6).

Multilateral donors, particularly the World Bank and the IMF, are often criticised for placing excessive focus on economic development and reconstruction. Development, in the broadest sense of a tangible improvement in people's lives, can play a role in encouraging people to invest in peace. Where people see real benefit from peace, Ball (2001) argues this can help them get through the difficult transition from war to peace. Economic development is therefore a critical aspect of reconstruction.

International donors and co-ordination

Bilateral aid, which gives individual country development agencies considerable power in conflict-affected environments, still accounts for the largest proportion of overall aid. Individual donor states and agencies will all have their own priorities and specialisms, and their level of interest and involvement in particular states and in different sectors will vary. Countries also have broader policy and strategic objectives which affect their willingness to commit aid to particular countries. Earlier in the chapter we discussed how thinking about development has changed since the mid 1900s. One aspect of this is an emphasis on the harmonisation of aid to reduce overlap and duplication of effort. This is part of a broader campaign to increase the effectiveness and efficiency of aid. However, donor co-ordination has proved elusive, particularly in the context of fragile and conflict-affected states.

Ball (2001) emphasises that effective co-ordination requires a high calibre of staff working within agencies which are also open to working together across organisational boundaries. As nominal relationships between agencies actually develop between people on the ground, Ball also suggests that the head offices of these agencies must be prepared to devolve authority and a measure of power to workers in the affected country to expedite such collaboration. The size of the bureaucracies involved may further militate against co-operation, with different procedures, requirements and organisational culture creating institutional barriers. Donors and agencies are often keen to protect their reputation or perceived comparative advantage in particular sectors. Seeing an aspect as 'their area', in which they may have invested significant resources in staff development, recruitment and building links with NGOs, they can be reluctant to work with others. Collaboration and co-ordination require a degree of institutional memory and the development of deeper relationships between agencies. This is hampered by the reliance of many donor agencies on international staff, who typically remain in each post for only two to three years. A strong cadre of local staff, who usually remain in post longer and have both situational knowledge and language skills, can help maintain this institutional memory. However, as Ball also notes, both donors and NGOs tend to favour staff from their own home countries or international staff in general, possibly fearing a loss of control if local stakeholders are too highly empowered and promoted.

The need for greater co-ordination and harmonisation has also affected institutional arrangements for raising, administering and distributing aid. Mechanisms for improving co-ordination include the use of basket funds, to which all donors to a particular sector or project commit funds, and which are run by one donor. This type of arrangement gives that one donor overall responsibility for the sector and the authority to negotiate with other donors, NGOs and the government. It therefore reduces the number of donors which governments and local actors need to meet and report to, an important consideration in situations where government and civil society may have both limited capacity and many demands on their time.

Relationship and differences between donors and NGOs

We have already discussed the issue of funding, and how reliance on national governments for funding may compromise the independence of NGOs. It is, however, important to explore the relationships and differences between donors and NGOs in a little more depth. The first and perhaps most significant difference is in the overall amounts of aid provided by the two. Just considering donor funding, it is clear that bilateral aid still represents the largest source of aid. Global Humanitarian Assistance, which uses data collected by the OECD DAC to show how much aid is bilateral or multilateral, estimates that in 2009, of the total aid given by DAC countries, multilateral aid accounted for less than 13 per cent. The total monetary value of multilateral aid from DAC members is estimated at US$15,022 million, whilst overall aid was $118,757 million. About 90 per cent of all overseas development assistance comes from the twenty-two OECD countries, with the United States, Germany, France, Japan and the United Kingdom as the biggest donors by volume. However, only around five countries (Norway, Luxembourg, the Netherlands, Sweden and Denmark) have reached the agreed global target of 0.7 per cent of gross national income, though others have plans in place to increase their contributions. These five countries account for almost 70 per cent of all aid.

David Keen's work *Complex Emergencies* (2008) explores the priorities and motivations for different groups of actors working in and around the humanitarian sector. This establishes a range of differences between the priorities of international governments, powerful elites within the affected society, and aid organisations. For bilateral donors, he argues that aid partly performs a function of containment. Encouraging war-affected populations to gather and remain in particular spaces effectively allows a form of containment, discouraging people from seeking asylum. It can also, as suggested earlier in the case of Kurds in northern Iraq, help in preventing the spread of conflict across borders. In this case, the spillover of Kurdish refugees into Turkey could have exacerbated tensions between the Turkish government and the ethnic Kurdish population.

Keen (2008) notes that the relationship between donors and NGOs is inherently unequal. Donors provide a significant proportion of the funds which NGOs rely upon, which makes them the more powerful actor in any relationship. However, whilst donors may be willing to use NGOs to help deliver development objectives, they are not always amenable to using the power they have on their behalf in negotiations with governments and other powerful actors. In particular, where aid is misappropriated or diverted, this is often labelled by donors as an 'implementation problem' – transferring responsibility to the NGOs, who rarely have the leverage and power to ensure aid gets through.

Within the NGO sector, there are many different types of organisation with a range of specialisms, budgets, staff profiles and relationships with donors. NGOs are seen as a way of bridging the gap between governments or donors and citizens. They form a key part of civil society, and they can be effective 'connectors' when considered from Anderson's 'local capacities for peace' perspective. To assume that NGOs are always local, representative or even contributing positively to peacebuilding would, however, be a mistake. When looking at the work of any particular NGO, especially those claiming to be 'local', there are always questions to be asked about which constituency or group the organisation claims to represent.

Donors are often criticised for preferring NGOs who speak their language, both literally and in terms of the buzzwords and fashions in aid. They also tend to compete for access to the 'best' local consultants – often well-educated individuals – and their organisations, who provide a 'local' perspective in terms which donors can easily translate to their programmes and reports.

However, there are issues with this approach. For example, it is questionable how 'local' the perspective is of one who speaks an international language (usually English), who has received an education often up to university level, perhaps overseas, who knows how to write project proposals and reports, and who tends to reside in a relatively wealthy urban area. No doubt such individuals have more ability to navigate local politics, to speak to aid recipients and negotiate with a range of partners, all necessary for today's modern NGO. But there is a very real risk that such NGOs and individuals skew the discussion and practice of development by becoming the 'usual suspects', sought after by donors who are essentially relying on an urban-educated elite to advise them how better to tackle poverty.

This rise of the professional NGO is partly a response to growing donor (and public) demands that aid be used efficiently and effectively. It is symptomatic of the professionalisation of the humanitarian sector discussed earlier in the chapter. However, it also reflects the adoption of new public management-type practices by NGOs keen to win donor funding. One danger identified by Smillie (1997) is that, despite rhetoric about local ownership and partnership, donors' investment in NGOs becomes primarily about creating effective deliverers of their policies. This tends to favour partners who are more experienced, better connected and more established and disadvantages smaller organisations, whose staff may be less well educated and based further from donor offices in capitals, and who often occupy volunteer as opposed to salaried posts.

It also militates against open and honest evaluation of NGO work by the organisations themselves. In a climate of competition for donor funds and favour, evaluation of a programme which did not work as expected is a tool for disciplining behaviour, something which can be used as an excuse to deny future funding rather than as a mechanism for reflective learning. Competition also reduces the incentive for NGOs to work together, though in situations of conflict and natural disaster-induced humanitarian crises some of the larger agencies have co-ordinated fundraising campaigns, often with the aid of UN and some of its agencies. The reliance on donor funding further skews accountability, so that NGOs become accountable to donors rather than to those they are committed to helping. The relationships between donors and NGOs are therefore constantly developing, with factors such as prior experience, capacity, and ability to speak donor language having a strong impact on the likely success of an NGO. For larger transnational NGOs, such as Oxfam or Save the Children, it is possible to have greater agency and power in discussions with donors, partly on account of their size and financial power and the public support for their work.

Summary points

1 Development as a subject dates from before the Second World War, but modern development approaches owe a debt to the Marshall Plan, which helped in the reconstruction of Europe after 1945.
2 There is no single view on development, and there is a complex set of relationships between modernisation, dependency, Marxist and neo-liberal approaches to development.
3 Development aid is provided through private, state and NGO means and can be divided into humanitarian and development aid, although this distinction covers interventions that are effectively both.

4   Bilateral aid is the largest mode of international aid, followed by private aid and remittances and multilateral aid. This dwarfs aid provided through NGOs.

5   There are many ways of administering aid and ensuring harmonisation amongst donors, but this remains a perpetual problem.

Discussion questions

1   How does the international development community engage with post-conflict countries?

2   How can we disaggregate the international community and are there differences between NGOs and donors?

3   What are the implications of the 'do no harm' thesis?

4   Is development intervention politically neutral?

5   How far has development become 'securitised' and does it matter?

References and further reading

Anderson, Mary (1999) *Do No Harm: How Aid Can Support Peace – or War*. Boulder, CO: Lynne Rienner.

Anderson, Mary (2001) 'Enhancing local capacity for peace: do no harm', in Luc Reychler and Thania Paffenholz (eds), *Peacebuilding: A Field Guide*. Boulder, CO: Lynne Rienner.

Ball, Nicole (2001) 'The challenge of rebuilding war-torn societies', in C. A. Crocker, F. O. Hampson, M. B. Anderson and P. Aall (eds), *Turbulent Peace: The Challenges of Managing International Conflict*. Washington, DC: United States Institute of Peace Press.

Hilhorst, Dorothea (2002) 'Being good at doing good? Quality and accountability of humanitarian NGOs', *Disasters*, 26(3): 193–212.

Jacoby, Tim (2010) 'Emerging patterns in the reconstruction of conflict-affected countries', *Disaster*, 34(1): 1–14.

Keen, David (2008) *Complex Emergencies*. Cambridge: Polity.

Smillie, Ian (1997) 'NGOs and development assistance: a change in mind-set?', *Third World Quarterly*, 18(3): 563–77.

Stein, Janice (2005) 'Humanitarianism as political fusion', *Perspectives on Politics*, 3(4): 741–4.

6 International intervention and peacekeeping

Interventionism, peacekeeping and privatisation have become increasingly important topics and are interlinked. A range of actors, from the UN to regional organisations such as the African Union, have mounted peace support operations, which often turn out to be long-term undertakings. The chapter considers how the presence of a peacekeeping, or even a peace enforcement, mission can affect development and security. It looks briefly at the history and major trends in international peacekeeping, outlining key debates on the political economy of peacekeeping, which links to the previous chapter's analysis and earlier discussion of the political economy of violent conflict. It will also discuss the move to regional interventionism, regional security and regional peacekeeping solutions, outlining the advantages of this approach, such as a possibly more nuanced understanding of particular conflicts, but also highlighting problems of capability, neutrality and legacy.

The development of peacekeeping

The United Nations estimates that, in March 2010, almost 124,000 personnel were deployed across sixteen missions, on four continents. This level of personnel – not all of whom are soldiers – shows just how important the UN has become as a force in the drive to create and maintain international peace and security. Though the UN was established in the aftermath of the Second World War and is now over sixty years old, this growth has not happened as gradually as one might expect. The UN Department of Peacekeeping Operations (DPKO) estimates that the numbers it has deployed have increased ninefold since 1999.

The conflict environments in which UN peacekeepers find themselves have changed considerably since the organisation's establishment, especially since the end of the Cold War and the turn of the millennium. To appreciate the challenges which the UN faces in maintaining global peace, and by extension the motives for creation of a plethora of other international security organisations with a peacekeeping capacity besides the UN, it is useful to consider the history of UN peacekeeping. It was established in response to particular pressures and challenges. However, these types of conflict have to a significant degree disappeared, led to stagnated protracted *de facto* settlements, or been rendered less frequent by increasing civil and intra-state war and processes of state failure and collapse. To understand the history of UN peacekeeping therefore allows us to appreciate a little better the history of attempts by the international community to deal with violent conflict, through containment, peacekeeping and, more recently, peace enforcement. This is all the more important in the context of development since, as discussed in the previous chapter, the drive to maximise the impact and effectiveness of aid means being able to implement programmes and evaluate them. In a conflict-affected or insecure context, this task becomes even more difficult than usual.

We begin with the UN as it is the largest provider of peacekeeping forces globally. A primary aim of the UN is to establish and maintain international peace by providing mechanisms for the resolution of disputes between states. It has the power to authorise and deploy military, civilian and police personnel to achieve this aim, but this power is contingent on the support of its members, particularly the five permanent members (the United Kingdom, the United States, France, China, Russia) and the ten non-permanent members of the Security Council. Peacekeeping missions are usually authorised by vote in the Security Council, reflecting the fact that it is this particular organ which is charged in the UN Charter with maintaining peace and security. The ability of the UN to establish a mission is also contingent on the willingness of member states to contribute the personnel, equipment and other support necessary to meet the mission's mandate.

The UN does not have a standing army of its own. There are restrictions on which countries can provide troops for a particular peacekeeping mission, reflecting a preference for the force to be as neutral as possible. Parties to a conflict would not be able to contribute forces to a UN mission, as this would compromise its neutrality and potentially its effectiveness. Similarly, countries seen as having an interest in particular conflicts are usually not considered suitable providers of troops. This includes the use of troops from a former colonial power in a former colony, although on occasion this provision has been ignored.

These limitations on who can provide troops, along with the economic attractions of peacekeeping for contributing states, have led to a relatively small range of states providing the bulk of peacekeeping forces – in particular, Pakistan, India, and Bangladesh. By deploying large numbers of peacekeepers on UN missions, these and other developing states are able to maintain large armed forces, outsource the costs of paying part of their forces, and also benefit from the training, equipment and allowances provided by the UN.

The cost of these missions is nominally borne by all UN member states, whose contributions are worked out according to a formula taking into account their size and ability to pay. The permanent members of the Security Council are also required to pay more on account of their responsibility for international peace and security. The United States, Japan, Germany and the United Kingdom are currently the biggest contributors, with the United States providing over a quarter of the budget (Bellamy *et al.*, 2010). The total spent on peacekeeping by the UN since its creation in 1948 is estimated at US$69 billion, with expenditure for 2010 alone expected to be $7.26 billion.

One of the defining features of any specific UN mission is its mandate. UN peacekeeping missions are intended to contribute to maintaining international peace and security, acting under one of two main chapters of the UN Charter. Chapter VI deals with peaceful solutions, or 'pacific settlement of disputes', requiring states which may have a dispute that could lead to war to enter into negotiation to seek settlement. It also allows such states to bring their disputes to the UN for arbitration, though the recommendations under Chapter VI are not legally binding. Perhaps the most famous resolution issued under the chapter which has not been enforced is Resolution 242, requiring Israel to withdraw from territories which it had occupied during the Six Day War with Arab nations in 1967. By contrast, Chapter VII, 'Action with respect to the peace, breaches of the peace and acts of aggression', allows the UN to undertake military action if necessary to restore international peace and security. Chapter VII permits the imposition of sanctions or blockades on states. It also confers the right to use the military forces which are put at the organisation's disposal by member states to carry out missions to restore peace and security. In reality, peacekeeping is often said to belong to 'chapter six and a half', a phrase coined by the second Secretary-General, Dag Hammarskjold, to describe its hybrid nature, often involving the UN playing a role somewhere between mediation, negotiation and the threat or use of force to restore peace and security.

UN missions are often described as resting on three ideal principles – impartiality, minimum force and consent (Bellamy *et al.*, 2010). The earliest UN missions were amongst those most clearly based on consent by the parties involved in a dispute. In June 1948 the UN Truce Supervision Organisation was set up to monitor the ceasefire in the Middle East after the creation of Israel. Though its mission has adapted to the shifts in the Israeli–Palestinian–Arab conflict complex in the region, the organisation, staffed primarily by military observers and acting as a go-between for parties to the conflict, exists to this day. It was not until 1956 that the first UN 'peacekeeping' operation was authorised, the UN Emergency Force (UNEF). This was developed to help end the Suez Crisis by providing neutral forces to police the ceasefire line between Israel and Egypt. In line with its desire to deploy only where countries gave consent, when Israel refused the UN permission to deploy on its territory, UNEF remained stationed only on Egypt's side of the border. Similarly, the UN mission authorised for Cyprus in 1964 was developed in response to complaints from representatives of both Greek Cypriot and Turkish Cypriot communities on the island, as well as Greece and Turkey themselves. Since an outbreak of violence in 1974, the island has been effectively partitioned, with a demilitarised buffer zone across its centre. Delicate and often tense negotiations over its future have remained generally peaceful in large part because of the presence of the UN force based permanently in Cyprus. This type of UN peacekeeping is based on consent by all state parties involved, and involves primarily policing and monitoring duties rather than war-fighting.

Aside from the instances of ceasefire monitoring described above, there are other missions which can be considered to be of the traditional peacekeeping type and which have achieved the aims set out in their mandate. For example, in April 1989, the UN Transition Assistance Group (UNTAG) was deployed to Namibia, tasked with monitoring the withdrawal of South Africa and helping run elections for an independent Namibian government. This is regarded as a successful mission by any measure and conforms to the ideals of neutrality and consent. It is, however, possible to discern a range of other types of peacekeeping mission which do not always conform to the ideals. Indeed, in some more recent cases, as we will discuss, there is arguably little or no peace to keep – instead peace must be built, made or enforced, with the UN playing a more or less significant role, often alongside regional peacekeeping forces. UN missions are increasingly multifaceted, incorporating policing, military and civilian functions. They also operate more in insecure environments, sometimes without the consent of one or more warring parties, which brings into question their neutrality. One type of mission in which the UN routinely engages, especially since the 1990s, is supporting the implementation of a peace agreement between parties. Another increasingly common type of operation is that used to legitimise, incorporate, augment or simply 're-hat' a peacekeeping mission dispatched by another organisation. Each of these tells us a little about the kinds of states the UN system seeks to encourage and how its strategies for ensuring international security have adapted over recent years. However, each can be seen in its own way as informed by particular understandings of what is necessary to create security and, in many cases, better conditions for development and conflict prevention. As we shall see, these overlap closely with the ideals of liberal peacebuilding, emphasising global economic governance and neo-liberal approaches to political and economic reconstruction. Just as donors and aid agencies have shifted emphasis to obtaining the right conditions and environment for development and for tackling the root causes of conflict, so peacekeeping is also seen as contributing to these aims.

Assisting in the implementation of peace agreements is a role which has become closely associated with UN peacekeeping. As discussed in Chapter 2, the dismantling of colonial empires led to many states, across Africa in particular, gaining independence. In the context of the Cold War, groups vying for control of these states appealed for and often enjoyed support from the Soviet Union or the United States. The so-called proxy wars which ensued continued in some countries past the end of the Cold War. During the period of decolonisation, and in a Cold War context, the ability of the UN to intervene in these conflicts had been severely hampered by the need for agreement of all five permanent members of the Security Council, including of course the United States and the Soviet Union. With the end of the Cold War and the breaking of this deadlock, a much more proactive role was envisioned for the UN. As support of Cold War patrons was withdrawn and donor pressure on developing states to undertake democratisation grew, some of these festering conflicts were at least partly resolved through peace agreements.

The role of the UN in such a process often includes the policing of demilitarised zones and the monitoring of ceasefires, necessary steps to create a space in which all sides to a conflict can feel they are secure during their participation in peace negotiations. UN troops can then be asked to ensure that forces remain confined to areas they agree to during negotiations, and that any promises of disarmament and demobilisation are kept. The UN deployed such a force to assist in the implementation of a peace agreement in Rwanda in 1993. However, this is universally regarded as an example of a failed mission. There was limited international support for the UN Assistance Mission for Rwanda – UNAMIR – particularly after the experiences of the United States and UN in Somalia (see below). Tasked with overseeing the implementation of the Arusha Accords, signed by the Rwandan government and the rebel opposition group, the Rwandan Patriotic Front, the force proved both too small and to be lacking a strong enough mandate to prevent the ethnic cleansing which quickly turned to genocide in 1994. At the height of the genocide, fewer than 300 UN peacekeepers remained, with the larger contingents – notably well-trained Belgian troops – withdrawn after the killing of ten Belgian paratroopers serving with the UN force. These soldiers were specifically targeted by those orchestrating the genocide precisely because they reasoned, correctly, that donor states have little stomach for African conflicts and are highly sensitive to casualties. The failings of the UN in Rwanda caused considerable soul-searching in the years following, informing attempts to reform the UN (as will be discussed) and the increasing focus on developing rapid reaction forces, often at regional level, which can respond more quickly to deteriorating situations.

However, the UN has not been entirely unsuccessful in this kind of peacekeeping. Mozambique is considered an example of success in supporting peace agreement implementation, partly due to the lessons it had learned from its earlier experience in Angola. During one of its assistance missions in Angola, UNAVEM II (1991–2), the UN was tasked under the Bicesse Accords with monitoring the ceasefire between the MPLA government and the rebel group UNITA and observing and verifying presidential and parliamentary elections. UNITA was backed by Cuba, the Soviet Union and apartheid South Africa, and led by Jonas Savimbi, but this external support diminished after the Cold War. When neither the MPLA candidate Dos Santos nor the UNITA candidate Savimbi achieved 50 per cent of the vote in the presidential election – Savimbi achieved 40 per cent compared with Dos Santos's 49.75 per cent – a second round of voting was declared. Before this could take place, Savimbi and his followers reinitiated war with the government, and civil war continued until Savimbi's death in 2002. Amongst the many reasons cited for the failure to implement the peace accords is the UN's inability to ensure sufficient numbers of UNITA fighters were grouped, disarmed and demobilised before elections. When Savimbi feared defeat in a second round of voting, this limited and weak demobilisation programme allowed his followers to return to violence quickly. UNITA's capacity to finance its operations through the shadow economy in diamonds was also key to its rapid return to war-fighting. This demonstrates, as discussed in Chapter 2, the importance of tackling the political economy of conflict as well as some of the more obviously military aspects.

In the case of Mozambique, the two main fighting groups, RENAMO and FRELIMO, had also enjoyed patronage from the superpowers during the Cold War. South Africa, under the apartheid regime, had supported RENAMO as part of its strategy of destabilising neighbouring regimes and preventing anti-apartheid fighters from South Africa basing themselves across the border. But by the early 1990s the increasing ties between the West and the formerly socialist-inspired FRELIMO government, combined with RENAMO's waning international support, laid foundations for peace negotiations. In 1990 a new constitution set out the transition to democracy, and between 1992 and 1994 the UN Operations in Mozambique (ONUMOZ) oversaw the implementation of the general peace agreement. This involved not only monitoring and verifying the ceasefire, including the separation and concentration of forces, but also demobilisation and the collection, storage and destruction of weapons. In addition ONUMOZ oversaw the withdrawal of foreign fighters, provided technical assistance, and monitored the electoral process. Comprehensive disarmament and demobilisation programmes before elections were held, and the UN co-ordination of support for the development of RENAMO into a viable political party, able to contest elections effectively, are counted amongst the reasons Mozambique's elections did not spark renewed fighting by the losing party.

The UN peacekeeping function has also been used as a way of legitimising interventions undertaken by other organisations. Both East and West Africa provide recent examples of this kind of peacekeeping. In 1990, a regional organisation, the Economic Community of West African States (ECOWAS), established a monitoring group (ECOMOG). Drawing mainly on troops from Nigeria, ECOWAS deployed this peacekeeping mission to Liberia in an attempt to contain a civil war in which the UN was highly reluctant to intervene. It was not until 1993 that the UN established an observer mission in Liberia to support ECOMOG by acting as a neutral arbiter in verifying compliance with ceasefire agreements. This force, however, remained small and focused on observation until being partially absorbed and replaced by a UN mission, UNMIL, in 2003, following the resignation of the Liberian president, Charles Taylor. On the opposite side of the continent, in 2004 the African Union established a mission to protect ceasefire monitors in the Darfur region of Sudan. As the ceasefire broke down and violence grew over the succeeding years, it quickly became clear that this force could not keep or enforce the peace and was itself a target for the forces involved. In 2007, the UN deployed an assistance mission in Darfur incorporating the AU peacekeepers, UNAMID. (For discussion of the advantages and potential problems associated with these regional approaches, see *Regional security and management of peacekeeping* below)

Finally, it is useful to consider briefly the situations in which the UN has deployed in states which have begun to disintegrate or collapse. Though we tend to think of multidimensional peacekeeping as a post-Cold War phenomenon, the UN mission in Congo from 1960 to 1964 was deployed into a situation which had many of the features associated with more recent civil wars and collapsed state environments. Congo had only recently gained independence and was nominally a sovereign state with one government, in Kinshasa. However, political infighting and scrambling for control over mineral-rich provinces meant that factions had begun to attempt to break away from the state or to seize control of it from others. The mission was a relative success, as by 1964 the state remained intact and stability had been restored, but the UN forces had broken with the principle of impartiality by fighting on the side of the government. This reduced the trust in the UN of developing states, which feared that it could be used outside of the classical 'standing between two sides' model.

A much more recent example of UN peacekeeping in a collapsed state is that of Somalia. UNOSOM was created in 1992, mandated to protect UN personnel and equipment and humanitarian supplies being delivered to the capital, Mogadishu. Within the first few months it became clear that the humanitarian situation was deteriorating rapidly and that armed groups were operating with relative impunity, especially in Mogadishu, and preventing aid from reaching civilians. The mandate was enhanced to reaffirm the role of peacekeepers in protecting aid convoys, and in December the Security Council authorised UNITAF, a US-led United Task Force, to use all means necessary under Chapter VII to protect humanitarian convoys and operations. In 1993, UNOSOM's mandate was again updated, with the objective of establishing security in Somalia. But despite achieving tentative agreement between the main faction leaders, the UN forces continued to come under attack from some, notably those loyal to General Aideed, the self-styled leader of Somalia. In an attempt to snatch Aideed, in response to UN Resolution 837 calling for his arrest, US forces found themselves outnumbered. The deaths of nineteen American soldiers, and injuries to over seventy more, led ultimately to the withdrawal of US troops in early 1994. With a much reduced force, and a lack of co-operation between the factions towards peace, the UN voted to withdraw UNOSOM II in 1995.

How has peacekeeping changed, and why does it matter?

The discussion above has indicated some of the ways peacekeeping has changed, particularly since the end of the Cold War, and why. It is, however, important to consider how the principles of UN peacekeeping have become compromised and the impact of this process on current and future attempts to maintain international peace and stability. The changes in international peacekeeping since the end of the Cold War have been described by scholar Hugo Slim as a move to 'second-generation peacekeeping' (Slim 1996). Rather than just peace 'keeping,' it is now possible to speak of peace 'building,' peace 'making' and even peace 'enforcement'. These suggest an increased politicisation and militarisation of such initiatives, which can be discussed collectively as peace support operations (PSO). As Slim points out, 'the new peacekeeping does not differ from traditional peacekeeping in its activities alone. In matters of principle, it frequently struggles to maintain or deliberately oversteps the three key peacekeeping principles of consent, impartiality and minimum force' (Slim, 1996). The identification of a mission as 'peace enforcement' signifies that the intervening force may not have the consent of all sides involved, or that it may deliberately support some at the expense of others in order to force an end to fighting between parties. This means intervening in a conflict where there is effectively no peace to keep. Peace enforcement is also more costly in both financial and human terms than other forms of peacekeeping. A former UN Under Secretary-General for Peacekeeping stated of the UN Operation Desert Storm in Iraq:

'one day's expenditure on that operation would have been more than enough to finance United Nations peacekeeping for the whole of 1991' (Goulding 1993: 462). As well as being costly, intervening in a conflict without the consent of all parties can make those involved in peace enforcement a target for those involved in the conflict by calling their neutrality into question. This has been demonstrated by the targeting of UN forces in the DRC (MONUC/MONUSCO) by Congolese militia groups, the Mayi-Mayi. The greater danger to civilians, police and troops deployed as part of UN missions where there is no negotiated peace, or where the agreement breaks down, can make it difficult to secure commitments by countries to send troops. Belgium's withdrawal from the mission in Rwanda after the deaths of ten of its peace keepers adds further weight to Thakur's wider observation that 'National public opinion is unlikely to support high-risk ventures in far-off lands for the sake of quarrelling foreigners' (Thakur and Schnabel 2001). Peace enforcement is pursued in complex conflicts where traditional peacekeeping is not possible. There may be multiple 'sides' involved, there may be no agreement on a ceasefire, and intervening forces may themselves become parties to the conflict, supporting particular forces against others. Many states have been extremely reluctant to provide the troops and even equipment needed for such operations.

Improving UN peacekeeping

Faced with these challenges, and reflecting on the failings of UN peacekeeping in particular, there have been attempts to reform the peacekeeping system and improve practices. In 1992, UN Secretary-General Boutros Boutros-Ghali presented a first step which has underpinned this process, *An Agenda for Peace: Preventive Diplomacy, Peacemaking and Peace-Keeping*. This set out the challenges facing the UN in ensuring international peace and security, noting the contribution the UN could make to international security using the resources and mechanisms at its disposal. It also defined peacekeeping (involving the deployment of a UN mission) as different to peacemaking (primarily Chapter VI actions) and preventive deployment. Of particular interest for development actors, Boutros-Ghali also emphasised the importance of peacebuilding. Similar to the 'do no harm' approach adopted by many development actors and discussed in Chapter 5, the *Agenda for Peace* commits the UN to look for ways of strengthening the structures, processes and institutions that help to maintain peace and prevent relapse into conflict. The form this new peace should take is intimated by Boutros-Ghali's contention that 'Democracy at all levels is essential to attain peace for a new era of prosperity and justice' (1992: §82).

The agenda therefore reaffirmed that the UN should continue to play a role in international peace and security. However, as we have seen from the examples above, the instances of peacekeeping during the 1990s were not always particularly successful. In cases such as Rwanda and the Balkans, notably the Srebrenica massacre, through its inaction the UN was accused of negligence and direct complicity in the killing of civilians. The role played by states and state armed forces – whether regular or irregular – in violence against the civilian population also raised the question of whether the UN could and should relax its principles and intervene without consent of all parties if necessary. These debates were spurred by two key documents.

The first, the Brahimi Report, was released in 2000. It reflected on the causes of the UN's past failures in peacekeeping and suggested ways in which future operations could be more effective. Underlying its main recommendations is a conviction that the UN cannot and should not attempt to resolve all conflicts. It made a repeated request that member states offer better support to the UN politically, financially and operationally, and it recommended that UN peacekeepers should be able to defend both themselves and their mandate, and to act to stop violence committed against civilians if they witness such instances. It made many other specific recommendations, including improved intelligence gathering and communications and an enhanced rapid reaction capability. This latter has proved particularly difficult to achieve, leaving a gap which regional organisations have attempted to begin to fill (see *Regional security and management of peacekeeping* below).

A second key document which has informed debates on the role of peacekeeping in maintaining international peace and security is the report of the International Commission on Intervention and State Sovereignty (ICISS): *The Responsibility to Protect*. This document, released in 2001, responded to a question raised by UN Secretary-General Kofi Annan: How could the international community reconcile respect for state sovereignty with the need to intervene to prevent human suffering and systematic human rights violations? The principle of the report, often abbreviated to R2P, argues that sovereignty confers rights – principally to non-intervention – but also responsibilities. Where a state is unable to protect its citizens, or is actively carrying out genocide, war crimes or crimes against humanity, the international community has a duty to intervene and the state loses its right to non-intervention. It also confers three responsibilities on the international community: to *prevent* conflict and other crises which put populations at risk; to *react* to human suffering, using a range of means including the supportive and non-military; and to *rebuild*, providing resources and support as necessary. The principle has, however, been greeted with some scepticism by states, particularly relatively small states, which fear it will be used by stronger powers as a pretext to intervene in their affairs. There is also a question of threshold: At what point do human suffering or human rights violations become systematic and so extensive that the R2P is triggered? Attempts have been made to translate the principle into policy and to deal with some of these thorny questions. The UN has been a key partner in this process, particularly under the current Secretary-General, Ban Ki-moon. In a 2008 speech he set out his vision for operationalising R2P based on three pillars (ICISS 2010):

1   Pillar One stresses that states have the primary responsibility to protect their populations from genocide, war crimes, ethnic cleansing and crimes against humanity.
2   Pillar Two addresses the commitment of the international community to provide assistance to states in building capacity to protect their populations from genocide, war crimes, ethnic cleansing and crimes against humanity and to assisting those which are under stress before crises and conflicts break out.
3   Pillar Three focuses on the responsibility of the international community to take timely and decisive action to prevent and halt genocide, ethnic cleansing, war crimes and crimes against humanity when a state is manifestly failing to protect its population.

R2P is still a relatively new norm, and arguably the issue of civilian protection has been superseded on the international agenda by terrorism and concerns with more traditional security issues such as nuclear proliferation. However, as far as development is concerned, it is notable for its emphasis on rebuilding and shares some of the same goals as many development agencies and actors. In particular, the focus on prevention includes dealing with the root causes of conflict, highlighting the need for political development, economic development and legal protections for citizens backed up by stronger rule of law. The ICISS report does emphasise the role which the United Nations can play, but its recommendations – like those of the Brahimi Report – are a reflection of frustration with the limitations of UN peacekeeping. It is partly in response to these frustrations that regional organisations have begun to take greater roles and responsibility for managing conflict and undertaking peacekeeping.

Regional security and management of peacekeeping

As discussed in Chapter 1, in the post-Cold War, and especially post-2001, security environment, conflicts are not considered to be purely the concern of those countries or regions where they occur. Processes of globalisation mean aspects of insecurity that exist in far-off lands are as capable of affecting the security of developed states as those closer to home. Given that achieving agreement on UN intervention, particularly in African conflicts, is notoriously difficult, the international community has sought instead to encourage regional organisations to handle conflicts in their areas. The EU, for example, commits itself and member states to 'support, over the long term, the enhancement of African peace support operations capabilities, at regional, sub-regional and bilateral levels as well as the capacity of the African States to contribute to regional integration, peace, security and development' (European Union 2005). This already established process has been injected with new energy in the context of the war on terror, amid fears of the links between terrorist groups, illicit resource networks and ungoverned spaces (Farah and Shultz 2004).

An early example of regional peacekeeping discussed briefly earlier, the ECOMOG intervention in Liberia, provides a useful illustration both of the reasons for growing interest in regional solutions and of the pitfalls of this form of peacekeeping. ECOMOG was formed in response to the international community's reluctance to intervene in the Liberian civil war. Other states in the region feared that the conflict there would spill over into other West African states, and the intervention was largely justified publicly on these and humanitarian grounds. It was heavily reliant on Nigerian troops and for the most part was led by Nigerian officers. The dominance of the force by Nigeria and anglophone states more generally caused resentment amongst the francophone members of ECOWAS, particularly Côte d'Ivoire, whose government had a close relationship with the rebel leader threatening to topple the government, Charles Taylor. It is often suggested that one of the strengths of regional peacekeeping is that those organising and carrying out the mission may have a better understanding of the conflict and valuable language skills which could enhance the effectiveness of the operation. In this case, however, the mission was heavily criticised for corruption and looting, earning the moniker 'Every Car Or Movable Object Gone'. It was also suspected that Nigerian elements of the force were supplying arms and other support to some of the factions fighting against Taylor's group. This example demonstrates how the effectiveness of regional peacekeeping organisations can be hampered by a perceived or actual lack of neutrality. It also begins to hint at some of the negative aspects of the political economy of peacekeeping.

However, though regional forces being deployed within their own region can cause problems, in some cases this approach may be the only way to secure consent for a mission to take place. In the case of Sudan, the government in Khartoum consistently rejected the notion of a UN peacekeeping force because, it argued, given the Security Council's dominance by Western states, this would be a cover for neo-colonial ambitions. The African Union, however, was able to secure permission for a small mission comprising African forces. Such missions by the AU are authorised by the organisation through the Peace and

Security Council. Initially comprising 150 troops intended to protect ceasefire monitors, this force grew to around 3,500 troops over its first year. As an African force, consisting mainly of Rwandan and Nigerian soldiers, it was more acceptable to the Sudanese government than a UN force. However, the mission quickly found itself under attack from rebel groups operating in the Darfur region, with thirty-five peacekeepers briefly kidnapped in 2005 and around twenty-five killed between 2005 and 2007.

The AU was praised highly by the UN and states such as the United States for its willingness to engage in peacekeeping in Africa, particularly given the Sudanese government's refusal to allow a UN force. Under this arrangement, the AU supplied troops, but it lacked the ability to transport them and their equipment to Sudan, relying on the United States and EU member states for logistical assistance. Financing for the mission was also inadequate. It was understood that international donors would pay, but difficulties in securing consent for a UN force meant that the AU mission continued after its funding had begun to dry up. By the time the force was replaced in 2007 by a joint UN–AU mission, UNAMID, there were complaints from contributing nations and individual peacekeepers that they had not been paid for months.

These kinds of arrangements between the UN and regional organisations with a peacekeeping capacity are regulated under Chapter VIII of the UN Charter. As part of efforts to enhance the ability of developing states to undertake peacekeeping, even if only as an interim measure whilst UN missions are being prepared and authorised, donor states have invested in the training and equipping of forces in countries contributing to peacekeeping. For example, the United States has instituted a continent-wide programme of African Contingency Operations Training and Assistance (ACOTA). A successor to the African Crisis Response Force and African Crisis Response Initiative, this trains selected African armed forces to undertake peace support and humanitarian relief operations. Other individual states have bilateral relationships with particular countries through which they provide military training and assistance. The European Union has also provided support to the African Union in its efforts to build up a rapid reaction capacity which could deploy at two weeks' notice in cases where genocide is happening or believed to be imminent.

Such efforts reflect the past failings of the UN and the international community, but even though regional organisations are improving their capacity to engage in peacekeeping – ECOWAS sent forces to Sierra Leone and Guinea-Bissau, and the AU deployed a further mission in Somalia in 2007 – challenges remain. In particular, the costs of peacekeeping are high, and for the foreseeable future, whilst Africa may provide the troops, it is likely that developed states will be expected to pay for and equip them. Similarly, in the case of logistics, it is not feasible or desirable to expect developing states to generate the capacity to move large numbers of troops and amounts of heavy equipment across the continent, and countries such as the United States are likely to continue to fulfil this role. Finally, there is the issue of the quality and discipline of personnel being supplied for these missions. As discussed in the case of ECOWAS, peacekeepers can engage in a variety of activities which support the continuation of conflict or support a war economy.

Crime, war economies and peacekeeping

The instances of peacekeepers committing abuses highlight their potential involvement in war economies and in processes which undermine human security, development and prospects for peace. The political economy of peacekeeping is an extremely important issue to consider when analysing the impacts and effectiveness of any particular mission.

The example given above relates to West Africa, but abuses and indiscipline are by no means limited to African personnel. Some of the biggest scandals have involved UN peacekeepers from a range of countries, including developing states, which are key providers of troops to UN missions, and donor states. The association of peacekeeping missions with prostitution, and in some cases human trafficking, is well documented, from the Balkans to the DRC and Haiti.

In the Balkans, prostitution and human trafficking have been linked to the presence of peacekeeping forces and large and well-established organised crime networks. Brothels, frequently staffed by women who have been trafficked or coerced into prostitution, are often located in close proximity to bases used by NATO personnel, and this is an observation which is replicated when examining other peacekeeping missions. By paying for sex with these women, peacekeepers, knowingly or otherwise, are creating a market for the trafficking of women and putting money into the hands of organised crime groups. In eastern DRC, peacekeepers have been accused of rape and of trading food and basic resources for sex with women and girls fleeing conflict. Given the conditions in which these displaced populations often exist, such food-for-sex transactions can hardly be considered consensual.

Furthermore, similarly to Anderson's (2001) argument about the implicit ethical messages produced by aid workers, the involvement of peacekeepers in sexual abuse adds to the message that sexual violence and exploitation are acceptable and that perpetrators can act with impunity. At the same time, the impact on HIV/AIDS and other STDs is relatively undocumented but clearly recognised as a threat. For example, Tripodi and Patel (2002) show that the spread of HIV/AIDS within African militaries has a direct effect on their peacekeeping capability and presents a threat to the populations they are supposed to be protecting. Whilst peacekeeping efforts may serve to provide hard security in terms of safeguarding state and regional security, at the same time their very deployment may be associated with rapid increases in HIV rates in the local population, producing a new threat. Given that peacekeepers are amongst the most mobile of populations, this must also have serious implications for the capability of the troops themselves, for their home populations and also for the next deployment zone.

Also in the DRC, peacekeepers have been found to have traded weapons to rebels in return for natural resources, and peacekeepers with the AU mission in Somalia are accused of selling weapons to rebels there. In both countries they have also been targeted by rebels, raising the prospect of peacekeepers arming the very groups from which they are ostensibly trying to protect themselves and civilians.

Abuses and crimes committed by UN peacekeepers are recognised by the UN as a problem which must be tackled if the blue helmets are to maintain their integrity and reputation. A detailed report by the UN Office of Internal Oversight Services in 2005 highlighted instances of the kind described above and raised questions as to how the UN would discipline and punish those responsible. The traditional response was to hand over the findings of such investigations to the home countries of those who had transgressed to take action through national courts and procedures. In 2009, the UN sent over 100 such reports to home countries, but critics have pointed out that these rarely receive a response and alleged perpetrators are seldom punished, or that punishments do not reflect the severity of the crimes, particularly against minors. It is also argued that, once a contributing country is made aware of one of its personnel being under investigation, the usual practice is to recall them from the mission, making it difficult for the UN to conclude investigations. Disciplining peacekeeping forces is therefore notoriously difficult. The UN has sought to tackle some of these concerns, setting up a Conduct and Discipline Unit in 2007 with offices in its main missions, but the stain on its reputation will be difficult to remove.

Peacekeeping, security and development

A key aspect of the role that peacekeepers play, particularly when implementing comprehensive peace agreements and undertaking peacebuilding, involves working to rebuild security sectors. Part of this is achieved through processes of DDR, especially attempts to re-establish a monopoly of the use of force in the hands of those authorised by the state. DDR and the management and facilitation of small arms and light weapons (SALW) programmes have also become part of many UN missions, and are often written explicitly into their mandate. However, in some cases other mandates have been designed which specifically refer to the need for the UN to engage in aspects of security sector reform. One review of UN missions on Kosovo, the DRC, Burundi and Haiti (Hänggi and Scherrer 2008) concluded on the evidence of these experiences that UN capacity to support SSR was minimal and poorly coordinated. It also suggested that the funding mechanisms for SSR were inadequate, with a lack of funds hampering attempts by the UN missions on the ground to gain credibility with local actors. To bring some of these general challenges into focus it is useful to look at two examples in a little more detail.

UNMIL, the UN Mission in Liberia, had support for security reform expressed as part of its mandate. Specifically, it was intended to assist in training, monitoring and restructuring the Liberian police force and to assist in creating a new restructured military in Liberia. Both were to be carried out in co-operation with ECOWAS and other interested states, notably the United States, which took a lead role. The ambitious programme was intended to be multi-sectoral and to address both the governance and the components of the security sector. However, critics charge that it has remained narrowly focused on the numbers of police and military forces which have undergone basic training at the expense of broader concerns of oversight, democratic control, sustainability of the programmes, and sustained engagement. One comprehensive and highly critical report (Malan 2008) suggested that SSR was too often not effectively budgeted for at the start, with the UN hoping for a lead donor to take ownership of the process and responsibility for funding. In the Liberian case the United States did take up this role, but was criticised for its slow disbursement of funds and its reliance on private contractors to carry out much of the vetting, recruitment and training of new personnel. Though the Liberian military and police are undoubtedly an improvement on those which existed before and during the country's civil war, by comparison the extended security sector – prisons, courts systems, the justice infrastructure, democratic oversight and improved rule of law – remain relatively weak and underfunded.

In the case of the DRC, the UN mission (MONUC, replaced in January 2010 by MONUSCO) was established in 1999, but SSR was added to the mandate only from 2008. This reflects the ongoing intervention in the DRC by regional powers up to 2003 and the focus from 2003 to 2007 on planning for and holding elections. After the elections, and following efforts by a range of states in the broad field of SSR in the DRC during this time, including South Africa, Belgium, the United Kingdom and the United States, it was felt that the United Nations should co-ordinate SSR assistance to avoid duplication of effort. The endeavours of the UN to support SSR in the context of the peacekeeping mission in the DRC therefore at first emphasised the need to provide security for elections and later the need for co-ordination in the face of multiple initiatives by bilateral and multilateral donors.

However, it had become clear by 2008 that the initial premises on which reform were based, such as the decision to reintegrate many rebel factions into the existing state army instead of building a new army from the bottom up, were misguided. Warlords maintained parallel command structures inside the DRC army after being ostensibly integrated, but continued in some cases to loot and to attack civilians whom they had previously terrorised as rebels. One of these factions, that of the Rwanda-linked general Laurent Nkunda, also threatened to try and topple the Congolese government, damaging the fragile relationship between the DRC and Rwanda in 2008–9.

The context in which SSR is being implemented, by a range of countries in a state the size of Western Europe and with limited infrastructure, has hampered UN attempts to create security at every turn. The most notable and visible failures have been in the east of the country. The authority of the government there remains limited by the activities of a range of rebel groups from the DRC and beyond. The UN force in the region has proved inadequate in ensuring security, and the Congolese armed forces have frequently been accused of rape, looting and human rights violations.

Congolese police and soldiers remain underpaid or even unpaid, damaging morale and encouraging looting and corruption. The lack of police capacity has led to the army being deployed for purposes of internal security, problematically given their poor reputation and the lack of effective mechanisms for vetting and excluding those who committed abuses during the previous conflicts. The UN's work in this area has been largely inadequate, though in the face of a situation which is arguably not post-conflict this is hardly surprising. What it has left is a dramatic disparity of quality and investment in training and equipment for different units within the police and the army, reflecting the fact that these have often been trained at different centres run by different donors – notably France, the European Union and Angola – with very different approaches (Dahrendorf 2008).

Summary points

1 UN peacekeeping is a very large undertaking with a number of key challenges. The UN does not have a standing army and is reliant on member countries providing troops.
2 The UN record on peacekeeping has been mixed, with some notable failures (Somalia) and some very notable successes (Sierra Leone).
3 The UN is just one of the key actors engaged in rebuilding security sectors following wars.
4 Like other processes in conflict-affected environments, peacekeeping affects the local political economy and security and development dynamics in specific ways.
5 The experiences of the UN provide notable examples of how good intentions can raise serious issues and a range of unintended consequences.

Discussion questions

1 What are the main issues in developing a peacekeeping capability within the UN?
2 Why are UN peacekeeping mandates so important and how have they affected UN operations on the ground?
3 To what extent are regional peacekeeping forces a solution to the shortcomings of UN peacekeeping?
4 Should the UN have a standing army to carry out peacekeeping operations?
5 How should the international community engage with and support regional peacekeeping?

Further reading

Bellamy, Alex J., Williams, Paul, and Griffin, Stuart (2010) *Understanding Peacekeeping*, 2nd ed. Cambridge: Polity.

Boutros-Ghali, Boutros (1992) *An Agenda for Peace: Preventive Diplomacy, Peacemaking and Peace-Keeping*. New York: United Nations.

Dallaire, Romeo (2003) *Shake Hands with the Devil: The Failure of Humanity in Rwanda*. London: Random House/Arrow Books.

Goulding, Marrack (1993) 'The evolution of United Nations peacekeeping', *International Affairs*, 69(3): 451–64.

ICISS (International Commission on Intervention and State Sovereignty) (2001) *The Responsibility to Protect*. Ottawa: International Development Research Centre.

Moore, Jonathan (ed.) (2004), *Hard Choices: Moral Dilemmas in Humanitarian Intervention*. Oxford: Rowman & Littlefield.

Ofuatey Kodjoe, W. (1994) 'Regional organisations and resolution of internal conflict: the ECOWAS intervention in Liberia', *International Peacekeeping*, 1(3): 261–302.

Shawcross, William (2001) *Deliver Us from Evil: Peacekeepers, Warlords and a World of Endless Conflict*. New York: Simon & Schuster.

7   Privatisation of security

A growing feature of the conflict landscape in developing countries is the privatisation of the use of force. This can take the form of the establishment of private armies or presidential guard-type forces which provide security for elites whilst the security of the population at large remains minimal. This is an illustration of how security has moved from being ideally a public good, or even a basic service which populations could expect by virtue of belonging to a state, to in reality a private commodity available only to those who can afford to pay. In the broader field of conflict and peacekeeping, security has also become privatised, with a burgeoning private industry involving companies undertaking a variety of tasks for both states and non-state actors.

The chapter will consider where privatised security fits into the debates discussed so far, exploring how private military companies (PMCs) and private security companies (PSCs) have been involved in both security and development-related activities in developing states, using examples from Iraq, Liberia and Sierra Leone. Having outlined where and how these companies are acting, and the types of roles they are fulfilling, the chapter will analyse the debates around whether they help or hinder development and security, focusing on issues of regulation, oversight and accountability. It will also include discussion on the US policy of using the Department of Defense as a means to bring about development, focusing on Iraq as an example of military-led development, but also on AFRICOM as an organisational solution to improving the security situation across Africa. However, we will also discuss the likelihood of using PMCs to deliver some of this security and the implications of using private contractors to deliver security and development.

What are PMCs and PSCs?

Private companies involved in the security sector can be nominally subdivided into private security companies and private military companies. The former usually provide a range of services, including risk analysis and close protection for individuals and strategically important locations. The latter may offer these services but will also typically provide combat-trained personnel who can be used in training or, in some cases, be deployed alongside the armed forces of a state or in isolation. The term 'private military company' is the one most often used in a more general way to refer to a company which supply some or all of the services above, and it is the one we will use in the rest of the chapter.

In brief, there is a very large number of companies in this area covering a wide range of capabilities of varying quality. Blackwater Worldwide (now Xe) is one of the best known and biggest. It says of its own services:

> We are not simply a 'private security company.' We are a turnkey solution provider for 4th generation warfare. We assist with the development of national and global security plans, train, equip and deploy public safety and military warriors, build combat live-fire indoor/outdoor ranges, MOUT [military operations in urban terrain] facilities and shoot houses, create ground and aviation operations and logistics support packages, develop and execute canine solutions for patrol and explosive detection, and can design and build facilities both domestically and in austere environments abroad.'[1]

In other words, a big company like DynCorp or Xe can cover a huge number of training, tactical and logistical services. MPRI (Military Personnel Resources Inc.), a division of L3 Communications, was founded by General Vuono, former US Army Chief of Staff during the first Gulf War, and General Soyster, a former director of US military intelligence. The company currently has more than forty offices worldwide and employs over 300 former generals.

The range of specialist organisations engaged in this activity within the United States, Western Europe, Russia and Israel is vast, encompassing lower end 'hot' operations, like close protection in Iraq and Afghanistan, through to sophisticated missile, air surveillance, intelligence and logistical services.

It was estimated that in Iraq there were around 185,000 private contractors to around 165,000 soldiers, Afghanistan has continued the increase in the private–public ratio. Marie-Dominique Charlier, a former political advisor to the ISAF commander in Kabul in 2008, describes the growing ability of those companies 'to influence military decisions on operational matters' of ISAF in Afghanistan. Quoting a Congressional Research Service report, she estimates that the numbers of PMC personnel in Afghanistan vary from 130,000 to 160,000, the second-largest deployment after Iraq. This means that the additional 30,000 troops constituting the 2010 surge were accompanied by around 56,000 contracted personnel (Charlier 2010).

The questions here are why there so many and how accountable are they to the US government?

Where do they come from? The historical development of private security

Before discussing how private security actors contribute to contemporary peacekeeping, security and development, it is useful to consider briefly the historical development and experience of such companies in the developing world.

Critics charge that private companies which provide services associated with conflict and peacekeeping, especially those that supply armed soldiers and military equipment to states and non-state actors, are nothing more than modern-day mercenaries. This image, of the soldier for hire, or of the soldier who becomes involved in a conflict because he is paid to do so, often seeking other forms of self-enrichment along the way, is a common one. It is informed by the often romanticised exploits of mercenaries in Africa such as British-born

---

[1]'About us', at www.blackwaterusa.com/ (accessed August 2005).

Mike Hoare and French-born Bob Denard, but mercenaries have existed as an aspect of armed conflict for centuries, from Europe to the Middle East. The individuals mentioned here are archetypal mercenaries, and the term itself has negative connotations reflecting a mistrust and suspicion of those who seek to become involved in conflict for financial gain. However, the privatisation of security has developed radically since the early 1990s, though this is not to say that the image of small bands of men, or soldiers of fortune, seeking to depose governments is entirely outdated. In 2004 a plot was uncovered to overthrow the government of Equatorial Guinea, in West Africa. The plot involved former British SAS and South African military personnel, and is believed to have had financial backing from a range of high-profile individuals in the United Kingdom, South Africa and Lebanon as well as the Equatorial Guinean opposition in exile. However, despite the media attention afforded to this incident, especially in the United Kingdom, mercenary activities of this kind are relatively rare. Much more common is the new face of privatised military power – the PMC.

PMCs have proliferated since the end of the Cold War and particularly since the turn of the century. This is due partly to a range of parallel processes. The end of the Cold War and the anticipation of a more peaceful world led to pressure for the downsizing of standing armed forces. This reflected the desire for a peace dividend to be brought about by reducing military budgets. Those who left security forces as a result of this process formed a ready pool of recruits for the PMCs that began to emerge. It is possible that the end of apartheid in South Africa also had a disproportionately large impact on the development of the private security sector, with some of the earliest and most infamous PMCs established in that country by former apartheid-era security professionals. One in particular is worth discussing briefly in detail, as its activities have had a significant impact on the development of PMCs into the slick corporate organisations we see today. It also sparked some of the first major debates about privatisation of security, its desirability, its impact on sovereignty, its ability to complement or replace the UN and regional actors in managing conflict, and how this new development might feature in a post-Cold War security environment.

The development of post-Cold War military companies

Perhaps the most famous private military company in the 1990s was Executive Outcomes, whose activities continue to inform the high level of suspicion surrounding the motives of such companies; their methods of recruitment; the activities they are willing to perform, and for which clients; and how their fees are paid by developing state governments in particular. Executive Outcomes was created in 1989 in South Africa, consisting primarily of demobilised South African soldiers. It included many from units disbanded at the request of Nelson Mandela's African National Congress (ANC), units which were considered particularly heavy-handed in their treatment of civilians or prisoners and in pursuing anti-apartheid activists. With a well-trained and battle-hardened force to draw upon, advanced techniques, and equipment including armour, helicopters and tanks, the company gained a reputation for effectively helping governments to secure resource-rich areas of their countries from rebel groups. In 1993 it was awarded a contract by the Angolan government to recover diamond mining areas controlled by the rebel group UNITA, which it did with efficiency, and by 1994 it had helped pressure UNITA into negotiations with the government by augmenting the relatively weak Angolan armed forces. In 1995 the company was employed by the government of Sierra Leone to secure the capital, Freetown, and to take back and protect diamond producing areas from the rebel Revolutionary United Front (RUF). Again this was achieved with perhaps surprising speed, though the price of this contract has been difficult to ascertain. It is widely believed that the links between the owners of Executive Outcomes and mineral companies such as Heritage Oil and Gas and Branch Energy allowed the company to arrange deals giving them access to oil and diamonds in Angola and Sierra Leone respectively (Harding 1997).

As the armed forces of developed states, particularly the United States, have become engaged overseas, and amidst financial pressures to cut the size of standing armies, the private security industry has burgeoned. Those demobilised find ready employment in PMCs at the end of their service, and PMCs in turn are able to offer much higher salaries than national armed forces. At the same time, and with the United States mindful of the experiences of Vietnam in Somalia, it is easier to avoid public outcry at the numbers of troops being killed if some of those undertaking dangerous assignments are privately contracted. This fear of body bags returning to the home states has often been forwarded as a key explanatory of the growth of PMCs, but it is difficult to support this contention in the cases of Iraq and Afghanistan, where states intervening have borne heavy casualties.

Amongst the most well-known PMCs are companies based in the United Kingdom (ArmorGroup, Aegis) and the United States (DynCorp, Halliburton). In the United States in particular, such companies are often termed defence contractors, but the overlaps with activities associated with PMCs can be extremely high. In recent years PMCs have become heavily, and controversially, involved in aspects of peacekeeping, peacebuilding and development. DynCorp has been used by the United States to deliver its Plan Colombia policy in South America, and along with other companies was deployed on US soil in the aftermath of Hurricane Katrina. However, it is more often associated with the ongoing operations in Iraq and Afghanistan.

What do people use mercenaries for?

Executive Outcomes is one particular example and demonstrated some of the roles PMC's could play. It is however usually used to highlight the ways that PMCs can become directly involved in combat, but increasingly PMCs play a variety of roles in insecure environments, including but not limited to the following.

> *Protection*   Providing protection for individuals, buildings, bases, personnel, equipment and convoys is a staple activity for private security providers. Local firms often supply guards for NGO premises in developing states, usually unarmed, whilst larger international organisations are more often contracted to provide guards for embassies and donor agencies. Private companies have also secured high-profile contracts from national governments to protect key individuals and staff deployed overseas. This is common for workers and civilian personnel in Iraq and Afghanistan, but the United Kingdom, for example, has used private contractors to guard some of its Foreign Office personnel and embassies for some years.
>
> *Training and advice*   Drawing on a pool of experienced personnel, PMCs are able to provide training and advice for civilians from NGOs, aid agencies and national governments, as well as police and armed forces. This can include the provision of risk analysis for NGOs and other actors operating in insecure environments to facilitate their work. Donor states have also used PMCs as part of their attempts to build up African peacekeeping capacity and to undertake security sector reform. Given its current military commitments overseas, the United States is increasingly unable to send its own military personnel on ACOTA and so delegates this role to private contractors. ACOTA training

has previously been conducted by the PMC Military Professional Resources Incorporated, which has been active in Benin, Ethiopia, Ghana, Kenya, Mali, Malawi, Nigeria, Rwanda and Senegal. The US commitment to undertake SSR in Liberia was also subcontracted, with DynCorp and Pacific Engineering Architects tasked with dissolving the Liberian army and creating a new force. The deals signed with these companies have been criticised by organisations such as the International Crisis Group for a lack of transparency. It is unclear how much they are being paid and the terms under which they are operating, which has also drawn criticism from the Liberian government.

Logistics Another staple activity for private companies in the security sector is in the provision of logistical services to military forces. Companies have secured multi-billion-dollar contracts to fulfil essential non-combat functions, including catering, providing postal services, and constructing and maintaining military bases. The privatisation of these functions is in line with the broader move by many donor governments to achieve greater efficiencies. Within the United States, big PMCs provide air logistics and land transport for military personnel, and there are a number of private firms that provide specialised and protected maritime logistical support.

Force multipliers The members of PMCs are overwhelmingly specialist former military or police. In particular, many consist of former special forces personnel or those engaged in activities such as surveillance, engineering, aircraft piloting or maintenance or even signals and intelligence. Many PMCs also have their own specialisms, including dog handling, mine clearance, maritime protection and anti-piracy, and clandestine surveillance.

Could PMCs contribute to peacekeeping?

The above tasks are relatively discrete and clearly defined. However, there has been much discussion around whether and how PMCs could contribute to peacekeeping. The same trends which have facilitated the growth in PMCs – downsizing of national military forces, the end of the bipolar world order, and the rise in civil wars – have placed considerable pressure on the UN. The failings of UN peacekeeping missions, notably to prevent or halt the 1994 Rwandan genocide or to prevent the Srebrenica massacre, have raised questions about whether such a large and bureaucratic organisation is able to respond with the speed, force and flexibility necessary. In recent years, PMCs have grown considerably in size and also gained experience in the kinds of roles which peacekeepers might be expected to perform. Given their potential to contribute to peacekeeping, the question arises as to how this would work in practice: Would PMCs be expected to undertake particular tasks within a broader UN staffed and led mission? Would they act as an advanced party to be deployed rapidly before potentially being fully or partly replaced by a later UN mission? Could they undertake an entire multidimensional peacekeeping operation, alone or operating as part of a consortium?

For their part, PMCs have indicated a willingness to be involved in all of these scenarios. Showing the scale of their ambition, in 2003 a group of PMCs released a concept paper offering their services to supplement the UN mission in Congo (MONUC). They claimed the deployment could be completed within a three-month period and suggested that their anticipated costs would be a fraction of those of the UN force. They argued that high-profile failings of UN forces, especially in the protection of civilians, demonstrated that it was unable to fulfil its mandate with the resources at its disposal. This possibility of such companies augmenting existing peacekeeping missions or providing specific services for them is much more feasible than the prospect of a mission staffed and managed entirely by a PMC. The need for the UN Security Council to authorise missions makes it highly unlikely that such an initiative would be approved, and though PMCs clearly have a range of skills and experience of value to peace support operations they are unlikely to be able to fulfil all of them. The possibility of rapid-response private security contractors who could deploy quickly with a small well-trained force to prevent genocide or conflict from escalating is also not out of the question. However, the UN has so far seemed unwilling to consider such a standing force, for reasons which will be discussed, and emphasis has instead been on rapid reaction forces based in conflict-prone regions such as sub-Saharan Africa.

Despite the continuing reluctance on the part of many international actors formally to acknowledge the place of private security contractors within global security, these actors are playing a growing role. To understand how this role has changed and what the implications of the trend are for security and development, it is useful to weigh up some of the main advantages and disadvantages of private security forces.

Benefits of private security forces

Perhaps one of the most frequently cited benefits of PMCs is that their availability makes it possible to work in insecure environments which might otherwise be somewhat 'off limits'. In Somalia since the mid-1990s, humanitarian agencies and NGOs, as well as donor representatives, have relied on private security forces to protect their staff and buildings and the aid they are attempting to distribute. In an environment where the rule of law is limited and where arms proliferation has led to large numbers of gangs using force to access even basic resources, agencies and personnel which attempt to go without protection are soft targets. Without the protection of private security providers, often informal and unregulated in contrast to the large corporate PMCs that are associated more with operations in Iraq and Afghanistan, these agencies would be unable to carry out their work.

Supporters of the private security industry often argue that PMCs are more cost effective than traditional militaries. They can provide a specifically tailored and selected force to deal with a particular task, and this is all the contracting organisation has to pay for. It is not cost effective, by contrast, to maintain a standing military force, comprising many components and specialist divisions, when these might rarely if ever be used. The ability of PMCs to put together such forces at short notice is partly a function of the next advantage, their access to skilled personnel.

Because of the large and high-value contracts they can secure for their services, PMCs are able to pay extremely large salaries to those with particular combat experience or skills, especially to those who are being deployed in dangerous environments. Mandatory retirement ages and the downsizing of national armed forces, likely to continue unabated given the current global economic recession, provide a steady stream of recruits for PMCs. The ongoing conflicts in Iraq and Afghanistan have also produced a large number of relatively young members of the armed forces who have considerable combat experience compared with those in their positions a decade or two ago. The linkages between PMCs and the networks of contacts senior PMC staff enjoy with armed forces, intelligence services, and other private defence companies also allow them to source expertise at short notice.

For larger PMCs in particular, the ability to respond rapidly to a request is a key point of differentiation from more bureaucratic organisations such as the UN. The UN needs to secure agreement first that action is necessary, then that a peacekeeping mission is appropriate. Even once this decision has been made, assembling the forces and other contributions necessary from member states can be a long process. PMCs, by contrast, are able to pull together missions relatively quickly, as they can subcontract any necessary skills and expertise which they do not already possess 'in house'. After the Rwandan genocide, one prominent PMC representative claimed that, whilst the UN was left standing by as the killings took place, his company could have deployed a small but effective force within weeks. It is possible that even a small force, if able to act against those committing genocide and in defence of civilians, could have considerably slowed or even stopped the progress of the killings whilst an appropriate UN response was still being debated.

What are the downsides to privatising security?

Critics often highlight the lack of distinction between humanitarian, civilian and military actors. The close association between many NGOs and donor states, as discussed previously, leads to those NGOs being viewed increasingly as an extension of donor foreign and security policy. Protection therefore becomes necessary if agencies are to reach target populations, but it brings risks. By seeking protection from a PMC, humanitarian and development NGOs are required to adopt an attitude to risk which is dictated by the company providing security. This may be more restrictive than what they might otherwise have adopted and so affects where and how they operate. At the same time, by contracting out their security, such organisations gradually lose the ability, or fail to develop the ability in the first place, to conduct their own risk assessments and make their own security arrangements. It is in the interests of the PMC to emphasise the dangers and their ability to mitigate those dangers, but in the longer term, or in particularly insecure country contexts, the likelihood is a more risk-averse posture and a very different relationship between the NGO and those they are trying to assist.

There is also a disparity between local and overseas staff. As with aid agencies and NGOs, local staff are often paid much less than their counterparts brought in from donor countries. Where local staff are paid less, particularly for less skilled jobs such as guarding infrastructure, there is an increased likelihood of corruption and engagement in criminal activities. In addition, local staff are often expected to undertake work which may be more hazardous or in the most insecure areas, as it is considered less dangerous for them than for foreign staff. As has been seen in Iraq, where local citizens are recruited by private security forces, they risk becoming targets for groups who oppose the national government or the national backer of their employing organisation. For those recruited from military forces and government agencies in developed states, high pay levels are used to compensate for the levels of danger involved in assignments, but for local staff, though securing paid work at all may be a luxury, the pay does not always reflect the danger of the job. Again as paralleled in aid work more generally, when the mission is complete, or if the situation deteriorates to a point where overseas staff are removed from the country, local staff are likely to be left behind and potentially subject to reprisals.

There are sometimes quite close links between private security providers and politicians or parties to a conflict. These links are visible for all sizes of private security providers and from the formal to the informal. Small, irregular and informal security companies and providers, especially those operating in developing states, are often linked with local strongmen. Where local groups which are little more than militias are paid to protect the staff of aid agencies or humanitarian NGOs, the funds or goods they receive in return can perpetuate their non-peaceful activities, contributing directly to conflict. Furthermore, reflecting the 'do no harm' approach discussed earlier, such actions send implicit ethical messages which can reinforce the idea that the way to protect yourself is through arms. Payment for the protection activities and the security services such groups supply is channelled back into operations by the group more broadly, and where a group is operating informally in the security sector it can often also be linked to organised crime, including people trafficking and racketeering.

Allegations have surfaced regularly of links between politicians involved in making decisions about war and those larger, more corporate PMCs awarded lucrative contracts to facilitate the conflict or to support peacebuilding and reconstruction. In particular, concerns have been raised about links between key individuals in the Bush administration and US companies awarded large contracts to provide services in Iraq and Afghanistan. Also in Afghanistan, a country whose private security sector has grown exponentially since 2001, senior Afghan government officials, including some close to President Karzai, have been accused of corruption in facilitating the awarding of security contracts to groups which they represent or in which they have financial stakes.

Accountability and oversight

A final key challenge to envisioning the future of PMCs in peacekeeping, security and development is in the arena of accountability, regulation and oversight. The sheer scale of the involvement of private contractors in the peacekeeping and reconstruction operations in Iraq and Afghanistan makes their continued use likely. Many development and reconstruction agencies rely to some extent on protection by military and private contractors, notwithstanding President Karzai's stated intention to have them disbanded or incorporated into a new Afghan force by 2011. Attempts to regulate and provide a legal framework for PMCs have therefore become crucial if these companies are to play a positive role in reconstruction and development. Although attempts have been made to regulate the industry and provide oversight, these have so far been largely inadequate.

In Iraq, PMC personnel were controversially granted immunity from Iraqi prosecution under Order 17, signed by the leader of the Coalition Provisional Authority, Paul Bremmer. This action, alongside the range of complaints about PMC employee conduct discussed above, has led to calls for clarification on the legal framework governing the actions of PMCs and their staff from within Iraq, the United States, international media and human rights and justice NGOs. The difficulty in regulating PMCs stems partly from the difficulty in defining what a PMC is for the purposes of international law. The 1948 Geneva Convention and a UN Convention on Mercenaries (1948) were concerned more with the classic small bands of soldiers of fortune seeking to enrich themselves by overthrowing governments. The corporate outfits which are now in operation are subcontracted by states, which makes even deciding whether captured PMC employees are regarded by international law as prisoners of war or as mercenaries or criminals problematic. As international law is intended to regulate the conduct and relations of states, calls for greater regulation have made little headway in clarifying the international legal position. However, interstate relations are regulated by international law, and should a private contractor operating on behalf of a state break international human rights or humanitarian law in another, it is feasible that the contracting state could face prosecution.

Concerns over the vagueness of regulation of PMC activity have also elicited responses from within the private security industry. Representatives of the large companies have insisted that they are able to self-regulate through effective codes of practise and based on existing international law. Industry organisations such as International Peace Operations

Association (IPOA) and the British Association of Private Security Companies (BAPSC) in particular have contributed to discussions on regulation. The procedures which they have suggested for investigating grievances and complaints have, however, been criticised by human rights groups as not transparent enough and as lacking in effective and adequate punishments. It is possible for states to prosecute those firms they have contracted, even if the offences occur outside of the home/contracting country. The US Military Extraterritorial Jurisdiction Act (MEJA) allows for this eventuality, but covers only personnel contracted by the Department of Defense.

The need for effective frameworks for accountability and oversight is manifest. PMC staff in Iraq and Afghanistan, in particular, have been accused of involvement in civilian deaths, of being too quick to use their weapons, and of prisoner maltreatment. The Abu Ghraib scandal is a particularly well-known case, in which, from 2004, US soldiers were accused of, and in some cases photographed, abusing prisoners in a facility outside Baghdad. Private contractors were also implicated in these events, which included torture and rape of detainees. In 2007, employees of one of the largest US contractors, Blackwater, killed eight civilians and wounded nine others in Baghdad whilst escorting a US diplomatic convoy. Blackwater claimed that a car failing to stop had been perceived as a threat, but subsequent investigations by the Iraqi government and the FBI have found the shootings unjustified. Blackwater's licence to operate was revoked the next day. It has since rebranded (it is now called Xe, pronounced 'Zee') and undergone a change of managerial staff.

Afghanistan has seen an acceleration of private contractors as part of the military effort. As a recent Congressional Research Report stated:

> The Department of Defense (DOD) increasingly relies upon contractors to support operations in Iraq and Afghanistan, which has resulted in a DOD workforce that has 19% more contractor personnel (207,600) than uniformed personnel (175,000). Contractors make up 54% of DOD's workforce in Iraq and Afghanistan. The critical role contractors play in supporting such military operations and the billions of dollars spent by DOD on these services requires operational forces to effectively manage contractors during contingency operations. Lack of sufficient contract management can delay or even prevent troops from receiving needed support and can also result in wasteful spending. Some analysts believe that poor contract management has also played a role in abuses and crimes committed by certain contractors against local nationals, which may have undermined U.S. counterinsurgency efforts in Iraq and Afghanistan.
>
> (Schwartz 2010)

In Afghanistan, as indeed in Angola and Sierra Leone during the 1990s, concerns have been raised about the ways in which contractors source weapons for their staff and those with whom they are working. In the Afghan case, whilst forbidden to import arms, they are frequently accused of illegally bringing weapons into the countries where they operate or buying them on the black market. In this vein, a US Senate Armed Services Committee hearing in 2009 found that Blackwater had employed a subcontractor in Afghanistan, Paravant, which had used weapons intended for the Afghan police, resulting in the accidental shooting of one of their contractors. By buying weapons on the black market or bringing them into the country, PMCs are contributing to the illegal arms market and to weapons proliferation. As discussed earlier, the shadow economy in one item, in this case guns, often intersects with the illegal trade in other goods. The involvement of criminal gangs in the illegal arms market also suggests that, by sourcing their weapons in this way, some PMCs are contributing to groups who threaten the security of the states in which they operate and the region more broadly.

Even when contractors operate relatively uncontroversial activities there are issues with accountability.

> The HNT contract is worth $2.16 billion and covers 70 percent of the supply chain for the U.S. effort in Afghanistan. The contract is critical to the basic survival of U.S. troops stationed throughout the country in remote and dangerous areas. By any measure, a contract of this significance would seem to demand exacting oversight by the Department of Defense. Both military and HNT contractor personnel reported that such oversight was virtually nonexistent.
>
> (SNSFA 2010)

There is a clear need for greater transparency in the awarding of contracts, in setting out the detail of what PMCs are expected to achieve, and in clarifying the relationships between various PMCs and other businesses (particularly those concerned with post-conflict reconstruction or natural resource extraction). Transparency is, however, extremely problematic in the private security industry, and often contracting states have found it difficult to untangle the complex web of associations between different companies. Where one company is damaged by scandal, as happened with Executive Outcomes, Sandline and Blackwater, the bulk of its staff may set up a new company under another name and operate free of any historical stigma. The larger companies also often control a network of smaller companies to which they subcontract projects and tasks, making it a complex undertaking to work out how much of the lucrative defence contracts on offer is going to each of the particular companies. As small companies are frequently sold, subcontracted or subsumed into other organisations, there are also concerns about the vetting and recruitment of staff. Whereas the policies of the parent company may be sound, in practice it is cheaper to employ local staff for many tasks, and the need to have forces ready quickly can preclude effective vetting in an environment where confirming identities and backgrounds is already difficult.

To get around this, many firms have formed oversight mechanisms within the industry along the lines of business associations. A number of the bigger companies belong to associations such as the International Peace Operations Association (IPOA) and the British Association of Private and Security Companies (BAPSC), which have internal guidelines and codes of conduct based on expulsion from that association as the hardest punishment. However, the weakness of this approach is shown when a major company is considered in breach of the guidelines. When IPOA wanted an investigation into Blackwater over the Al-Nisour Square incident in Baghdad, the company left the association and established their own – the Global Peace and Security Operations Institute.

Despite a continual stream of controversy, involvement in congressional hearings, several attempts at expulsion by the Iraqi government, and a change in name driven by the poor publicity, Xe continues to be a major US government contractor. It is currently in the top five contractors used by the State Department, and around 90 per cent of its income derives from government contracts, including extensive involvement in counter-narcotics deployment.

The above concern with vetting and recruitment practices is particularly acute in situations where military, police and other formal and informal security providers have been involved in human rights abuses and violations. The need to fill quotas for staff quickly, particularly given that one of the industry's selling points is its ability to deploy rapidly, can lead to recruitment being rushed. Where individuals known by local populations to have committed abuses are recruited into private security forces, or indeed newly reconstituted national security forces, there is likely to be continuing mistrust by citizens. It also signals that past crimes will not be accounted for and that those in positions of power and responsibility may act with impunity.

Perhaps the most concerning aspect of privatisation is that it turns security into a commodity and potentially into the preserve of those who can afford it. In the same way that private security guards acting to deter crime in wealthy suburbs can displace crime to less well-protected areas, using PMCs to secure targets, people and areas considered of high value displaces insecurity to other areas.

International intervention and private companies: the case of AFRICOM

The United States Unified Command for Africa – AFRICOM – was officially activated on 1 October 2008. A 'command' is the highest organization within the US Department of Defense, in which policies, programmes and personnel are focused on either a geographical region or a functional area of responsibility. AFRICOM is really an internal consolidation of US activity and a reorganisation of Defense Department personnel with the aim of making US policy towards Africa more effective. Among the central themes of AFRICOM's mission are building security partnership capacities, conducting theatre security cooperation, building important counter-terrorism skills and, as appropriate, supporting American government agencies in implementing other programmes to promote regional stability. As such, AFRICOM's primary aim is to support Africans in addressing the security problems of the continent, particularly war prevention.

On face value this is non-contentious. However, in practice it has turned out to be an extremely divisive measure that has proved controversial amongst African states, to the extent that only Liberia was willing to host the HQ; Camp Lemonier is located within a French military base in Djibouti. This is partly the result of the United States failing to enter a dialogue with Africa over AFRICOM, but also because of the weakness of many African states, which have not agreed amongst themselves. This has contributed to Africa's own inability to address issues such as piracy in Somalia. At the same time, Africa's 'regional hegemons', particularly South Africa and Nigeria, may be concerned about the erosion of their own power. The idea of replacing local hegemons (Nigeria and South Africa) with international hegemons (such as the United States or US-controlled companies) may not be a positive step forward. If the United States wishes to support Africans in maintaining their own security, then engagement with the most militarily capable states on the continent must be a key part of that strategy.

Many African analysts hold that AFRICOM represents an example of US paternalism, which excludes Africans from any agency in their own security. In addition, AFRICOM is seen as the United States pursuing its own interests in counter-terrorism and the procurement of African raw materials, which is not only undermining any moral position it may have held but also preventing African states from developing realistic security policies. The African security community itself has consistently raised four core areas that are problematic: regional destabilisation through undermining regional powers and structures; the potential for undermining African states; subordinating African interests to US ones; and undermining the AU – not least by not consulting the organisation in the early stages of AFRICOM.

The situation has been complicated by the role of PMCs within this framework. The most frequently cited example is that of the SSR work carried out by DynCorp in Liberia. The US government contracts with PMCs to provide services, and, quite rightly, that means those companies are accountable to the US government. However, this situation may produce problems if the PMC is not answerable to the local government of the state in which it is operating. As a result, the government of Liberia could not make changes to the mission of DynCorp or anything it was doing whilst training the Liberian armed forces. The government was forced to go to the US administration, which would then go to DynCorp. This raises serious accountability issues in case of underperformance, mismanagement or breaches in human rights. The government of Liberia has no power to sanction US DynCorp staff within its own country.

Other international actors

An alternative view is from the French perspective. French policy has a different set of aims based around the protection of francophone Africa from anglophone incursions. This is based partly on a security policy involving defence co-operation agreements and the regular deployment of marines and legionnaires to the continent. From a French perspective, US support for Kagame in Rwanda, an anglophone in a francophone country, represented a threat to these interests. The development of a US presence in Djibouti, another historical ally, has further intensified this perceived threat, and the French have modified their approach. Instead of acting as a neo-colonial power, France now works primarily through the European Union, allowing the French to engage in areas where there may be historical difficulties (Rwanda) or in anglophone Africa. Seen in this context, the development of AFRICOM is an extension of US power and a potential danger to francophone interests on the continent. France sees AFRICOM both as being about oil and as an extension of the 'war on terror' through institutionalisation of the pan-Sahel Initiative. Consequently, France and francophone Africa is unlikely to come around to AFRICOM any time soon.

Clearly the United States may have good intentions, but AFRICOM is almost a textbook example of how the United States manages in many ways to misunderstand how other parts of the world think. The main mission of AFRICOM itself is to conduct security operations to secure Africa 'in support of US Foreign Policy aims', and the United States fails to recognise that this in itself may be interpreted as a security threat. In short, it also seems clear that AFRICOM represents something of a missed opportunity to reconfigure US engagement with Africa in the wake of the end of the Cold War and the involvement in Iraq and Afghanistan. It further implies that the lessons of recent US engagement suggest that a military approach may not be the best way to engage with an entire continent.

Oil, China and terrorism

Any discussion of AFRICOM's aims takes oil, China and terrorism as its three main points and then raises issues of imperial overstretch in Iraq and Afghanistan. In practice, this may mean that the employment of private military companies is the only way in which the training and support can realistically be carried out under the AFRICOM mandate. This heady mixture of economic gains and private security effectively means that there is a serious sovereignty question concerning the US-sponsored presence. Historically weak regimes have used PMCs to secure commercially viable areas of their country, leaving the rest beyond the reach of the state. An approach predicated on this has, as its logical conclusion, a privatised continent of governments that lose their links with both people and country and concentrate on economic resources guarded by private companies paid for by the United States (and securing them for US interests).

There is, of course, a wider international relations debate about the securitisation of policies towards weak states. Importantly, even if the supposed alternative aims of AFRICOM are not true, the securitisation of traditional development and humanitarian activity in Africa may derail existing approaches to development, including those of US institutions such as USAID. The securitisation of all activities in Africa and interventions being led by the military sends a conflicting set of signals to those people trying to improve the lot of civil society and developing democracies. In the short term there could be some military stabilisation, but in the long term this may have more detrimental effects.

It is certainly clear that AFRICOM needs to change fundamentally its approach to dealing with its African and international partners and, above all, to treat them like partners. Without local ownership, any security gained will be short-lived. Furthermore, this may be exacerbated by the extensive use of PMCs to carry out the core mission. If this is married to a central set of aims that are strategic, relying on denying China and terrorism and on securing oil reserves, then any wider gains in terms of democracy or humanitarian approaches may be endangered. At the same time, if AFRICOM is here to stay, then the question must be whether or not it is redeemable as a credible agency and whether or not the plan to take the current portfolio of activity and the proposal to support state organisations to develop security institutions enjoys any confidence amongst African states.

Are PMCs a blessing or a curse – or both?

Private companies operating in the security sector can therefore be seen as a blessing or a curse. On the one hand, they can deploy quickly and with well-trained, well-equipped forces, without having to go through the many layers of bureaucracy and the difficulties of putting together a force that characterise UN intervention. They can end a conflict quickly and potentially decisively by cutting off rebel funding. They can vastly enhance elements of a state's own armed forces for a short period to inflict military defeats on rebels used to facing demoralised, underequipped and underpaid soldiers and reservists. However, the true financial costs involved are often unclear, with countries leveraging their future income – and development possibilities – in order to secure victory in the present. There is also little guarantee this victory will last once the company leaves – Angola returned to civil war after the end of the Executive Outcomes contract. In short, in the 1990s such companies were seen as able to end conflict, even if only temporarily, to provide an incentive for rebels to pursue negotiated peace, but they were demonstrably unable to provide peace – a much more multifaceted process. Their preoccupation with securing high-value areas such as capital cities and resource-rich locations also brought into question the extent to which they could be successful in providing security to broader populations or where one focal point for violence is lacking, such as in the Rwandan genocide. Since 2001, PMCs have grown in both size and number and are becoming a regular feature of both intervention and post-conflict reconstruction. However, the speed of this transformation is not without its challenges.

PMCs have been used in Iraq and Afghanistan to provide security for individuals and organisations, transport convoys, and key military, economic and government infrastructure. They have also been employed to train the police and armed forces, with the expectation that, as these forces improve, the levels of international troops and private contractor involvement can be reduced. Estimates by the US Congressional Research Service in 2010 suggested there were 30,000 armed private contractors in Iraq and 25,000 in Afghanistan, costing the United States in particular billions of dollars a year. These are the registered official contractors; the rapid growth of the industry had led to an increase in smaller unregistered agencies, which may employ as many as 70,000 in Afghanistan alone.

Where PMC regulation and oversight is ineffective, it becomes difficult for developed states involved in development and reconstruction to argue that developing state governments must enhance their own rule of law. There is also a dilemma as to how long PMC training programmes for national security forces should last. Critics have often charged that donors are too quick to tick training boxes and then withdraw before recruits are ready to take over, but PMCs have contradictory motivations. To finish quickly would, if training proves successful, be a good advertisement for their company and potentially attract new business; on the other hand, the longer the training and other contracts last, the more these companies can earn. The important role which states contracting such organisations should then play is in providing clear transparent requirements, with benchmarks to show that programmes have achieved objectives. Given the stretched nature of many armed forces engaged in post-conflict reconstruction and development, and financial pressures to downsize militaries to create a more flexible response capability, it is likely that PMCs will continue to play a significant role.

Summary points

1   Much of the current security terrain is occupied by private military contractors.
2   Private security involves a broad group of actors, ranging from professional companies undertaking specialised security tasks to individual mercenaries.
3   The main issue with private contractors is accountability to responsible authorities, which is difficult to enforce.
4   As international interventions become more stretched and more complex, it seems likely that there will be an increased reliance on PMCs.
5   Privatising security brings with it a political responsibility with regard to who and which groups can afford to pay for protection and which can't.

Discussion questions

1   Should private companies be involved in security operations?
2   How might you regulate private companies to develop accountability mechanisms for their actions?
3   What criteria could be used to judge the effectiveness or success of PMC operations?
4   Could the ad hoc employment of rapid-response PMCs be a viable solution to the UN's lack of a standing army?
5   How might interventions such as AFRICOM make use of PMCs in a positive way?

Further reading

Avant, Deborah (2005) *The Market for Force: The Consequences of Privatizing Security*. Cambridge: Cambridge University Press.
Gaultier, Leonard, *et al.* (2001) *The Mercenary Issue at the UN Commission on Human Rights: The Need for a New Approach*. London: International Alert; www.international-alert.org/pdf/unhr.pdf (accessed 6 March 2011).

Harding, Jeremy (1997) 'The mercenary business: Executive Outcomes', *Review of African Political Economy*, 24(71): 87–97.

Holmqvist, Caroline (2005) *Private Security Companies: The Case for Regulation*, Policy paper no. 9. Stockholm: SIPRI.

Musah, Abdul, and Kayodi Fayemi (eds) (2000) *Mercenaries: An African Security Dilemma*. London: Pluto Press.

Shearer, David (1998) *Private Armies and Military Intervention*, Adelphi Paper no. 316. Oxford: Oxford University Press.

Singer, Peter (2003) *Corporate Warriors: The Rise of the Privatized Military Industry*. Ithaca, NY: Cornell University Press.

8 Security and justice after conflict

This chapter outlines the complex area of justice and security following conflict. In some ways these can be seen as two separate subject areas, but they are inextricably entwined. First we look at the large subject of disarmament, demobilisation and reintegration (DDR), which forms the core of activities that immediately follow conflict in most places. This incorporates issues such as what to do with combatants, both rebel or insurgency movements and swollen militaries formed to fight them, and the types of activity designed to assist combatants to return to their communities. The chapter then goes on to examine the nature of security and justice in post-war situations, including the growth of crime and other security problems, along with the establishment of systems to tackle justice issues. This is a huge topic that covers a lot of complex ideas about the nature of justice and the law and what is applicable in a state emerging from conflict. Different perceptions of justice and the role of the international criminal court, international justice, transitional justice and local perceptions of justice are considered. Finally the idea of security sector reform is analysed as a means to bring together some of these issues and how it is used to make sense of the sometimes complicated lexicon used to describe peacebuilding, truth and reconciliation commissions, post-conflict reconstruction and public and individual security.

When do conflicts end?

There is currently a lot of debate and a lot of literature dealing with 'post-conflict reconstruction'. It may be surprising, therefore, to discover that there is something of a debate about when the post-conflict phase actually starts and when conflicts end. This is frequently portrayed by international aid agencies as a *conflict cycle*, which is essentially a four-stage process, as outlined in Table 8.1. This outline of the conflict cycle makes a number of assumptions, including a similarity across different conflicts but also linearity within conflicts, which means that conflicts all follow a similar development process. However, it also raises a number of questions, not least how the international community measures the start and end of conflicts and what levels of violence are to be expected after a ceasefire. In addition, there is an underlying assumption here that peace equates to no violence and is a 'normal' condition for most societies. This is disputed in some of the literature (see Chapter 3).

What is clear from Table 8.1 is that this particular chapter is essentially dealing with a set of actions that are occurring after the formal ceasefire in most cases – i.e., late on in the cycle. Even then, there are notable exceptions, particularly in Iraq, where there is continued violence, and also in Afghanistan, where the government and international allies are fighting

Table 8.1 The conflict cycle

Stage	Nature of conflict	International response	Peace operations
Escalation	Gradual escalation of violence, culminating in formal start of armed conflict	Diplomacy aimed at conflict prevention	Conflict prevention activities, primarily diplomatic
Armed conflict	Battle death casualties under formal conflict conditions	Mitigation	Humanitarian and 'peacemaking' interventions, including armed intervention
Post-ceasefire	Gradual decline in absolute levels of violence and change in nature of violence	Termination, DDR	Peacekeeping operations and peace enforcement operations
Peace	Few or no conflict casualties	Recovery	Peacebuilding operations, small arms and light weapons control

a counter-insurgency war whilst simultaneously engaging in 'post-conflict' activities such as peacebuilding, DDR and small arms control.

What is special about the post-conflict context?

The study of post-conflict states is blessed with a wide and varied lexicon of terms that overlap, contradict and confuse whilst trying to describe varying forms of collapse. Whether fragile, weak, collapsed or neo-patrimonial, these dysfunctional states all suffer from vulnerability to external shocks, internal conflict, competing economic and political structures, and an inability to exercise effective legal control within their borders. A post-conflict state exhibits all of these features but in extreme circumstances. What post-conflict security implies is a context in which there has been a serious conflict which has come to an end, the state may have completely collapsed along with security, and there is a desire to reconstruct it.

Engaging in security and justice in post-conflict environments poses special challenges but may also bring particular opportunities. Post-conflict states may be weak or even non-existent, political situations may be fragile and continue to be violent, and economies may, at best, be precarious. For a policymaker, a blank slate may be attractive for reconstruction, since there is usually a local will to accept all forms of external support, even in sensitive areas like security, which may be lacking in countries not experiencing collapse. This may, however, be complicated when the environment is not actually 'post-conflict' at all, as in Afghanistan and Iraq.

The main difference between post-conflict interventions and 'normal' interventions is that the former needs to deal with the legacy of past conflict (Bryden and Hänggi 2005). This could be true of any post-authoritarian state, however it is defined. Rather, the main distinguishing features of post-conflict environments are usually the need to provide immediate security; the need to manage and disarmam, demobilise and reintegrate combatants; and the need to downsize security actors. At the same time, post-conflict intervention is usually carried out in highly unstable political environments where the 'war mentality' may still be present, armed groups are usually powerful, there is no democratic tradition, small arms and light weapons are readily available, and the state may have completely or partially collapsed.

The social environment

Armed conflict is extremely damaging to the social fabric of any country affected. Apart from the obvious loss of human capital caused by casualties, conflicts tend to break down the traditional networks and family structures on which people rely in their everyday lives. There is a tendency for entire communities to be uprooted and become internally displaced persons (IDPs), and this also tends to produce rapid urbanisation as people flee the countryside for the relative security of towns and cities. In northern Uganda this was manifest in the phenomenon of 'night commuters', whereby people would not sleep in their homes, but would come into the main cities and sleep wherever they could, returning to their fields in the morning.

Apart from the issues of IDPs, conflict tends to exacerbate inequalities within society, since those affected are disproportionately rural and poor. The rich may be able to relocate internationally and then return following the war, whereas the only options available to the poor may be to walk to relative safety as internal or external refugees. The large-scale migration of people, the collapse of the state, and the traditional and formal (police) means of maintaining human security are also associated with considerable increases in the incidence of HIV/AIDS and associated violence against women.

Rebuilding this social fabric is extremely complex and is a long-term undertaking. Education, water, sanitation and basic security at the local level are critical as the basis of a recovery strategy, but these need to be accompanied by support for the collective trauma produced by conflict and the need to deal with atrocities and human rights abuses in a lawful manner.

The importance of gender

Gender is particularly important in post-conflict environments. When discussing gender here, we are not talking just about women, but about the relationship between women and men within society. In most conflicts, the early phases are characterised by men fighting, but this changes as women may start off being victims but then become perpetrators. This has significant effects on social structures where women have traditionally had a subservient role within the household. Consider the Maoist movement in Nepal. Women play a very traditional role in the household in most of Nepal and have not generally been recruited into the security services. However, the Maoist ranks include several influential, educated and experienced women with command and combat experience. In the post-war environment this may mean that not only will many of those women will be unwilling to take up traditional roles again, but there needs to be a reassessment of the nature of the police and the military in terms of accommodating women into the ranks of integrated security services. This is a significant cultural and societal change that should not be underestimated.

At the same time, whilst domestic violence remains a very serious issue across large parts of the world, it is a particular danger in post-conflict environments. Many analysts believe that gender-based violence actually increases after conflicts, even when women have been deliberately targeted during the conflict. This incorporates rape, torture, beatings, marital rape and also psychological violence, none of which is halted by a formal peace agreement. For example, in Nepal both sides targeted women despite a high level of female participation within the Maoist movement, and this has continued following the conflict. In many ways the Nepali peace represents an opportunity for women, but it also takes place within a view of the male participants that women are simply going to return to traditional roles (see Watson and Crozier 2009).

The economic environment

Armed conflicts have a tendency to destroy economies, reducing production and consumption of goods, but also severely reducing wealth and livelihoods. Depopulation of rural areas often leads to critically reduced production of food, whilst the destruction of infrastructure means that the economy is in no position to recover rapidly. At the same time, there is a brain drain effect, as those who can leave the conflict zone, frequently to go overseas.

This is a hugely difficult area but is important. One of the easiest ways to provide anyone with a disincentive to pick up a weapon is to give them a job. However, the frequently expected 'peace dividend' following ceasefire agreements usually takes a long time to develop, and it may be the international community itself that provides the main source of jobs for several years after a conflict through the presence of international troops and aid agencies. Investment takes a lot longer, and apart from some goods – notably the manufacture of alcohol and cigarettes – manufacturing takes a long time to recover if it manages to do so at all.

The security environment

Violence does not usually end with the signing of a ceasefire agreement. Whilst the main protagonists may be sincere in their desire for a peaceful solution to a conflict, it is difficult to control all local commanders, many of whom may be seeking to do well personally out of the situation. At the same time, there are bound to be tensions at a local level between former combatants. However, the main source of violence in most post-ceasefire situations is usually criminality. When a conflict is over but the state may be lacking effective security forces, particularly police, criminal gangs see opportunities to fill the vacuum. Large international operations around drugs, for example, are relatively footloose and can locate very quickly into areas of the world economy where smuggling cannot be properly counteracted.

In terms of human security, the absence of local police in particular, coupled with the location of migrant communities usually in camps, means that some groups, particularly women and children, suffer from forms of violence that are relatively low on the radar of the international community. Domestic violence is a real problem in most post-conflict environments and can be very difficult to deal with. In the aftermath of the Sierra Leone war, one of the innovations developed by the country's police was the hiring of more women and the establishment of family support units to tackle this specific problem. This was so successful that the model has been exported to other parts of West Africa.

Post-conflict security

Having outlined the overall context of post-conflict security and justice, it is instructive to unpack the security aspect to look at some of the complexity that may exist beneath the surface. The first element in this is to consider the complexity of state and human securities. The contrast between them is set out in Table 8.2. Post-conflict security interventions need to build on both of these. Clearly states need to exist, but they are not just bureaucratic expressions or institutions. States need legitimacy, and they are more likely to be legitimate if they can demonstrate that

Table 8.2 Contrasting state and human security

State security	Human security
Protecting political structures and territory	Protecting human well-being
Regime survival, state and sovereignty	Survival of people rather than states – sometimes regardless of or against states
Based on 'freedom from fear' – war, terrorism, territory	Based on 'freedom from want' – basic needs, security of individuals, emancipation
State-building as a technical-institutional process	Protection of 'human rights' and human dignity

they are representative but also that they can meet legitimate human security concerns. Where states struggle to develop legitimacy is where they claim a monopoly of force (and therefore of security) but lack the capacity to protect against smuggling, drug gangs or non-state actors that affect the security of the population.

This is a particular concern in post-conflict environments, where rates of violence may actually be comparable with rates during fighting, even if the source of the violence (crime) is different. At the same time, indirect deaths through disease, malnutrition or poor medical care are also likely to remain high and further undermine state legitimacy. Against this background many post-conflict countries also face an increased risk of structural conflict through demographic changes. A so-called youth bulge can produce a situation whereby there are a disproportionate number of young, unemployed males in society – just the demographic that is the most likely to enter violent crime. This may also be exacerbated by a high concentrations of IDPs in camps or shanty towns, where other crimes, particularly theft and sexual violence against women tend to be higher.

This, then, adds to a long list of threats to human security in post-conflict situations – violations of human rights, job and income security, violent crime, non-governed spaces, state terrorism, food insecurity, disease, population displacement, environmental degradation and loss of cultural or social identity – an extremely complex list of factors to build into an overall intervention strategy in security and justice. The international community has developed a set of requirements for dealing with these aspects built around a number of key principles:

- conflict resolution and suppression (stopping conflicts starting again);
- long-term political stability (usually through comprehensive peace agreements and attempts to address underlying problems);
- economic development (the most difficult);
- 'democratic' government (in a variety of guises);
- societal transformation (not trying to go back to the pre-war society but developing new ways of working – e.g., gender relations);
- respect for human rights and the law (see below).

Within this overall framework sit the core approaches to security and justice outlined above. These include DDR (see below) but also strategies on small arms and light weapons, resettlement programmes, improvement of service provision and peacebuilding activities. They also imply an approach to the development of social justice that raises some critical questions about how to achieve all of these elements – in particular about control and external drivers of change, accountability, and operational priorities and long-term aims, all of which we will come to below.

Disarmament, demobilisation and reintegration

DDR is one of the most common types of external intervention in post-conflict environments. Essentially the idea is very simple:

1   *Disarmament* refers to the collection, documentation, control and disposal of small arms, ammunition, explosives and light and heavy weapons of both combatants and civilians.
2   *Demobilisation* refers to the formal and controlled discharge of identified and active combatants from armed forces and other non-state armed groups.
3   *Reintegration* refers to the process by which former combatants acquire civilian status and gain sustainable employment, livelihood or income in a civilian capacity.

So far, so good, but the picture is further complicated by a wide variety of other aspects that have to be included. In particular there are a whole range of alternatives for the 'R' element, among them:

- *reinsertion*, which refers to a form of transitional assistance designed to cover the basic needs of the ex-combatant as they establish themselves. This could involve transitional security costs as well as food, shelter, medical help, training, employment or tools;
- *rehabilitation*, which is a common element in most DDR-related programmes and is critical in achieving positive results. It refers primarily to the means through which former combatants can overcome psychological issues, drugs and drink problems (which are very common), and issues related to the communities expected to bear the return of combatants following conflict;
- *resettlement, repatriation, etc.*, which refer to the bundle of issues surrounding the whole package of settling former combatants who may have been removed from their communities for some time.

In addition to the 're' elements of DDR, there is the possibility of integration rather than rehabilitation. This is where the two opposing armed forces give up their former formations and come together in what is usually termed a 'national army'. This happened, for example, in the case of South Africa, where the former ANC fighters and the South African Defence Force merged into a new force that was a genuine South African military. Similar processes have taken place in a wide variety of contexts, ranging from Burundi to El Salvador, and they may involve merging armies, intelligence agencies and the police. The advantage of integration programmes is that they may form the basis for confidence in change within a state previously seen as being oppressive (apartheid South Africa) and also the recognition that not everyone is able or willing to return to the community from which they came.

The first DDR programmes date from the United Nations Observer Group in Central America in 1989, although the activities individually are not new. Since the 1980s there have been more than sixty documented DDR programmes. Over this time there has been a shift in emphasis away from purely military approaches and towards more developmental ideas, particularly on rehabilitation elements. In fact, in many post-conflict environments DDR programmes have been a major source of international funding for a wide range of activities.

DDR programmes have become an integral part of the post-conflict process and are critically important for a number of reasons:

- they form a symbolic act relating to the willingness of participants to develop peaceful approaches;
- they are an integral part of the peace process and the overall reduction in the numbers of small arms and light weapons;
- they are the main means through which former combatants can stop being combatants and regain some form of normal life.

However, DDR has been criticised for being a process that is frequently carried out independently of broader peacebuilding initiatives. For example, it does not usually address weapons that are circulating within the civilian population, and, historically, many programmes have had symbolic and public weapon-burning ceremonies that have effectively destroyed obsolete rather than operational weapons. In addition, DDR processes have resulted in increased flows of weapons over borders in conflicts that have a regional character, and this has been made worse by combatants receiving help in more than one country – e.g., a combatant in Sierra Leone being demobilised there, but then moving into Liberia and going through the same process, and then on to the DRC, etc. This situation was worsened by some of the techniques used for demobilisation, particularly paying combatants an allowance.

Badly done DDR and gender

This is important because, where it has been done badly, DDR has usually made things worse. Demobilising combatants with emotional or psychological issues and handing them money creates a situation whereby combatants have no means to support themselves other than to turn to crime or violence. At the same time, it has been recognised that women can comprise a significant element of any combatant body and yet they may have different DDR needs. Women often become directly involved in fighting, as in Liberia. However, many more women perform essential logistical support tasks, such as cleaning, cooking, childcare and portering, as well as having a sexual role in either a voluntary or a forced status. In most DDR programmes, though, women are almost invisible and have been treated as no more than dependents of the men. There are numerous reasons for this, including the registration of combatants, which is usually provided in conjunction with local commanders. DDR programmes themselves are usually designed for men and thus may have little relevance for women. For example, in Sierra Leone there was an undue emphasis on military integration for the men or, alternatively, income generation through retraining in skills such as carpentry. Reproductive health was not really represented, and many women who had been forcibly used as sex slaves within the RUF found it difficult to register as heads of households and therefore to access benefits.

International law and, now, international DDR guidelines state that women should not be discriminated against on the basis of their sex. UN Security Council Resolution 1325 specifies that DDR programmes should take account of the different needs and experiences of women and men and therefore need to reflect the involvement of women. This effectively means that women and girls will have to be encouraged to register and programmes should cope with their demands in their own right rather than as dependents.

DDR in Afghanistan has had a number of unintended consequences for women (see Rossi and Giustozzi 2006). From the beginning it was about male Islamic combatants attached to the Taliban, and there was very little understanding of how the programmes would affect women and households. First, former combatants are frequently left at home for months before reintegration packages take hold. The subsequent tensions within households increase the risk to women through the likelihood of domestic violence on account of frustration. Second, women and children were usually left behind to tend animals and look after the farm. On their return many men have failed to take up these roles again, and therefore women's tasks have expanded overall without any corresponding increase in male workloads.

An important question to ask here is who is eligible for DDR? This is a contentious issue in many contexts. The starting point is always that those eligible should be all combatants and support services of any armed group. However, drawing boundaries around this group is not easy. Child soldiers, for example, are frequently regarded as being ineligible and may enter a different process. In addition, not everyone who can hand in a weapon is a legitimate combatant, and there needs to be an assessment strategy that verifies eligibility. Typically, this would exclude those too young or who have not served for long enough, and would aim to weed out those who had not served in an armed force. Women constitute another complex group in this process.

Issues in DDR

The first step in the DDR process is disarmament, which is clearly highly symbolic. This is usually managed by military or former military personnel, frequently from a neutral country or organisation. Whilst it is an important aspect of national arms control, there are issues with getting hold of the right weapons rather than obsolete weaponry and also in maintaining the confidence of those disarming. For example, there were concerns during the Zimbabwean peace process that, once the ZIPRA and ZAPU forces were gathered at the assembly points, the Rhodesian security forces would launch an attack. This was mitigated by UK intervention and security guarantees. In Nepal, following the insurgency, the Maoist guerrillas were allowed to keep their weapons in their cantonments, but these were locked away in central storage with the UN and the Maoists retained a key. The safety of all parties and a proportional and fair disarmament process should always be core concerns.

The demobilisation phase of the process officially transfers combatants to civilian status and involves their formal discharge from armed formations. This should be linked with formal honouring ceremonies such as lowering flags to highlight the 'peace with honour' elements of discharge. Wherever possible, discharge should not be accompanied by cash lump-sum payments, since these may be perceived as 'cash for weapons'. Any payment to support reinsertion of former combatants into society should be linked to training or work undertaken and paid gradually over a period of time. This is not a quick process.

The reintegration process is easily the most complex element of DDR. Essentially it can be broken down into a series of components:

- providing information and counselling on available reintegration opportunities;
- supporting the former combatants and their dependents in participating in local communities;
- offering targeted support to groups in need of specialised care (children, the chronically ill, the disabled, women and youth);
- increasing the capacities of the receiving communities to integrate the demobilised.

The real core of any reintegration effort is the information, counselling and referral system. A shortage of job opportunities is essentially a security risk, and therefore it is critical to develop alternatives to violence-based livelihoods for former combatants. This might entail training or broader education, including literacy classes and vocational training. It may also involve integration possibilities – i.e., moving from one army to new security forces. This should also provide support to those who need help with mental or physical issues as a result of conflict.

Critically, it is common for local communities to reject some former combatants, as a result either of atrocities during the conflict or for some other reason (like crime), so maintaining a dialogue with the communities is extremely important. It is often assumed that these communities are passive in the DDR process, but without their participation the entire enterprise will fail. It is necessary that accepting communities should benefit, to avoid accusations that DDR processes reward belligerents rather than those who were law-abiding.

Gender remains a difficult issue in the DDR process. For example, women may have been active combatants, or they may have played logistical support roles either voluntarily or as a result of coercion. They may also be dependents of male combatants. Many DDR programmes have provided inadequate support to these groups, partly as a result of the requirement to hand in a weapon in order to participate in a DDR programme. In addition, it has been the case within some programmes that women have had poorer access to information sources and may even be prevented by their own commanders from being put forward for the better employment opportunities. The concentration of young men in such groups and the availability of alcohol and drugs, as well as the usurping of normal social roles, mean that many young men in particular may resort to domestic violence or drug abuse, both common problems within DDR programmes.

Reconstituting justice

Since the 1980s, along with DDR programmes, societies making a transition from an authoritarian regime to democracy, or from conflict to peace, have chosen to deploy a variety of mechanisms to deal with the legacies of human rights abuses by previous regimes or during conflict. These measures are collectively known as transitional justice, in order to differentiate them from the longer-term development of regularised state and non-state justice systems. The United Nations defines transitional justice as the 'full range of processes and mechanisms associated with a society's attempts to come to terms with a legacy of large-scale past abuses, in order to ensure accountability, serve justice and achieve reconciliation' (UN 2004: 4).

Such interventions would typically include elements of:

- criminal prosecutions;
- truth and reconciliation commissions;
- reparations for victims;
- tribunals;
- vetting; and
- institutional justice reform.

These activities involve prosecution, accountability and also truth-telling, all of which contribute to overall accountability and the rule of law but also in the reconstruction of the public narrative of what happened during the years of conflict. Traditionally, transitional justice has been seen as a separate process to DDR, but increasingly the two are being treated as interlinked, aimed at overcoming the illegitimate use of force and the capacity of societies to integrate former combatants. The establishment of the International Criminal Court (ICC) provides another international mechanism for accountability linking DDR and transitional justice.

What constitutes a 'war crime' or a 'violation of human rights'?

There are several sources of definition for this type of crime. The ICC offers a series of definitions of the offences subject to transitional justice within the Rome Statute of 2002 and defines a war crime as:

- wilful killing;
- torture or inhuman treatment, including biological experiments;
- wilfully causing great suffering or serious injury to body or health;
- extensive destruction and appropriation of property not justified by military necessity or carried out wantonly;
- compelling a prisoner of war (POW) or protected person to serve in hostile forces;
- wilfully depriving POWs of a fair trial or treatment;
- unlawful deportations or confinement;
- taking of hostages;
- killing or wounding a combatant who has laid down arms;
- using any form of gas or chemical warfare;
- committing outrages of personal dignity, in particular humiliating treatment; and
- intentionally using starvation of civilians as a method of warfare.

The statute goes on to discuss the issue of serious violations of international customs that are applicable to armed conflicts, in particular directing attacks against the civilian population in the knowledge that such attacks may cause significant incidental or collateral damage, damage property or kill civilians. It clearly states that the excessive use of force where it is likely that there will be civilian casualties also constitutes a violation, as does the deliberate bombing or shelling of urban areas or villages – something that is commonplace in several contemporary wars.

The definition of crimes against humanity may overlap, but are different, even though they may be associated with transitional justice:

- murder;
- enslavement;
- deportation and forced migration;
- imprisonment;
- torture;
- rape, sexual slavery, enforced prostitution, forced pregnancy, sterilisation or any form of sexual violence;
- persecution of any identifiable group or collectivity on political, racial, religious or gender grounds;
- enforced disappearance of persons; and
- other inhuman acts.

This second list is further enhanced by the specific laws against genocide set down in the 1948 Convention on Genocide, where genocide is effectively seen as an extreme version of crimes against humanity.

Approaches to transitional justice

It is useful to review the main approaches to transitional justice to provide a comprehensive picture of the issues that arise in this field. A full discussion of all approaches is beyond this book, but this chapter will concentrate on:

- the ICC;
- prosecutions and tribunals;
- truth and reconciliation commissions;
- reparations; and
- institutional reform and local justice.

The International Criminal Court

The ICC is effectively an expression of the liberal view of universal human rights enshrined in the UN. These rights seek to protect the individual from justice that is the sole preserve of the state. The core idea of the 'liberal peace' is that human rights are universal and that they should be enforced as such, regardless of the wishes of states. This idea was developed further by outlining a consensus on universal human values and also creating an international legal mechanism for independent enforcement of those values – the ICC – where the international community can represent individual citizens against states as well as prosecuting individuals for war crimes and issuing warrants for their arrest.

The Rome Statute was signed by 120 countries. Only seven countries stood in opposition to the ICC, importantly among them the United States and also Sudan, which has been identified as a one-time haven for some of those subject to ICC warrants, including Joseph Kony of the Lord's Resistance Army. At the same time, the ICC is innovative partly because it also embraces non-state signatories, namely 250 NGOs that provide a voice for those not represented by states.

As a result, the outcome of the Rome Statute reaches beyond the conventional range of international law and widens the process of referral to international justice mechanisms beyond the community of states and particularly the permanent members of the UN Security Council. By establishing an office of an independent prosecutor the statute provides an avenue for individuals and non-governmental actors, not necessarily represented by states, to pursue formal international justice.

The ICC is theoretically empowered to investigate acts of genocide, war crimes, crimes against humanity and 'aggression', but there are significant brakes on its power to do this in practice. Apart from pressure from the United States as a non-signatory, the ICC has no means of enforcement but depends on signatory states to comply. This means that, if an ICC warrant is issued, it has to rely on the justice mechanism of the representative state – a real problem if the state is the perpetrator. Whilst this can be partially overcome by bringing perpetrators to court in the ICC in the Netherlands, it does mean that states still hold the upper hand in legal terms.

When in 2003 President Museveni of Uganda called for the first warrant to be issued on Joseph Kony, the leader of the rebel group the LRA, it became a test case for the ICC. Unfortunately Kony remains at large, and the involvement of Museveni in the warrant has created some criticism, since it has characterised the LRA as the sole perpetrator of violence and entirely in the wrong, whereas the Ugandan army has been involved in extensive violence in the north of Uganda for some years. Thus it is perceived that the use of the ICC system is biased towards state violence in this case. To date the jury remains out on the effectiveness of the ICC.

Prosecutions and tribunals

The first group of approaches refers broadly to prosecutions – i.e., formal proceedings against someone in a criminal court, usually involving suspected human rights violations or other international crimes. The nature of these proceedings can vary considerably, from those held in the ICC in the Netherlands or another neutral country (e.g., Arusha in Tanzania in the case of Rwanda) through to big, set-piece international courts in-country, as used in Sierra Leone. Such proceedings tend to focus on leaders and those who can be clearly identified as influential in the style of atrocities. They also tend to involve international legal staff and judges, and measurement is made against international law.

The use of criminal punishment through prosecution is frequently cited as the most effective method of preventing further conflicts and human rights violations. The publicity of such proceedings is designed to produce a deterrent effect through demonstrating that perpetrators can and will be punished under international law and also showing the victims that post-conflict governance involves a willingness to enforce the rule of law.

In practice, however, such trials are subject to significant difficulties, not least the fact that they cannot punish everyone. The two most recent examples of this type of action, in Sierra Leone and Rwanda, both lasted several years and managed to try only a small proportion of those who had actually perpetrated the crimes. In fact they went on for so long that several of the accused died whilst in custody, never seeing their cases tried in court.

At the same time, in situations where the judicial system has either collapsed or been compromised by close association with previous regimes, there are questions about who is going to do all the legal work involved and who is going to pay for it. Indeed, there are questions about the level of domestic accountability of the legal system if it is simply imported. From the victims' perspective it may be more credible to involve a local judicial system, but this is not often possible. An additional issue here is that of international justice versus local ideas of justice. Whilst there remains an issue of avoiding 'victor's justice' and merely taking revenge, there are real issues of difference between the law and what local people regard as justice. The best way to illustrate this is through an example.

In the special court in Sierra Leone, several members of various rebel groups were being prosecuted for war crimes, but then a former minister, Samuel Hinga Norman, was arrested and set to stand trial for the same offences. To many people in Sierra Leone, Norman was a hero. He had organised the local village militias into defence forces that had fought the rebels and in many cases had managed to protect civilians. However, they had fought a vicious war in the same manner as the extremely violent RUF, and it was on this basis that Norman was arrested. There were several demonstrations outside the court building in Freetown and protests from several people involved in the war citing Norman as a hero. In the event he died whilst in custody before his case was completed.

The relevance of this case is that local people may sometimes have different perceptions of justice to those upholding international law.

Truth and reconciliation commissions

In the last twenty years there have been more than twenty commissions established in a wide range of countries. An increasing number of local actors have sought to develop non-judicial mechanisms for accountability and narrative construction and as a means of making a positive contribution to building trust and reconciliation. The most common form of commission is the 'truth' commission, or truth and reconciliation commission (TRC), whereby local authorities seek to develop and establish an accurate, or at least accepted, historical record of events. This is carried out mainly through the identification of particular individuals and institutions responsible for the violations and then interviewing them to provide a rich seam of material for cross-reference.

The best-known example of this has been the South African Truth and Reconciliation Commission, where members of the former apartheid regime recounted various acts of abuse perpetrated by the previous government. It has also been used effectively in Chile and Argentina to find out what happened to those who had disappeared under previous military regimes.

There is no easy way to develop reconciliation, and the very fact that TRCs frequently lend those giving evidence a form of immunity from further prosecution may actually increase the legacy of bitterness in the peace process. There is a balance here between the importance of developing an official and accurate collective memory of what happened and a desire for accountability and prosecution. It may be that some crimes are so great – as in the South African case – that some specific individuals can later be prosecuted in criminal proceedings. It may also be the case that – as in Rwanda – there is little pretence at getting to the truth as opposed to a particular version of events.

Reparations

A hugely contentious subject, the practice of paying reparations to victims of abuse after a conflict reflects two main needs:

1   to provide recognition of the victims and their losses; and
2   to show that the new post-conflict government is taking past abuses seriously and therefore cementing a stronger trust between state and citizens.

A third reason is clearly that the payment of reparations prevents the perception that perpetrators gain through being perpetrators – i.e., they gain financially as they go through the DDR process, whereas those who were not combatants do not. The absence of reparations payments in a post-conflict context, particularly where the DDR process does indeed provide some form of support for former combatants, can greatly increase the risk of local communities not accepting reinserted combatants and therefore represents a risk to the process as a whole.

Institutional reform and local justice

This is another huge subject but is critical to the longer-term functioning of the state justice system. Transitional reform effectively relates to the prevention of future human rights violations and violence through tackling the structural conditions that led to conflict in the first place. Justice – or perceived lack of justice – frequently sits at the core of this. Typically, institutional reform can involve the redesign of oversight mechanisms, training, capacity-building, etc., but it also entails the vetting of those within the system and the credibility of, for example, police officers who served in the previous regime. Those guilty of human rights abuses or widespread corruption, for example, are frequently rooted out and replaced with younger officers.

There is a key question within the reform process about the balance of the new system. For example, most people in the countryside and who cannot afford lawyers do not receive formal justice from state providers, but from local forms of non-state or quasi-state justice systems. In parts of Africa this may be the local chief, who has a brief to dispense local justice that is cheap, understandable and immediately available. In many other parts of the world this same system may be operated by village elders or religious authorities. This type of 'traditional justice' is clearly attractive, but it does raise issues that can create difficulties. Traditional justice systems have been biased against some segments of society, particularly women and youth. In Africa, the exclusion of women and youth from local justice and the abuse of these systems by local chiefs was a major contributor to more than one conflict, particularly in Sierra Leone. Whilst traditional justice systems are clearly important, there are serious questions concerning their incorporation into the overall justice system.

Having said this, the impact of local justice mechanisms can be astonishing. The impact of the *gacaca* system developed in Rwanda following the genocide led to the establishment of some 11,000 local courts in 2002 designed to try low-level suspects of genocidal acts. Nearly 800,000 perpetrators of genocide have been tried within these community courts, usually publicly in front of the local population, including victims. The idea is that prosecutors will investigate the crimes tried under *gacaca* and then take them to higher, formal courts. This has the advantage of pre-trial of hundreds of thousands of suspects but also a truth-telling exercise whereby victims and family members get to ask perpetrators what happened.

In this way, the institutional elements of reform are closely related to both DDR and SSR.

Security sector reform and justice

SSR represents one sort of template for the institutional reform of the justice sector. In essence, it entails the transformation of the entire security system and the provision of state and human security within a framework of democratic governance. The template is based on civil control over security services – the military, non-state security actors, the judicial system, the police, intelligence operations, customs and all other related elements. SSR encourages non-state interaction and a strong involvement of civil society, as well as oversight to overcome the fears of the general population with regard to the security services, which are made accountable to relevant oversight mechanisms subject to parliament. It attempts to integrate justice systems into police and human security mechanisms and to transform an abusive system into one that accepts and upholds human rights. According to the OECD DAC:

> Security system reform (SSR) seeks to increase *partner countries' ability* to meet the range of security needs within their societies in a manner consistent with democratic norms and sound principles of governance, transparency and the rule of law. SSR includes, but extends well beyond, the narrower focus of more traditional security assistance on defence, intelligence and policing.

(OECD 2005)

Saferworld, the international NGO, defines SSR as:

> a reform process applied in countries whose development is hampered by structural weaknesses in their security and justice sectors and often exacerbated by a lack of democratic oversight. SSR encompasses a broad variety of assistance programmes, such as: the development of norms of 'good practice' in the security sector; the control, collection and destruction of small arms; enhancing civilian control over the military; and community-based policing and justice reform.
>
> (ISIS 2006)

There is much that can be written on SSR, but the basic core activities are summarised in Table 8.3. The activities are extremely wide-ranging and can be divided into a number of sub-groups. At the highest level there is a concern to determine national, overarching strategies, particularly describing the nature of perceived threats – what is a security system needed for? At the next level, SSR aims to reform the overall nature of the security and justice institutions – the oversight mechanisms and rule of law that govern the activities of the security sector as well as individual braches within it, such as the military and criminal justice area.

Note that there is a sub-set of activities in the immediate aftermath of conflict embracing DDR and also small arms control (SALW) and transitional justice. It involves taking stock of issues that may arise from the peace agreement itself, including those who would seek to break the basic consensus surrounding peace, so-called spoilers. Finally, there are a number of cross-cutting themes that underpin a number of activities, particularly gender and anti-corruption.

SSR is intrinsically linked with DDR in terms of taking a fair view of security and justice and vetting those who may have been guilty of human rights abuses under previous regimes. For example, in El Salvador following the end of conflict, the police were the chief target of SSR since they had been instrumental in perpetrating a number of human rights abuses against civilians. The idea of the SSR programme was therefore to weed out those who had been involved and effectively start again, developing a fresh ethos through constructing a new training school where all police officers had to train. Over time this approach managed to instil a spirit of protection of human rights rather than abuse.

Table 8.3 Core activities in security sector reform

Overarching activities		
e.g., security reviews, threat and needs assessment, SSR and national security strategies		
Security and justice institutions	*Civilian management and oversight*	*Post-conflict SSR activities*
Defence reform	Executive management and control	DDR
Intelligence reform	Parliamentary oversight	SALW
Border security reform	Judicial review	Transitional justice
Police reform	Oversight by independent bodies	Peace agreement
Criminal justice reform	Civil society oversight	issues
Prison reform		Integration
		Spoilers
Cross-cutting activities		
e.g., gender, child protection, anti-corruption		

Core principles and associated challenges of implementing SSR

The OECD DAC has agreed on a number of working principles. SSR should be:

- people-centred, locally owned and based on democratic norms and human rights principles and the rule of law, seeking to provide freedom from fear;
- seen as a framework to structure thinking about how to address diverse security challenges facing states and their populations through more integrated development and security policies and through greater civilian involvement and oversight;
- founded on activities with multi-sectoral strategies, based on a broad assessment of the range of security needs of the people and the state;
- developed adhering to basic principles underlying public sector reform such as transparency and accountability;
- implemented through clear processes and policies that aim to enhance the institutional and human capacity needed for security policy to function effectively.

There are also a number of associated challenges involved in the implementation of SSR.

- It can be difficult to find local ownership for SSR, especially where it is most needed – for example, where security forces are part of the problem or where SSR may have the potential to change current power relationships.
- SSR is expensive and human resource intensive – it requires the co-operation of several actors and expertise from a number of different governmental departments and non-governmental institutions.
- SSR includes a wide range of activities and can be deployed in support of a variety of key objectives. This can often lead to inconsistencies and unevenness in implementation. The challenge is to provide a consistent and coherent overall framework with some form of prioritisation to avoid a mixed bag of ad hoc activities.
- SSR takes a long time to bring about changes, which may deter donors from engaging in this type of work.

However one defines SSR, the core idea rests with two central issues: operational efficiency of the security services (i.e., providing security for the population) and democratic control over those means of security, whether in formal security institutions or non-state providers (i.e., creating security that does not threaten the population and is answerable to it). Any reform in this area is important but sensitive.

Summary points

1   The post-conflict environment creates a series of challenges that require a number of specific policy approaches in the security and justice arenas.
2   DDR is a complex process that involves a series of stages. The last stage of rehabilitation is the most complex and can take years or even decades.
3   Involvement of local communities in the reinsertion of former combatants is directly related to the issue of transitional justice.
4   To facilitate reconciliation, former combatants should not be seen to benefit from taking up arms.

5   There are complicated choices to be made within the area of transitional justice, including balance between local/international justice and accountability/revenge.
6   Justice is an integral part of the overall security system and is critical for the protection of human security. This provides a direct link to security sector reform.

Discussion questions

1   What are the main issues that make working in a post-conflict security environment particularly fragile?
2   What are the main features of DDR? What are the key issues that complicate DDR as a model?
3   How has the international community developed DDR to overcome some of the deficiencies of the earlier model?
4   In what ways does transitional justice differ from normal justice? Does this produce any specific issues?
5   How has the international community supported transitional justice and do you think it has been successful?
6   How does justice fit into security sector reform?
7   What issues can you identify with security sector reform in terms of achieving its core aims?

Further reading

Ball, Nicole (2001) 'The challenge of rebuilding war-torn societies', in C. A. Crocker, F. O. Hampson, M. B. Anderson and P. Aall (eds), *Turbulent Peace: The Challenges of Managing International Conflict*. Washington, DC: United States Institute of Peace Press.

Bryden, Alan, and Hänggi, Hainer (eds) (2005) *Security Governance in Post-Conflict Peacebuilding*. Münster: Lit.

De Grieff, Pablo (ed.) (2007) *The Handbook of Reparations*. Oxford: Oxford University Press.

Muggah, Robert (ed.) (2009) *Security and Post-Conflict Reconstruction: Dealing with Fighters in the Aftermath of War*. London. Routledge.

OECD (Organisation for Economic Co-operation and Development) (2005) *Security System Reform and Governance*. Paris, OECD; www.oecd.org/dataoecd/8/39/31785288.pdf (accessed 27 February 2011).

UN (2000) *The Role of the United Nations Peacekeeping in Disarmament, Demobilization, and Reintegration: Report of the Secretary General*. New York, United Nations.

UN (2004) *The Rule of Law and Transitional Justice in Conflict and Post Conflict Societies: Report of the Secretary General*. New York, United Nations.

9 Future issues in the pursuit of security and development

This textbook has been designed to give readers a general introduction to an extremely complex subject in a very accessible way. As such, there are several key issues that we have been unable to include or to discuss in any great detail. This chapter aims to provide a discussion of the current debates in the policy world, reflecting on the increasing linkages between security and development.

Violent conflict has always presented a core development challenge, but it is only relatively recently that the two have come together in policy terms. This is despite the origins of modern development policy being located in the Bretton Woods institutions, which were established in the wake of the Second World War to rebuild Europe following that devastating conflict. However, there are several areas of the world that have been trailing behind the rest of the international community as a result of persistent violence and human insecurity. These areas are characterised by widespread poverty, stagnant human development indicators and poor economic and political development, and they lie disproportionately in Africa.

One of the key issues in policy terms is that large multilateral development organisations such as the World Bank and the International Monetary Fund have traditionally seen security, and indeed politics, as being outside their core competencies. This is mirrored at the national level, where aid agencies such as the United Kingdom's Department for International Development (DFID) and USAID in the United States also regard involvement in conflicts and security as being outside their core mandates, which relate to economic and social development. However, most organisations now recognise that poor security significantly compromises the ability of development programmes to improve the lot of the mass of population, and overseas development assistance is increasingly being used to support post-conflict interventions, institution-building within security structures, justice and policing, and the inclusion of non-state violent actors in security services. In many ways most development agencies have come to recognise that addressing the issues arising out of conflict requires an understanding of the interrelationships between politics, security and development.

This chapter outlines the background to the book and the core issues that have been laid out within the preceding chapters. It does not seek simply to repeat what has been said, but to set the main argument in the context of current policy and to identify some of the dilemmas of contemporary policymakers. In particular, it recognises that the post-1945 international system assumed, along with most international relations literature, that the primary threats to security were focused on the state, in the sense that they were wars between states (interstate wars) or were civil wars between different factions within a state. In reality, however, one of the main changes since the end of the Cold War has been an acceleration of conflicts that do not involve states directly or possibly involve them as only one of a number of players. Interstate wars have declined, whereas conflicts involving non-state actors, such as rebel movements and international criminal gangs, have rapidly increased and form a major threat to the security of a vast number of people. In addition, the evidence shows that ending wars, even when we can define what they are, is a difficult process, and several conflicts continue a long time after their formal ceasefires and mutate into different forms of conflict and insecurity.

In particular, conflict as it is experienced on the ground consists of a number of inter-linked cycles of violence forming a continuum of conflicts, from formal military wars through to the illegal trafficking of arms, natural resources, people and, most particularly, drugs. There are key vertical and horizontal connections between different conflicts: local conflicts are inevitably linked to bigger, more global networks and can easily escalate into political or cross-border violence as localised groups ally with transnational networks. Countries with weak state institutions – typically 'failed states' – are incapable of dealing with these shifting sands of conflict, where the difficulties of combating violence are exacerbated by poverty and poor governance, but also where the conflict has the greatest ability to compromise development.

International responses to conflict

Given the complex nature of conflict, the World Bank, amongst others, identifies three core challenges to the international response to conflict (World Bank 2011). These three issues hamper international efforts to reduce and mitigate conflict.

1   An excessive focus on post-conflict recovery means that the vast amount of funds available for post-conflict reconstruction is not mirrored by a corresponding level of funding for conflict prevention or to aid countries actually engaged in conflict. In other words, the international community tends to wait until conflict has happened until it acts. Many of those countries subject to conflict are left to prevent further conflict without external aid, or are faced with the prospect of conventional reconstruction during a conflict, which is never an attractive option.
2   The research and policy community has tended to treat different forms of violence as separate phenomena. This means that much analysis tends to ignore the linkages between different forms and levels of conflict, which, as we have seen, is critical in understanding how combatants can be simultaneously fighting for several different reasons. It also does not recognise the continuum of violence and thus underestimates, for example, the levels of conflict following peace agreements, as violence changes from formal conflict into criminal and social violence, even when it involves the same combatants.
3   The international architecture is largely designed to support individual nation-states and is ill-equipped to deal with the sorts of cross-border conflict that we have outlined in this book. A further complication here is that international actors are historically not good at dealing with non-state actors, particularly those contesting sovereignty. At the same time, it is true to say that in several contemporary conflicts the state is not valued so much per se as for the resources it can bring. In other words, one of many war aims for combatants may be to gain control of the state, and the state itself is reduced to a resource rather than a sovereign power.

To these three obstacles to successful contemporary conflict intervention outlined by the World Bank, we could add a fourth. One of the main issues in dealing with conflict is that of disputes between international actors themselves. In particular, there is an assumption that dealing with conflict is not part of the mandate of development agencies. Even its own report on conflict produces much discussion about whether this is the right thing for the World Bank to be doing. In the field this can also translate into defence institutions and development agencies simultaneously undertaking reforms that are not linked, even where staff from the same country do not speak to each other, let alone share and develop strategies for reform. This can be catastrophic where security governance relies on both civilian and military cooperation, and yet can easily be undermined by development agencies undertaking civil service reforms and military agencies focusing just on technical support without the governance aspects.

Characteristics of violent environments

The literature on violent environments is huge and often confusing. Broadly, the quantitative literature has been based partially on variables that are easier to measure (economic growth, resources, poverty, terrain) since it is much more difficult to measure, and therefore incorporate, variables such as grievances, ethnicities and historical enmity. One of the key quantitative analyses, by Collier and Hoeffler, directly compares greed and grievance, whilst using several statistical proxies for grievance. This method has raised several issues but has certainly not produced clear or decisive results, even when the proxies have favoured particular outcomes.

On the other hand, there is much case study material and qualitative analysis available that emphasises the specificity of the individual cases and their particular issues. This case study literature does, however, consistently highlight a number of issues that form a tentative conflict pattern. Among these issues are political injustice, secession, social exclusion, external pressures, and inequity between social and political groups. In particular, several case studies highlight the deliberate exclusion of some groups from political, economic and social resources as a key element in conflict, whether linked to regional, ethnic or historical factors. One of the key features of these variables is that they can be difficult to isolate and may not be susceptible to cross-country measurement. At the same time, even where statistics are present, they may not be accurate, given that conflict analysis is necessarily interested in areas that are subject to difficulty of access and therefore of gathering statistics.

Key challenges for analysis

Clearly there are several different challenges facing conflict analysts. This section outlines some of these core issues and the complex variables surrounding them. The list is not exhaustive, and it is in the nature of such lists that they change rapidly as the current situation changes around them.

1   The first major challenge is how to examine the interaction between some of these variables and the various types of conflict experienced by people on the ground. In particular, there is very little analysis of how different groups interact with each other or how they influence the direction of conflicts. There is an underlying assumption that all conflicts are similar and so can be reduced to a single set of explanatory variables. Within this there is a sub-assumption that all combatants within any given conflict are motivated by similar factors. In reality this is clearly not the case.

The Maoist conflict in Nepal, for example, involved a whole series of groups fighting for very different aims but under a shared label. To this complex mix may be added other sub-cycles of conflict involving anything on a spectrum from secession groups to drug gangs.

2   The failure to address the similarity hypothesis has also affected the policy arena. We have already mentioned the tendency to address all conflict issues at the level of the nation-state. This can be a real issue in areas where the nation-state is not necessarily the polity with which combatants identify. They may identify more readily with a local – i.e., sub-national – entity, or they may (and usually do) ignore international boundaries entirely. In such a situation a regional approach to conflict management may be far more appropriate, but regional institutions such as ASEAN or the AU are constructed in the image of other international organisations – i.e., they are built on nation-states. As yet, there is no solution to this difficult issue. Institutions exist, but the capability of the constituent parts of those institutions (states) is too low to develop effective regional actors.

3   A further challenge for the conflict analyst is that violence is constantly adapting to circumstances – it evolves in response to opportunities and threats. As mentioned above, there is a strong spectrum of conflict types that are closely related and may feed into each other. This means that, in any given circumstance, once one type of conflict is suppressed, a different type is able to rise up and take its place. Rather like Cerberus, the Greek guard dog of Hades, each time a head is removed another grows to take its place.

4   One clear feature of countries that have experienced conflict is that they are very likely to experience conflict again. This can manifest itself in a number of different ways.

   a   First, there is a high risk of relapse into a state of conflict and a renewal of hostilities linked to the war.
   b   Second, there is a high risk of fragmented and sporadic (and therefore unpredictable) conflict at a localised level as former groups of combatants divide into sub-groups.
   c   Third, there is significant evidence of new forms of violence associated with organised crime operating in grey areas of the global economy, usually involving illegal drugs, guns and other easily smuggled goods linked to local predatory groups connected with transnational criminal gangs.
   d   Fourth, local groups may easily be politicised during election and may be mobilised to support political groups. In this sense, democratic elections may actually encourage localised violence.

5   Having emphasised here local conflicts, there is a need to look more carefully at the linkages between local conflicts, global groups and regional economies. It has long been known that individual conflicts can prove contagious, in the sense that they may frequently spill over regional borders. A central challenge is therefore how best to develop regional approaches to conflict prevention and management when the key players in most regional organisations are themselves weak or fragile states.

6   A clear characteristic of all countries that have experienced violence is that conflict has a detrimental effect on development outcomes, and yet these are crucial in reconstructing post-conflict settlements. Large-scale violence associated with wars, conflicts and organised crime also has a disproportionately large effect on the most vulnerable sectors of society. At the same time, the demobilisation of combatants requires that they be

given an alternative to violence; such alternatives are often, however, destroyed by conflict. The development of an economy in a post-conflict environment is probably one of the most significant areas of intervention: in giving potential combatants jobs, their incentive to pick up arms is significantly reduced.

7 Lastly, there are many important challenges relating to institutions. Much international intervention has concentrated on reconstructing institutions following wars, whereas there is a clear correlation between poor institutions, state fragility and conflict. This suggests that institutions could play an important part in preventing as well as overcoming the effects of conflict, and yet there is very little work on the idea of state resilience in the face of challenges. Indeed, there is disagreement over what a resilient state may look like and in what ways it might mitigate the effects of conflict.

The role of the international community

Much of this book has been concerned with the questions surrounding what the international community can do about the effects of conflict. We have tried to show that, whilst this is critical, it is also extremely complex, and there are several potential unintended consequences of external intervention within conflicts that are little understood. In particular, intervening just to reconstitute a previous form of government (implied in the continual use of the prefix 're' – reconstruction, rebuilding, etc.) could potentially re-create the same conditions that led to conflict in the first place. The question is then altered to 'How do we understand the nature of the conflict in order that we can construct a lasting peace?' This is a very different and perhaps more complex question.

Humanitarian aid and development actors

The issues surrounding refugees and IDPs, and how to cope with them, are amongst the key challenges for development actors and those working in conflict-affected states. However, the factors that lead to individuals and/or whole communities becoming refugees, or to their displacement within their own state, are many and varied. To appreciate fully the complexity of the problems caused by refugee flows and displacement, and their impacts on conflict dynamics and processes of development and security, is beyond the scope of this book, but there are several key issues that feed directly into the security and development debate.

1 Refugees and IDPs can place considerable strain on local resources and services, including medical and educational services. This can be especially acute because of the relatively high proportion of youth and elderly amongst displaced populations and the poor state of their health before, during and following displacement. The limitations of capacity and resources in many host states make international assistance vital in caring for refugees, but providing longer-term support in protracted crises inevitably creates a burden on local and national economies.

2 An influx of displaced people to a new area, within or across borders, can result in the exacerbation of local intergroup tensions. Where refugees share characteristics such as ethnicity, religion or other form of kinship with a local population in a host state, or where they define themselves in opposition to a locally relevant identity, their influx can challenge existing intergroup dynamics and cause considerable physical insecurity.

3   Refugee groups which experience a lack of access to basic services or minimal physical security after displacement may as an alternative turn to local warlords and militias. If the latter groups are able to provide security, then the refugees themselves become a security threat through their reciprocal loyalty, support and perceived legitimacy.

4   Where displaced populations exist in urban settings, groups seeking a feeling of greater security and links to others from their homeland may set up their own communities or concentrate within particular areas or neighbourhoods. This may in turn reinforce divisions between the displaced and the 'indigenous' population, or between different groups within the indigenous population.

5   There may also be opportunities for armed forces to recruit 'volunteers' from within camps and among IDP populations. Violent groups offer a potential avenue for refugees to support themselves through association with a fighting force. For male refugees this may entail fighting or taking an active part in operations; for women the roles may include acting as a support mechanism for the fighter – cleaning, providing care, cooking, raising children or, in some circumstances, co-option into acting as a bush-wife to one or more fighters. Joining an armed group also offers refugees who are fleeing conflict a way of fighting against those whom they blame for displacement. On a more basic level, it may simply represent a way of escaping the dependent existence within a refugee or IDP camp.

6   Refugees and IDPs also attract resources from states, NGOs and international agencies. Humanitarian aid in refugee crises can be instrumental in the emergence or exacerbation of conflict through feeding militants and sustaining their supporters, contributing to the war economy and providing legitimacy for the combatants. It should be clear that, within many refugee camps, politics is not neutral. In other words, there is always a hierarchy, and control over aid goods is one way of reinforcing that authority. It could also be asserted, as Duffield does, that humanitarian aid can lead to displacement spending, as money that could have been used to purchase food can be used to buy weapons.

7   On a regional and international scale, refugees are often moved using the same networks and agents involved in human trafficking, the smuggling of economic migrants, and the trafficking of illicit resources such as arms, drugs and conflict resources. These systems and processes benefit transnational criminal networks, considered a threat to states which may be neither exporters nor recipients of refugees.

The problem of refugee camps

Most of the challenges facing displaced people stem from their lack of certainty as to whether and for how long they will be staying in the same place. Families who consider themselves to be displaced only temporarily will find it difficult to invest in the areas they occupy, whether through lack of resources or unwillingness to commit to a new location in case they are again displaced or are able to return home. There is limited possibility of their building more permanent housing or planting crops. This means that many displaced people continue to live in inadequate housing long after their initial move, whether in temporary camps or in urban areas.

This creates a serious development and security problem. Camps are frequently established in relatively harsh environments where it may be difficult to create alternative survival strategies to external aid. Even when opportunities exist, many refugees end up in poorly paid and temporary employment. Such groups are excellent recruiting grounds for violent criminal gangs, both at a local level within the camps and at a regional level within areas controlled by non-state actors such as warlords.

Humanitarian actors and politics

International aid agencies may be seen as an extension of a peacebuilding agenda that sees creating effective states as critical to long-term development. This views humanitarian organisations as part of, and potentially subordinated to, the overarching agenda of the transformation of states, societies and interstate relations through the spread of 'liberal' values and systems built on free markets and multi-party democracy. Many of those working in this area, whether for NGOs, multilaterals or bilateral donor agencies, think of development in a way that privileges values and rights they consider 'universal' – i.e., the UNDP focus on human development, the idea of 'human rights' and the aims of the MDGs. The issue here is not with the idea of human rights, but how they might be realised. In particular, humanitarianism has become focused not only on humanitarian relief but also on the spreading of development, democracy and human rights, even whilst most humanitarian agencies profess to be apolitical.

The preoccupation of donors with quickly instituting democracy may also be potentially incompatible with ensuring stability and legitimate, accountable government. In the interim period after conflict, donors may be dealing with unelected parties, warlords or rebel groups, and elections are frequently seen as a way of choosing a legitimate government which will then have the mandate to negotiate on behalf of the state. Elections may also form one of the conditions in a negotiated peace process. The experiences of many post-conflict states show that elections can become flashpoints for violence. This is true even of states not experiencing large-scale civil conflict, but the dangers can be exacerbated even in relatively stable states such as Kenya. Elections and democratisation, in its donor-preferred liberal form, encourage competition between political parties and their supporters, effectively transferring conflict from violence to politics. However, in a highly militarised society, where groups may fear for their own safety, or their position if they are not adequately represented in government, elections become an existential matter. There is no guarantee that groups who are defeated at the ballot box will accept the results – a danger which is magnified when demilitarisation has been only partial. At the same time, the formation of political parties may appeal to the lowest common denominator – i.e., 'Don't vote for them, vote for me. I am like you.' This has the effect, as parties founded on regionalism, ethnicity or class are formed, of institutionalising previous social divisions into the political system.

International donors and co-ordination

Bilateral aid still accounts for the largest proportion of overall aid, which gives individual country development agencies considerable power in conflict-affected environments. Individual donor states and agencies will all have their own priorities, and their level of interest and involvement in particular states and in different sectors will vary. Countries also have broader policy and strategic objectives which affect their willingness to commit aid to certain countries. Some countries have different accountability mechanisms for how they spend aid. In practice this has been a huge issue, since a recipient country could be faced with multiple donors with multiple reporting systems and multiple requirements in terms of accountability. As a result, it has been known for very capable civil servants within recipient countries to spend a disproportionate amount of their time just making sure that there is compliance with donor procedures. This had become such an issue that in March 2005 the international community issued the Paris Declaration of Aid Effectiveness, which detailed a series of indicators of harmonisation and alignment. However, it is not clear how far this has had an impact beyond a core group of (mainly European) donors, who have developed harmonised aid modalities around general budget support and sector-wide approaches to development aid. In the field, and particularly in post-conflict situations, it is imperative to reduce duplication and overlap and to ensure the most effective delivery of aid to where it is most needed.

Nicole Ball (2001) emphasises that, for co-ordination to occur effectively, a high calibre of staff is required to work within agencies which are also open to operating together across organisational boundaries. As collaborative relationships between agencies develop between people on the ground, she also suggests that the head offices of these agencies must be prepared to devolve authority and a measure of power to workers in the affected country. The size of the bureaucracies involved may further militate against co-operation, with different procedures, requirements and organisational culture creating institutional barriers. Donors and agencies are often keen to protect their reputation or perceived comparative advantage in particular sectors. Seeing an area in which they may have invested significant resources in staff development, recruitment and building links with NGOs as 'their own', they can be reluctant to work with others.

Collaboration and co-ordination require a degree of institutional memory and the development of deeper relationships between agencies. This is hampered by the reliance of many donor agencies on international staff, who typically remain in each post for only a few years. A strong cadre of local staff with both situational knowledge and relevant language skills can help maintain this institutional memory. However, both donors and NGOs tend to favour staff from their own home countries or international staff in general, possibly fearing a loss of control if local stakeholders are too highly empowered and promoted. An additional element here is that, whilst staff posted out to run aid programmes may be well qualified academically, they lack practical experience. This has led, within some aid agencies, to an overemphasis on the technocratic elements of development programming rather than a professional decision-making capability on the ground, as well as an increased reliance on external providers, either from NGOs or the private sector, to manage and deliver aid.

Relationship and differences between donors and NGOs

The relationship between donors and NGOs in the contemporary aid world is critical. Whilst bilateral aid clearly dwarfs NGO funding, NGOs remain important in the overall delivery of aid to specific groups and can greatly enhance the ability to reach vulnerable groups. At the same time, this independence is only partial, since many NGOs rely on core funding from government agencies. This is not an issue in itself, but serves to show that aid delivery is not only complex but is also the result of a complicated series of interlinked networks. The relationship between donors and NGOs is inherently unequal. Donors provide a significant proportion of the funds upon which NGOs rely, which makes them the more powerful actor in any relationship. However, although donors may be willing to use NGOs to help deliver development objectives, they are not always willing to use the power they have on their behalf in negotiations with governments and other powerful actors. In particular, where aid is misappropriated or diverted, it is often labelled by donors as an 'implementation problem' – transferring responsibility to the NGOs, who rarely have the leverage and power to ensure aid gets through.

Within the NGO sector, there are many different types of organisations with a range of expertise, budgets, staff profiles and relationships with donors. NGOs are seen as a way of bridging the gap between governments or donors and the citizens. They form a key part of civil society, and can be effective 'connectors' when considered from Anderson's (2001) local capacities for peace perspective. Local NGOs can play a critical role in providing 'fairness' or 'impartiality' where the direct involvement of a state agency would be sensitive or unacceptable. For example, negotiations between former Maoist combatants in Nepal and the Nepali government are being partly facilitated by a partnership between a local NGO, the Nepal Institute of Policy Studies, and an international NGO, Saferworld. Whilst this is financed largely by the UK government through the DFID, this intervention is ostensibly neutral, which is important given the sensitivity of such discussions.

To assume that NGOs are always local, representative or even contributing positively to peacebuilding would, however, be a mistake. When looking at the work of any particular NGO, especially those claiming to be 'local', there are always questions to be asked about which constituency or group the organisation claims to represent. Donors are often criticised for preferring NGOs who speak their language, both literally and in terms of the buzzwords and fashions in aid. They also tend to compete for access to the 'best' local consultants, often well-educated individuals and their organisations, who provide a 'local' perspective in terms which donors can easily translate to their programmes and reports.

However, there are problems with this approach. The perspective is of an individual who speaks an English, is well educated, knows how to write project proposals and reports, and tends to reside in a relatively wealthy urban area is not particularly 'local'. No doubt such individuals may have more ability to navigate local politics, to speak to aid recipients and negotiate with a range of partners, all necessary for today's modern NGO. But there is a very real risk that such NGOs and individuals skew the discussion and practice of development by becoming the 'usual suspects', sought after by donors who are essentially relying on such an urban-educated elite to advise them how to better tackle poverty.

This rise of the professional NGO is partly a response to growing donor demands that aid be used efficiently and effectively. It also reflects the adoption of new management practices by NGOs keen to win donor funding, resulting in organisations that are concerned primarily with effective ways of delivering aid despite a discourse that espouses local ownership and partnership. This tends to favour partners who are more experienced, better connected and more established and to disadvantage smaller organisations, whose staff may be less well educated, based further from donor offices in capitals, and often occupy volunteer as opposed to salaried posts.

Peacekeeping and privatisation

Peacekeeping has become a critical operation for the international community, particularly the UN, which estimates that, in March 2010, almost 124,000 personnel were deployed across sixteen missions on four continents. This level of personnel, both military and non-military, shows just how important the UN has become as a force in the drive to create and maintain international peace and security. Though the UN was established in the aftermath of the Second World War II, this growth has not happened as gradually as one might expect. The UN DPKO estimates that the numbers it has deployed have increased ninefold since 1999.

In addition, the conflict environments into which UN peacekeepers are deployed have changed considerably since the organisation's establishment, especially since the end of the

Cold War and the turn of the millennium. The UN really started its peacekeeping mission in the 1960s as an agent employed in keeping two formal militaries or groups apart. However, these types of conflict have essentially disappeared or have led to protracted *de facto* settlements. What has increased is the level of civil and intra-state war and processes of state failure and collapse. The history of UN peacekeeping is therefore closely linked with attempts by the international community to deal with violent conflict, through containment, peacekeeping and peace enforcement. This is all the more important in the context of development, as the drive to maximise the impact and effectiveness of aid means being able to implement programmes and evaluate them. In a conflict-affected or insecure context, this task becomes even more difficult, and UN peacekeepers play a critical role in providing an enabling environment for that to happen.

The UN faces a number of challenges in providing peacekeeping forces.

1   The UN has a mandate to establish and maintain international peace by providing mechanisms for the resolution of disputes between states and the power to authorise and deploy military, civilian and police personnel to achieve this aim. However, this power is contingent on the support of its members, particularly the five permanent and ten non-permanent members of the UN Security Council. Usually, peacekeeping missions are authorised by vote in the Security Council, requiring considerable political work.

2   The ability of the UN to establish a mission is also contingent on the willingness of member states to contribute the personnel, equipment and other support necessary to meet the mission's mandate. The UN does not have a standing army of its own.

3   There are restrictions on which countries can provide troops for a particular peacekeeping mission, reflecting a preference for the force to be as neutral as possible. Parties to a conflict would not be able to contribute forces, as this would compromise the mission's neutrality and potentially its effectiveness. Similarly, countries seen as having an interest in particular conflicts are usually not considered suitable providers of troops. This includes the use of troops from a former colonial power in a former colony, although on occasion this provision has been ignored.

4   These limitations on who can provide troops, along with the economic attractions of peacekeeping for contributing states, have led to a relatively small range of states providing the bulk of peacekeeping forces – in particular, Pakistan, India and Bangladesh. By deploying large numbers of peacekeepers, these and other developing states are able to maintain large armed forces, outsource the costs of paying for part of their forces, and also benefit from the training, equipment and allowances provided by the UN.

5   However, the reliance on troops from this narrow group of countries means that the UN – usually members of the Security Council – also has to provide logistical support in the form of helicopters and airmobile capability as well as the means to transport troops. For example, when Rwandan forces were deployed to Darfur in the mid-2000s, US aircraft flew from Germany to transport them.

6   The cost of these missions is nominally borne by all UN member states, whose contributions are worked out according to a formula taking into account their size and ability to pay. The permanent members of the Security Council are also required to pay more on account of their responsibility for international peace and security. The United States, Japan, Germany and the United Kingdom are currently the biggest contributors, with the United States providing over a quarter of the budget (Bellamy *et al.*, 2010). The total spent on peacekeeping by the UN since its creation in 1948 is estimated at US$69 billion, with expenditure for 2010 alone expected to be $7.26 billion.

Perhaps the defining critical feature of any specific UN mission is its mandate. UN peacekeeping missions are intended to contribute to maintaining international peace and security, acting under one of two main chapters of the UN Charter. Chapter VI deals with peaceful solutions, or 'pacific settlement of disputes', requiring states which may have a dispute that could lead to war to enter into negotiation to seek settlement. It further allows such states to bring their disputes to the UN for arbitration, though the recommendations of the UN under Chapter VI are not legally binding. By contrast, Chapter VII allows the UN to undertake military action if necessary to restore international peace and security and to impose sanctions or blockades on states. It also confers the right to use the military forces which are put at its disposal by member states to carry out missions to restore peace and security. Peacekeeping is often said to belong to 'chapter six and a half', a phrase coined by the second UN Secretary-General, Dag Hammarskjold, to describe its hybrid nature, often involving the UN playing a role somewhere between mediation, negotiation and the threat or use of force to restore security. In practice the clarity or otherwise of the mandate has been critically important. It has been positive when UN troops have been allowed the scope to act, as in Sierra Leone, but disastrous when they have stood by and watched extreme violence, as happened both in Rwanda in 1993 and in Srebrenica during the wars in the former Yugoslavia, when UN troops were unable to prevent a massacre of civilians in a designated UN 'safe area'.

Privatising violence

A growing feature of the conflict landscape in developing countries is the privatisation of the use of force. Private armies or presidential guard-type forces may provide security for an elite whilst the security of the population at large remains minimal. This is an illustration of how security has moved from being ideally a public good, or even a basic service which populations could expect by virtue of belonging to a state, to being in reality a private commodity, available only to those who can afford to pay. In the broader field of conflict and peacekeeping, security has also become privatised, with a burgeoning private security industry consisting of companies undertaking a variety of tasks for both states and non-state actors.

Before 1990 the overwhelming majority of PMCs were from the United Kingdom and were present in Africa, the Middle East, Latin America and the Far East. In the 1950s Sir Percy Sillitoe, a counter-espionage expert, handled security for De Beers and hired mercenaries to stop illegal diamond trading in Sierra Leone. In 1967 David Stirling, the founder of the United Kingdom's SAS, founded Watchguard to train guards and special forces in the Persian Gulf. The company was then expanded to provide military advisory training teams to overseas clients, frequently as an adjunct to the UK government itself and employing predominantly former UK personnel. Out of Watchguard came Saladin Security, Kulinda Security, KMS (Keenie Meenie Services) and KAS Enterprises, which provided anti-poaching operations in South Africa. Another similar company was Defence Systems Limited, which used former Gurkha troops to protect Lonrho assets in Mozambique during the Rhodesian and Mozambican wars.

Mercenary companies, therefore, are not new even in their modern form. In recent years companies such as Executive Outcomes from South Africa and Group 4, Control Risks Group, LifeGuard Management, Blackwater, MPRI, Dyncorps and Aegis have become far more public. Whilst several of these companies are relatively small in military terms, some of the bigger companies can field considerable manpower in areas where they are required to be combat active. In early 2010 it was estimated that some 70,000 mercenaries were active within Afghanistan.

These companies may provide desperately needed services that are not easily available elsewhere. In particular, when a rapid scaling-up of activities (a 'surge') is required, mercenary companies may provide a quick way of raising trained troops. Most employees of reputable private military companies come with considerable training behind them and are able to access a number of specialised skills that may be in short supply. Many private contractors are run and managed by former special forces personnel or other specialists from the police or other security services. These skills are valuable, since it can take a long time to train an individual to the required level of expertise and it is expensive to maintain a large military staff during peacetime.

The flexibility and speed of response of PMCs is one advantage, but there is considerable political capital in employing mercenaries to undertake tasks where it may not be politically acceptable to declare the interest of the state or where it may be politically unacceptable to take large numbers of casualties within conventional services. Put bluntly, it may be more politically acceptable to fly the body of a mercenary back home than a serviceman or woman draped in a national flag. In addition, there is evidence that national governments have used mercenaries on the ground where the involvement of service personnel may have been politically difficult. The UK government has done this in the Middle East for some years, and the US government employed MPRI to undertake tasks in Croatia, when, publicly, they were still able to tell the public that there were no US ground troops present. In these situations, mercenaries can be extremely effective.

However, despite these political benefits, there are some issues with the extensive use of such providers. Firstly, whilst the best of these companies are capable of providing extremely good quality and well-trained troops, the large surge in employment has resulted in more variable quality and questions about the motivation and training of some of the troops involved. There have been high-profile reports from both Iraq and Afghanistan, with public accusations of mercenaries killing civilians, harmful video footage of trigger-happy mercenaries on YouTube, and the pronouncements of governments against the use of companies such as Blackwater. There may also be an argument that the employment of these companies in a development sense may be harmful because they provide just a short-term solution. This raises serious questions about how to place mercenary companies into a legal and regulatory framework that is effective and can use the short-term benefits to enhance long-term aims.

As stated above, the main issue with private contractors is their lack of accountability. Whilst there have been attempts to develop working regulatory frameworks, the extraterritoriality and temporary nature of most of this sector means that it has proved almost impossible to make accountable legislation work. It does not help when several governments who are signatories of documents decrying mercenary activity also happen to be amongst some of the employers of their services. The closest practical attempt to develop legislation was probably carried out by the UK government and its issuing of a Green Paper on the legislation of private military companies, but to date this has not been enacted in law. A rather more draconian effort was introduced in South Africa in the mid-1990s, but this resulted in many of those involved relocating their business interests, illustrating that effective legislation and therefore accountability could probably be effective only at a global level.

Justice and security in post-conflict environments

Within this book we have taken a huge subject – justice – and condensed part of it into a chapter. The post-conflict environment we used as the context for this work assumed that we were dealing with a post-conflict environment post-peace agreement. However, it is important to note here that, whilst we can attempt to deal with the fallout from a conflict through peace commissions, DDR, tribunals, transitional justice and, in the longer term, SSR, it is a characteristic of post-conflict environments that violence does not stop with peace agreements. Rather, the type of violence and the sources of insecurity for most of the population tend to move away from formal or semi-formal conflicts and towards more decentralised, local violence linked to localised disputes or criminality. This may be further complicated by those who have been demobilised following conflicts and the nature of the demobilisation. In the absence of alternative employment, these groups are frequently easy prey for those seeking to benefit from the lack of firm governance. At the same time, the options available to former combatants, particularly women fighters, are critical in determining the character of the post-conflict settlement.

Whilst we have introduced the nature of security and justice in post-war situations, including the growth of crime and other security problems and the establishment of systems to tackle justice issues, there are complex ideas about the nature of justice and the law and what is applicable in a state emerging from conflict. In particular, the different perceptions of justice, and the role of the ICC, international justice and transitional justice, are always contentious.

Most iterations of the conflict cycle make a number of assumptions, including a similarity across different conflicts but also a linearity, which means that conflicts all follow a similar development process. However, it raises a number of questions, not least how the international community measures the start and end of conflicts and what levels of violence are to be expected after a ceasefire. There is an underlying assumption here that peace equates to no violence and is a 'normal' condition for most societies. Whether fragile, weak, collapsed or neo-patrimonial, dysfunctional states all suffer from an unpredictable vulnerability to external shocks, internal conflict, competing economic and political structures, and an inability to exercise effective legal control within their borders. A post-conflict state exhibits all of these features but in extreme circumstances. The state and security may have collapsed completely.

The most commonly cited difference between post-conflict interventions and 'normal' interventions is that the former needs to deal with the legacy of past conflict. The main distinguishing features of post-conflict environments are usually the need to:

- provide immediate security;
- disarm, demobilise and reintegrate combatants; and
- downsize security actors.

At the same time, post-conflict intervention is usually carried out in highly unstable political environments where armed groups are usually powerful, and where individuals within those armed groups expect to benefit from their participation of violence. A neglect of post-conflict security institutions may leave space for non-state actors and, potentially, criminal groups to enter and use the large number of unemployed but experienced fighters as a recruiting pool. However, it is imperative that the need for a technically better set of security services is accompanied by democratic control. By this we can include several definitions of what we mean by the term 'democracy', but essentially we are discussing the civil control of security services subordinated to civil authorities and not representing a basic threat to the general population. This requires a considerable level of governance skill and institutional development. In the end, a recovery from a conflict and a reduction in the likelihood of further conflict requires deep reform of the type proposed by SSR, and therefore political will.

Conclusion

This book has concentrated a lot of material into a very small space and has hopefully opened up a series of future questions for discussion. We have provided a glossary of terms and acronyms used in the security and development world and also a bibliography that provides far more reading both in academic terms and with regard to contemporary policy.

One of the core aims of this book has been to outline the very close links that exist between policy and academic work in this area, but this raises an epistemological dilemma regarding analytical approaches to conflict, security and development in poor countries. In particular, we have illustrated just how complex the real-world dynamics of security can be in places like Sierra Leone and Nepal and how they might not fit comfortably with some of the analytical models commonly used by political scientists. This is not to say that we disagree with the very well-developed methodologies that exist within the social sciences, but that we have deliberately adopted an intellectual stance that espouses analytic eclecticism. That is, we deliberately take elements from different research traditions to shed light on complex situations rather than simplifying a complex situation to fit a theoretical lens.

This is deliberate because we are conscious of the close link between scholarship and policy in this area and also of the danger of social scientists losing sight of what they are studying and being dazzled by 'elegant' theories. This means that they might be in danger of falling into the situation outlined by Lindblom and Cohen, where 'suppliers and users of social research are dissatisfied, the former because they are not listened to, the latter because they do not hear much they want to listen to' (1979, 1). Depressingly, as academics who work on the boundary between academic research and policy, we hear this lament continuing thirty years after this sentence was set down.

Consequently, in terms of future studies of security and development, we would certainly recommend the adoption of an eclectic stance on methodology for a number of reasons.

- It prevents the narrow approach of asking only part of the question required and therefore addressing only small, carefully regulated issues with simplistic assumptions.
- As such, it is better able to address the complex and messy real-world situations we have outlined within this book.
- It posits a pragmatic approach that allows researchers to get around the metaphysical aspects of theoretical divides and to engage in a practical, problem-solving way with the real world.
- It regards data as critically important, but is able to recognise that there are significant issues with data deriving from conflict zones and is therefore able to supplement data-driven analysis with qualitative approaches that add narrative and causal stories.

We are not arguing that analytical eclecticism is superior to any specific research methodology. Rather, we are following Aristotle in suggesting that taking a pragmatic approach to mixing approaches could add up to more than the sum of the existing parts and provide a clearer picture of what it is we are really interested in as social scientists.

There are a lot of key issues and core questions that remain unresolved in this subject area, which is partly why it is such an interesting area in which to study and to work. However, it also means that there are a lot of future issues that the international community will have to deal with. Probably the one central issue that has remained throughout all of the changes on the ground is the continuing animosity between agents and funders dealing with development and those looking at security. The central challenge here is to develop the idea of security as a broad church encompassing a number of different approaches, including development.

On 16 September 2010 Andrew Mitchell MP, the United Kingdom's secretary of state for international development, made a speech about conflict and development at the Royal College of Defence Studies in London. In this speech he argued that, as part of the government's strategic defence security review, there should be a reassessment of the United Kingdom's response to overseas conflict which would put development at the heart of an integrated approach to protect both the world's most vulnerable people and the United Kingdom from external threats. The emphasis on linking the work of the DFID with the Ministry of Defence and the Foreign and Commonwealth Office further cemented the view that this policy explicitly links security with development. Clearly this also has repercussions for other major international donors, including the United States and the European Union.

The linking of security and development should be seen as part of a bigger issue relating to how security problems in poor countries affect their growth. As Mitchell said:

> Tackling conflict overseas is very much in our national interests – even in a time of financial consolidation. But it is also in the interests of the world's poor. In too many parts of the developing world prosperity will remain a distant dream unless and until we succeed in tackling many of the conflicts that block development. It is surely no coincidence that no fragile country has yet achieved a single Millennium Development Goal, the UN-agreed lodestars for UK development assistance.

This potentially represents an important development in future policy. At a time when the United Kingdom is contemplating an end to overseas aid to India, there are similar stories across a number of middle-income countries where overseas aid is relatively unimportant and a need for concentration in those countries where aid can have the most impact. Given this, why not prioritise conflict-affected countries? After all, eight out of ten of those countries ranked lowest on the human development index have recently been or are currently at war. All of the top ten failed states in the world are experiencing conflict, and eight of these are in Africa. Among major root causes are a dangerous cocktail of dysfunctional governance; political, economic, and social inequalities; extreme poverty; economic stagnation; poor government services; high unemployment; and environmental degradation.

Ignore these countries and they will fall even further behind the majority of countries, but focus on them properly and they could stop acting as political and economic vacuums where predatory forces take power. Adding a security dimension to overseas aid could affect strategic decisions about allocation, either in determining that security should be seen exclusively in domestic UK or US terms, and therefore that development should support it, or that security is seen in broader terms and 'hard' security is only part of the threat. This latter requires a series of difficult decisions and a clear agenda setting out priorities in the area where development and security overlap.

By highlighting this link between conflict and development, therefore, the international community may be in a better position to show that aid money helps keep the world safe. An agenda based on a broader definition of security and its relationship to development could set out a new strategic logic for aid that could make sense both for the donors and for the poorest and most vulnerable.

Glossary

administration The organised apparatus of the state for the preparation and implementation of legislation, regulation and policy. Also called **bureaucracy**.

agency The ability to shape events through acting or – usually – exercising leadership.

agenda-setting Developing favourable conditions for power through shaping public discussion. Stalin notoriously controlled agendas of the Communist Party in the Soviet Union for these ends.

aggression An unprovoked, offensive act of hostility, attack or violence on an individual, a group or at government level. The United Nations defines aggression as the 'use of armed force by a state against the sovereignty, territorial integrity or political independence of another state, or in any manner inconsistent with the Charter of the United Nations' (UN General Assembly Consensus Resolution 3314, 14 December 1974).

alliance A coalition of individuals, groups, organisations or states based on formal or informal agreement, open or secret, formed to assist one another to secure identified objectives according to specified and mutually accepted criteria.

alternative dispute resolution (ADR) A range of activities other than legislation, which may involve conciliation or mediation of some kind, that may be used to resolve conflicts.

anarchic order Order in the absence of a co-ordinating authority; organisation without government.

anarchism A stateless society based on individual freedom without the constraints of an overarching authority.

appeasement A policy of granting concessions in response to aggressive demands with the intent of gaining some greater good or asset, usually peace. Appeasement is usually portrayed as a willingness to accede to an immoral actor or entity, as in the 1938 Munich Agreement between Chamberlain and Hitler.

arbitration A mechanism for resolving conflicts, normally involving a third party as an independent arbiter. Both parties submit their grievances and demands, fix a procedural process, and willingly submit to the outcome.

arms control Reducing or controlling the production and flow of arms through external monitoring, aimed at reducing conventional (and nuclear) war. In contemporary warfare, it is extended to cover control over small arms and light weapons (SALW).

authoritarianism A system of government in which leaders are not subjected to the test of free elections. It is usually centred on one individual or a small group surrounding a dictatorship.

authority Power based on consensus (when legitimate) regarding the right to issue commands and make decisions.

binational state   Two nations co-existing within one state.

bipolar   An international system in which there are two dominant nation-states – for example, the period of the Cold War.

bourgeoisie   A Marxist term referring to those who own the means of production – a middle class.

bureaucracy   Administration characterised by specialisation, professionalism and security of tenure.

capitulation   A conditional surrender or yielding of rights by a party engaged in a conflict. Capitulation is usually in the form of an official document.

ceasefire   A halt in offensive military actions amongst parties engaged in violent conflict. Ceasefires sometimes lead to more stable military or political agreements, but they serve to reduce immediate tensions and form a critical step to further peace efforts.

charismatic authority   Authority based on the admiration of personal qualities of an individual, or the cult-like adoration of a charismatic leader such as Joseph Kony in Uganda.

checks and balances   Government in which power is divided between the executive, legislative and judicial branches of government, and so each checks and balances the other, unlike in dictatorships, where one individual acts as he pleases.

citizenship   Legal membership in a community known as a nation-state.

civil society   A sphere of society somewhere between the state and the household. This 'public space' includes networks of institutions, groups and organisations through which citizens voluntarily represent themselves.

code of law   A comprehensive set of interrelated legal rules, linked to the 'rule of law'.

coercion   Power based on forcing compliance through fear and intimidation.

collective security   A commitment by a number of individuals, groups or states to join in alliance against external threats.

conciliation   The voluntary referral of a conflict to a neutral external party that either suggests a non-binding settlement or explores ways to bring about conflict resolution. Conciliation can also contribute to maintaining agreements and preventing future conflicts over other issues and is therefore an ongoing process. The impartiality of the third party is key.

conflict   From the Latin for 'to clash or engage in a fight', a confrontation between parties aspiring towards incompatible or competitive means or ends. Conflict may be violent or non-violent, and essentially all societies contain some form of conflict. In IR terms, we usually discuss interstate, intra-state and state-formation conflicts as well as global conflicts aimed at transnational criminal or terrorist networks.

conflict management   Ongoing intervention to prevent escalation of conflicts, particularly into violence.

conflict prevention   Action to redress grievances with the aim of avoiding conflict, stopping violence from recurring during a peace process or avoiding escalation.

conflict resolution   A variety of approaches aimed at resolving conflicts through the constructive solving of problems, distinct from the management or transformation of conflict. Conflict resolution is extremely broad and can refer to a process, a result and an academic field of study, as well as an activity in which people engage in without giving it the specific label.

conflict transformation   Changes in the general framework of the conflict, the participants, the core issues or some other basic element that shifts the conflict or process on to a different trajectory.

contracting out   Privatising activities through hiring commercial companies to provide public or merit goods and services such as security.

corporatism   Liberal democratic form of government, with the state as a dominant centre and everything else subordinated – for example, fascist Italy under Mussolini or Peronist Argentina.

coup d'état   An illegal seizing of power by the military or a faction of the military and some other political and security force.

custom   A generally accepted practice or behaviour developed over time.

customary law   Rules of conduct developed over time and enforceable in court, frequently by a customary ruler or traditional authority such as a village elder or a traditional chief.

decentralisation   Transfer of authority from central to local political authorities.

decommissioning   Disposing of arms following a peace agreement.

deconcentration   Relocation of central government agencies to the provinces.

demilitarisation   The removal of military forces from civilian areas, either internationally or through confining them to barracks. In the long term, it refers to the reduction of military influence from political life and a reduction in military spending.

demobilisation   The process of shifting former combatants away from conflict groups and either into a formal military (integration) or civilian life (reinsertion).

despotism   An individual ruling through fear without regard to law and not answerable to the people – a dictatorship.

deterrence   From the Latin *deterrere*, 'to frighten from', the act of making a potential enemy think that the consequences of an attack will outweigh the benefits.

devolution   A system in which the central government devolves (or delegates) power to regional governments.

dictatorship of the proletariat   A revolutionary seizure of power by the 'vanguard' of society, the Communist Party or similar, which then rules in the name of the working class. It was common in left-leaning revolutionary movements during the post-colonial era and re-emerged with the Maoist success in Nepal.

diplomacy   A system of formal or informal communication, but regularised through norms and common practices, that allows states and sometimes other armed groups to conduct their business with each other peacefully.

disarmament   Putting usable arms out of immediate reach of combatants and under the controlled jurisdiction of a party agreed within the ceasefire or peace agreement; reducing weapons stockpiles over time.

displaced person   A person forced to leave their home through no fault of their own, usually through threat of or actual violence. The term usually identifies internally displaced people as those fleeing from one part of country to another part of the same country. Crossing a border could lead to a displaced person becoming a refugee.

distributive laws   Laws designed to distribute public goods and services to individuals in society.

downsizing   Reducing the size and scope of an actor, either in government or of an armed force, for example.

elite   A small group of people with a disproportionate amount of public decision-making power. The elite frequently benefit from the political settlement following wars and can exist at both the central and the local level.

equality of opportunity   The equalisation of life-chances for all individuals in society, regardless of economic position, gender, race, ethnicity or geographical location.

escalation An increase in quantity, intensity or scope of violent exchanges among parties. Its opposite is **de-escalation**, which happens during a peace process.

ethnic group A group whose common identity may be based on linguistic, racial, national or religious affiliation.

executive A small group of officials, usually from the elite, who direct the policy process, make key decisions, and control the departments and agencies of government.

faction A group of individuals organised to further their own interests, usually within a larger group – for example, a group loyal to one specific leader in a larger group.

failed state A nation-state that is unable to provide basic services to its citizens, including security. Note that a failed state may be a collapsed state, like the DRC, or an authoritarian regime that has hijacked the state and will not provide services to citizens, like Zimbabwe under Mugabe.

formal legal institutions Institutions, ministries and agencies that are explicitly created by a constitution and therefore are constituted by law and mandated with specific roles.

free riders Those who enjoy a collective good without contributing any payment for it.

gender Power relations that exist between men and women in society. Note that gender does not equate with 'women'.

genocide Acts that deliberately seek to wipe out a racial or ethnic group. Genocide was defined as a crime by the Convention for the Prevention and Punishment of the Crime of Genocide of 9 December 1948 and further elaborated in Statute Article 2(2) of the International Criminal Tribunal for Rwanda.

gerontocracy Rule of old men.

guerrilla warfare *Guerrilla* is the Spanish for 'small war', and the term refers to an unconventional style of warfare fought by insurgents or irregulars against formal, conventional militaries. There are several styles, but one of the best known is the Maoist strategy of rural insurgency based on community networks, used in China, Vietnam and, more recently, Nepal.

head of government The person in charge of the **executive**.

head of state An individual who represents the state but does not exercise political power, for example the queen of the United Kingdom.

human rights Rights ascribed to all human beings and defined by the UN as being universal and inalienable; rights that everyone has by just being human.

human security An approach which argues that people should be at the centre of security, challenging the notion that states are the correct referent object when thinking about what a security threat is and how it can be tackled.

ideology A system of beliefs and values that explains society and prescribes the type and role of government.

influence The ability to persuade others to share in a desired aim or objective.

informal institutions Institutions that are integral to the political process, but which are not established by a constitution. They may be traditional authorities, customary authorities, or attributed to individuals such as chiefs.

insurgency Paramilitary, guerrilla, or non-violent uprisings directed against a nation-state or apparatus from within in order to achieve political objectives.

internally displaced person An individual who has to leave their home, usually because of violence, insecurity or natural disaster, but who does not cross an international border.

international law The body of rules governing the relationships of states with each other and the behaviour of states within that framework.

International Monetary Fund   One of the Bretton-Woods institutions (along with the World Bank) created following the Second World War to prevent another collapse in the world monetary system through the stabilisation of national currencies.

international order   The combination of institutions, governance mechanisms, actors and norms used to manage the framework of international states and to enforce international law.

intervention   In development terms, the involvement of an international or donor organisation in the development of a particular country – for example, UN peacekeeping forces.

judiciary   The formal branch of government with the power to resolve legal conflicts, comprising courts, lawyers, magistrates, etc.

junta   A Spanish word meaning 'a group of individuals forming a government', especially after a revolution or coup d'état. The term has overtones of illegitimacy.

legitimacy   Belief in the 'rightness' of rule or the right to exercise authority. Legitimate authority negates coercion within the population, whereas illegitimate authority necessitates the use of terror within populations.

liberal democracy   A system of government characterised by individual freedom, democracy, universal adult suffrage, political equality, majority rule and the rule of law.

mediation   A voluntary process facilitated by a third party that produces a non-binding outcome of a conflict or dispute.

modernisation   The gradual replacement of traditional authority with legal authority, or the theory that all states are on the same path to the modern state.

movement party   A type of political party which emerges from a political movement, such as a national liberation movement, as in Uganda.

multi-party system   A party system in which there are three or more major contenders for power and frequently taken as the aim of many post-conflict interventions.

nation   A country focused on the idea of a nation-state and nationhood through shared beliefs, language and identity.

national interest   Interests specific to a nation-state rather than to an individual, particularly survival and maintenance of power.

nationalism   Loyalty to the nation or nation-state and strong support for its interests.

nation-state   A state with a single predominant national identity.

negative-sum outcome   A lose–lose situation whereby a course of action results in all parties losing out.

normative   Political analysis based on values, ideas and commitment to a particular view of the world.

oligarchy   Rule of a small group of individuals above the law; group dictatorship.

paradigm   A scientifically non-proven set of beliefs about the world that constitute 'common sense' or the accepted way the world works.

parliamentary sovereignty   The supreme authority of parliament as the executive power.

patriarchy   The domination of society by men.

peacebuilding   A process for working towards the peaceful coexistence of former combatants.

peace enforcement   The employment of force against any non-compliant actor to ensure 'negative peace' – that is, the absence of violent conflict through intervention, usually as part of a broader peacekeeping process.

peacekeeping   The external involvement of external militaries, usually under the UN or a regional authority, with the aim of preventing further violent conflict or to enforce peace.

policy community   The network of individuals and organisations deeply involved in a particular area of policy and responsible for much generation of new ideas.

political alienation   Exclusion from political networks or sources of power; extreme disempowerment.

political culture   Attitudes, values, beliefs, and common practices that individuals in a society hold regarding their political system.

political economy   The study of the relationship between economics and politics within the nation-state.

political patronage   Government or other appointments made as a result of nepotism or political links – for example, generals running petrol companies, family members running security forces.

political police   Forces reporting directly to a political leader and used as political thugs rather than as law enforcement officers. They are usually armed and uniformed paramilitary organisations.

political process   The interaction of formal and informal political structures and actors in making and administering public and political decisions.

political socialisation   Transmitting political culture through generations.

positive-sum outcome   An outcome where all parties can be satisfied – a 'win–win' situation.

power   The ability to enforce policy, orders and objectives and get other individuals to act as ordered.

proletariat   Marxist term for the working class. Their only means of production is labour, which they have to sell to the **bourgeoisie**.

realism   Also known as *Realpolitik*, realism is a theory of international relations based on the state's ability to resolve disputes based on power.

reconciliation   A process that attempts to alleviate lingering animosity between previously conflicted parties. It is a key element of peacebuilding.

redistribution   The process of reallocating wealth or power to achieve an economic or social objective or a more equitable social outcome.

refugee   A person seeking asylum in another country as a result of the prospect of imminent harm or persecution.

representative democracy   A system of government based on the election of decision-makers by the people.

responsibility to protect   An approach which emphasises the duty of states to ensure their citizens are protected from insecurity, and the responsibility of the international community to intervene when a state wilfully disregards or fails in this duty.

rule of law   A system that ensures that all actors are subject to a recognised and institutionalised set of rules and regulations enforced equally across society.

security community   A group of like-minded actors, groups, states or organisations that act in concert in relation to security.

security complex   A group of actors engaged in security activities for good or ill, frequently comprised of mixed groups incorporating formal governments, local authorities, traditional authorities, criminal gangs, NGOs and others.

social justice   The equalisation of wealth and power to reach a more equitable outcome.

spontaneous order   As in a state of anarchy without oversight, the pattern of mutual co-ordination that emerges as individuals pursue their own interests.

stateless society   A society without a recognised or legitimate sovereign government, such as Somalia.

structuralism   A theory of international relations emphasising the impact of world economic structures on the internal political, social, cultural and economic structures within states.

structural violence   Embedded political, social or economic hierarchies that act to put particular groups of people at high risk of breaches of human security or groups that are systematically excluded from formal networks and are therefore oppressed by the structure itself.

terrorism   From the Latin *terrere*, meaning 'to frighten', terrorism is the undertaking of violent actions against secondary targets to further political aims. Terrorists usually deliberately select non-combatants as targets to maximise fright in order to gain concessions.

totalitarianism   A modern form of despotism or dictatorship in which the state undertakes to remake society according to an ideological design.

traditional authority   Authority based on customary law, such as chiefs, village headmen, etc.

treaty   A legally binding document signed by conflict participants and ratified by nation-states under international law.

tribe   A community of people linked by a foundation myth and a shared ancestry or belief system.

truth and reconciliation commission   A temporary body that attempts to address reconciliation and reparation through the investigation of human rights abuses and past violence.

war crimes   Violations of the accepted laws of war or recognised customs and conventions. Most war crimes are perpetrated against non-combatant populations and include murder, torture, deportation, rape, the taking of hostages, and forced labour. Other war crimes are plundering, unjustified destruction of property, the use of certain weapons, and the improper usage of symbols of truce.

World Trade Organisation   A Bretton Woods institution created after the Second World War to provide the ground rules for international trade and commerce.

zero-sum game   A situation where the gains of one party are inversely related to the losses of another party. In other words, as one side benefits, the other side suffers proportionally.

References and bibliography

Abrahamsen, R. (2000) *Disciplining Democracy: Development Discourse and Good Governance in Africa*. London: Zed Books.

Achvarina, V., and Reich, S. (2006) 'No place to hide: refugees, displaced persons, and the recruitment of child soldiers', *International Security*, 31(1): 127–64.

Ahmed, Ismail, A., and Green, Reginald H. (1999) 'The heritage of war and state collapse in Somalia and Somaliland: local level effects, external interventions and reconstruction', *Third World Quarterly*, 20(1): 113–27.

Albrecht, Peter, and Jackson, Paul (2009) *Security Transformation in Sierra Leone 1997–2007*, Birmingham: Global Facilitation Network for Security Sector Reform, www.ssrnetwork.net/publications/gfn_ssr_publications.php (accessed 24 February 2011).

Albrecht, Peter, and Jackson, Paul (eds) (2010) *Security Sector Reform in Sierra Leone 1997–2007: Views from the Front Line*. Berlin: Lit.

Alden, C. (1995) 'Swords into ploughshares? The United Nations and demilitarisation in Mozambique', *International Peacekeeping*, 2(2): 175–93.

Allin, D. (2002) *NATO's Balkan Interventions*, Adelphi Paper 347. Oxford: Oxford University Press.

Anderson, Mary (1998) '"You save my life today, but what for tomorrow?" Some moral dilemmas of humanitarian aid', in J. Moore (ed.), *Hard Choices: Moral Dilemmas in Humanitarian Intervention*. Oxford: Rowman & Littlefield.

Anderson, Mary (1999) *Do No Harm: How Aid Can Support Peace – or War*. Boulder, CO: Lynne Rienner.

Anderson, Mary (2001) 'Enhancing local capacity for peace: do no harm', in Luc Reychler and Thania Paffenholz (eds), *Peacebuilding: A Field Guide*. Boulder, CO: Lynne Rienner.

Anderson, R. (2000) 'How multilateral development assistance triggered the conflict in Rwanda', *Third World Quarterly*, 21(3): 441–56.

Auty, R. M. (1993) *Sustaining Development in Mineral Economies: The Resource Curse Thesis*. London: Routledge.

Auvinen, J., and Timo K. (2000) 'Somalia: the struggle for resources', in E. W. Nafziger, F. Stewart and R. Väyrynen (eds), *War, Hunger, and Displacement: The Origins of Humanitarian Emergencies*. Oxford: Oxford University Press.

Avant, Deborah (2005) *The Market for Force: The Consequences of Privatizing Security*. Cambridge: Cambridge University Press.

Ayoob, M. (1997) 'Defining security: a subaltern realist perspective', in K. Krause and M. Williams (eds), *Critical Security Studies: Concepts and Cases*. Minneapolis: University of Minnesota Press, pp. 121–46.

Bakewell, O. (2000) 'Uncovering local perspectives on humanitarian assistance and its outcomes', *Disasters*, 24(2): 103–16.

Baldwin, David (1997) 'The concept of security', *Review of International Studies*, 23(1): 5–26.

Ball, Nicole (2001a) 'The challenge of rebuilding war-torn societies', in C. A. Crocker, F. O. Hampson, M. B. Anderson and P. Aall (eds), *Turbulent Peace: The Challenges of Managing International Conflict*. Washington, DC: United States Institute of Peace Press.

Ball, Nicole (2001b) 'Transforming security sectors: the IMF and World Bank approaches', *Conflict Security and Development*, 1(1): 45–66.

Ball, Nicole (2003) 'Demobilising and reintegrating soldiers: lessons from Africa', in Sunil Bastian and Robin Luckham (eds), *Can Democracy Be Designed? The Politics of Institutional Choice in Conflict-Torn Societies*. London: Zed Books.

Ball, Nicole, and van de Goor, Luc (2006) *Disarmament, Demobilization and Reintegration: Mapping Issues, Dilemmas and Guiding Principles*, Clingandael Research Paper. The Hague: Netherlands Institute of International Relations.

Ballentine, Karen, and Sherman, Jake (eds) (2003) *The Political Economy of Armed Conflict: Beyond Greed and Grievance*. Boulder, CO: Lynne Rienner.

Barnett, Michael, and Duvall, Raymond (eds) (2005) *Power in Global Governance*. Cambridge: Cambridge University Press.

Bayart, Jean-François (1993) *The State in Africa: The Politics of the Belly*. London: Longman.

Bayart, Jean-François (2000) 'Africa in the world: a history of extraversion', *African Affairs*, 99(395): 217–69.

Bayart, Jean-François, Ellis, Stephen, and Hibou, Beatrice (eds) (1999) *The Criminalization of the State in Africa*. Oxford: James Currey.

Bayley, David (2006) *Changing the Guard: Developing Democratic Police Abroad*. Oxford: Oxford University Press.

Bayliss, John, and Smith, Steve (eds) (2008) *The Globalization of World Politics: An Introduction to International Relations*. Oxford: Oxford University Press.

Bellamy, Alex J., Williams, Paul, and Griffin, Stuart (2010) *Understanding Peacekeeping*, 2nd ed. Cambridge: Polity.

Berdal, Mats (1996) *Disarmament and Demobilisation after Civil Wars: Arms, Soldiers and the Termination of Armed Conflicts*. Oxford: Oxford University Press.

Berdal, Mats (2004) 'The UN after Iraq', *Survival*, 46(3): 83–101.

Berdal Mats (2005) 'The UN's unnecessary crisis', *Survival*, 47(3): 7–32.

Berdal, Mats, and Keen, David (1998) 'Violence and economic agendas in civil wars: some policy implications', *Millennium*, 26(3): 795–818.

Berdal, Mats, and Malone, David (eds) (2000) *Greed and Grievance: Economic Agendas in Civil Wars*. Boulder, CO: Lynne Rienner.

Berg-Schlosser, Dirk, and Kersting, Norman (eds) (2003) *Poverty and Democracy: Self-Help and Political Participation in Third World Cities*. London: Zed Books.

Bermeo, Nancy (2003) 'What the democratization literature says – or doesn't say – about postwar democratization', *Global Governance*, 9: 159–77.

Beswick, D. (2009) 'The challenge of warlordism to post-conflict state-building: the case of Laurent Nkunda in Eastern Congo', *Round Table: The Commonwealth Journal of International Affairs*, 98(402): 333–46.

Bhatia, Michael (2003) *War and Intervention: Issues for Contemporary Peace Operations*. Bloomfield, CT: Kumarian Press.

Bøås, Morten (2005) 'The Liberian civil war: new war/old war?' *Global Society*, 19(1): 73–88.

Bøås, Morten, and Jennings, Kathleen (2005) 'Insecurity and development: the rhetoric of the "failed state"', *European Journal of Development Research*, 17(3): 385–95.

Bøås, Morten, and Dunn, Kevin (2007) *African Guerrillas: Raging against the Machine*. Boulder, CO: Lynne Rienner, pp. 1–38.

Booth, Ken (ed.) (2005) *Critical Security Studies and World Politics*. Boulder, CO: Lynne Rienner.

Boutros-Ghali, Boutros (1992) *An Agenda for Peace: Preventive Diplomacy, Peacemaking and Peace-Keeping*. New York: United Nations.

Brauman, Rony (1998) 'Refugee camps, population transfers and NGOs', in Jonathon Moore (ed.), *Hard Choices: Moral Dilemmas in Humanitarian Intervention*. Oxford: Rowman & Littlefield.

Bryden, Alan, and Hänggi, Hainer (eds) (2005) *Security Governance in Post-Conflict Peacebuilding*. Münster: Lit.

Brynen, R. (1990) *Sanctuary and Survival: The PLO in Lebanon*. Boulder, CO: Westview Press.

Brzoska, Michael (2003) *Development Donors and the Concept of Security Sector Reform*, Occasional Paper no. 4. Geneva: Geneva Centre for the Democratic Control of Armed Forces; www.dcaf.ch/publications/Publications%20New/Occasional_Papers/4.pdf (accessed 23 February 2011).

Buur, Lars, Jensen, Steffen, and Stepputat, Finn (2007) *The Security–Development Nexus: Expressions of Sovereignty and Securitization in Southern Africa*. Uppsala: Nordiska Afrikainstitutet.

Buzan, Barry, Wæver, Ole, and Wilde, Jaap de (1998) *Security: A New Framework for Analysis*. Boulder, CO: Lynne Rienner.

Cabinet Office (2008) *The National Security Strategy of the United Kingdom: Security in an Interdependent World*, Cm 7291. London: HMSO.

Callaghy, Thomas (1994) 'Civil society, democracy, and economic change in Africa: a dissenting opinion about resurgent societies', in John W. Harbeson, Donald Rothchild, and Naomi Chazan (eds), *Civil Society and the State in Africa*. Boulder, CO: Lynne Rienner.

Caplan, Richard (2002) *A New Trusteeship? The International Administration of War-Torn Territories*, Adelphi Paper 341. Oxford: Oxford University Press.

C.A.S.E. Collective (2006) 'Critical approaches to security in Europe: a networked manifesto', *Security Dialogue*, 37(4) 443–87.

Cawthra, Gavin, and Luckham, Robin (eds) (2003) *Governing Insecurity: Democratic Control of Military and Security Establishments in Transitional Democracies*. London: Zed Books.

Cerny, Philip (1998) 'Neomedievalism, civil war and the new security dilemma: globalisation as a durable disorder', *Civil wars*, 1(1): 36–64.

Chandler, David (2008) 'Review article: theorising the shift from security to insecurity – Kaldor, Duffield and Furedi', *Conflict Security and Development*, 8(2): 265–76.

Charlier, Marie-Dominique (2010) 'Afghanistan's outsourced war', *Le Monde Diplomatique*, 9 February; www.rawa.org/temp/runews/2010/02/09/afghanistans-outsourced-war.html (accessed December 2010).

Chesterman, Simon (ed.) (2001) *Civilians in War*. Boulder, CO: Lynne Rienner.

Clapham, Christopher (1996) *Africa and the International System: The Politics of State Survival*. Cambridge: Cambridge University Press.

Clapham, Christopher (ed.) (1998) *African Guerrillas*. Oxford: James Currey.

Cliffe, Lionel, and Luckham, Robin (1999) 'Complex political emergencies and the state: failure and the failure of the state', *Third World Quarterly*, 20(1): 27–50.

Collier, Paul (2003) 'Civil war as development in reverse', in Paul Collier *et al.*, *Breaking the Conflict Trap: Civil War and Development Policy*. Oxford: Oxford University Press and the World Bank, pp. 13–32; http://econ.worldbank.org/prr/CivilWarPRR/text-26671/.

Collier, Paul (2009) *War, Guns, and Votes: Democracy in Dangerous Places*. New York: HarperCollins.

Collier, Paul, and Hoeffler, Anke (2000) *Greed and Grievance in Civil War*. Oxford: Centre for the Study of African Economies; www.csae.ox.ac.uk/workingpapers/pdfs/20-18text.pdf (accessed 24 February 2011).

Collier, Paul, and Hoeffler, Anke (2001) *Greed and Grievance in Civil War*, Policy Research Working Paper no. 2355. Washington, DC: World Bank.

Collier, Paul, and Hoeffler, Anke (2002) 'On the incidence of civil war in Africa', *Journal of Conflict Resolution*, 46(1): 13–28.

Collier, Paul, and Bannon, Ian (2003) *Natural Resources and Violent Conflict: Options and Actions*. Washington, DC: World Bank.

Collier, Paul, and Hoeffler, Anke (2004) 'Greed and grievance in civil war', *Oxford Economic Papers*, 56(4): 563–95.

Collier, Paul, Hoeffler, Anke, and Rohner, Dominic (2009) 'Beyond greed and grievance: feasibility and civil war', *Oxford Economic Papers*, 61(1): 1–27.

Conflict, Security and Development (2005), 5(2): special issue on security governance.

Cramer, Christopher (2006) *Civil War Is Not a Stupid Thing: Accounting for Violence in Developing Countries*. London: Hurst.

Crawford, Timothy, and Kuperman, Alan (eds) (2005) *Ethnopolitics*, 4(2): special issue: debating the hazards of intervention.

Cronin, Audrey (2002) 'Behind the curve: globalization and international terrorism', *International Security*, 27(3): 30–58.

Dahrendorf, Nicola (2008) 'MONUC and the relevance of coherent mandates', in Heiner Hänggi and Vincenza Scherrer (eds), *Security Sector Reform and UN Integrated Missions*. Geneva: DCAF, pp. 67–112.

Dallaire, Romeo (2003) *Shake Hands with the Devil: The Failure of Humanity in Rwanda*. London: Random House/Arrow Books.

De Berry, Jo (2001) 'Child soldiers and the Convention on the Rights of the Child', *Annals of the American Academy of Political and Social Science*, 575(1): 92–105.

De Grieff, Pablo (ed.) (2007) *The Handbook of Reparations*. Oxford: Oxford University Press.

De Waal, Alex (1994) 'Dangerous precedents? Famine relief in Somalia 1991–93', in Joanna Macrae and Anthony Zwi (eds), *War and Hunger: Rethinking International Responses to Complex Emergencies*. London: Zed Books.

De Waal, Alex (1997) *Famine Crimes: Politics and the Disaster Relief Industry in Africa*. Oxford: James Currey.

DFID (Department for International Development) (2005) *Fighting Poverty to Build a Safer World: A Strategy for Security and Development*. London: DFID.

DFID (2005) *Why We Need to Work More Effectively in Fragile States*. London: DFID; www.jica. go.jp/cdstudy/library/pdf/20071101_11.pdf.

Dowty, Alan, and Loescher, Gil (1996) 'Refugee flows as grounds for international action', *International Security*, 21(1): 43–71.

Duffield, Mark (1997) 'NGO relief in war zones: towards an analysis of the new aid paradigm', *Third World Quarterly*, 18(3): 527–42.

Duffield, Mark (2001) *Global Governance and the New Wars: The Merging of Development and Security*. London: Zed Books.

Duffield, Mark (2008) *Development, Security and Unending War: Governing the World of Peoples*. Cambridge: Cambridge University Press.

Duffield, Mark, Macrae, Joanna, and Curtis, Devon (2001) 'Editorial: politics and humanitarian aid', *Disasters*, 25(4): 269–74.

Eaton, Dave (2008) 'The business of peace: raiding and peace work along the Kenya–Uganda border', parts I and II, *African Affairs*, 107(426): 89–110; 107(427): 243–59.

Edwards, Michael, and Gaventa, John (eds) (2001) *Global Citizen Action*. Boulder, CO: Lynne Rienner.

Elbe, Stefan (2003) *Strategic Implications of HIV/AIDS*, Adelphi Paper no. 357. Oxford: Oxford University Press.

Ellis, S. (1999) *The Mask of Anarchy: The Destruction of Liberia and the Religious Dimension of an African Civil War*. London: Hurst.

Englebert, Pierre, and Tull, Denis (2008) 'Postconflict reconstruction in Africa: flawed ideas about failed states', *International Security*, 32(4): 106–39.

European Union (2003) *A Secure Europe in a Better World: European Security Strategy*. Brussels, December.

European Union (2005) 'Council Common Position 2005/304/CFSP of 12 April 2005 concerning conflict prevention, management and resolution in Africa and repealing Common Position 2004/85/CFSP', *Official Journal of the European Union*, L97, 15 April.

Evans, Gareth (2004) 'When is it right to fight?', *Survival*, 46(3): 60.

Farah, Douglas, and Shultz, Richard (2004) 'Al Qaeda's growing sanctuary', *Washington Post* 14 July, p. A19.

Fearon, D., and Laitin, D. (2003) 'Ethnicity, insurgency and civil war', *American Political Science Review*, 97(1): 75–90.

Finkelstein, Lawrence (1995) 'What is global governance?', *Global Governance*, 1(3): 368.

Forster, Anthony (2005) *Armed Forces and Society in Europe*. Basingstoke: Palgrave.

Frynas, J. George, and Wood, Geoffrey (2001) 'Oil and war in Angola', *Review of African Political Economy*, 28(90): 587–606.

Fukuyama, Francis (1992) *The End of History and the Last Man*. London: Hamilton.

Galtung, Johan (1969) 'Violence, peace, and peace research', *Journal of Peace Research*, 6(3): 167–91.

Gaultier, Leonard, *et al.* (2001) *The Mercenary Issue at the UN Commission on Human Rights: The Need for a New Approach*. London: International Alert; www.international-alert.org/pdf/unhr.pdf (accessed 6 March 2011).

Gleditsch, Nils Petter, *et al.*, (2002) 'Armed conflict 1946–2001: a new dataset', *Journal of Peace Research*, 39(5): 615–37.

Goldstone, Jack (2002) 'Population and security: how demographic change can lead to violent conflict', *Journal of International Affairs*, 56(1): 3–21.

Goodhand, Jonathan, and Hulme, David (1999) 'From wars to complex political emergencies: understanding conflict and peace-building in the new world disorder', *Third World Quarterly*, 20(1): 13–26.

Gordenker, Leon, and Weiss, Thomas (1995) 'Pluralising global governance: analytical approaches and dimensions', *Third World Quarterly*, 16(3): 357–77.

Gordenker, Leon, and Weiss, Thomas (eds) (1996) *NGOs, the UN, and Global Governance*. Boulder, CO: Lynne Rienner.

Goulding, Marrack (1993) 'The evolution of United Nations peacekeeping', *International Affairs*, 69(3): 451–64.

Goverde, Henri, *et al.* (2000) *Power in Contemporary Politics: Theories, Practices, Globalizations*. London: Sage.

Hampson, Fen Osler, and Malone, David M. (2002) 'Improving the UN's capacity for conflict prevention', *International Peacekeeping*, 9(1): 77–98.

Hänggi, Heiner, and Scherrer, Vincenza (eds) (2008) *Security Sector Reform and UN Integrated Missions: Experience from Burundi*. Münster: Lit.

Harding, Jeremy (1997) 'The mercenary business: Executive Outcomes', *Review of African Political Economy*, 24(71): 87–97.

Held, David, and McGrew, Anthony (2002) *Governing Globalization: Power, Authority, and Global Governance*. Cambridge: Polity, pp. 1–21.

Hettne, Björn, and Söderbaum, Fredrik (2005) 'Intervening in complex humanitarian emergencies: the role of regional cooperation', *European Journal of Development Research*, 17(3): 449–61.

Hilhorst, Dorothea (2002) 'Being good at doing good? Quality and accountability of humanitarian NGOs', *Disasters*, 26(3): 193–212.

Hill, Chris (2001) 'The EU's capacity for conflict prevention', *European Foreign Affairs Review*, 6(3): 315–34.

Hills, Alice (2003) 'Dissolving boundaries? The development marketplace and military security', *Contemporary Security Policy*, 24(3): 48–66.

Hoffman, Danny (2004) 'The civilian target in Sierra Leone and Liberia: political power, military strategy and humanitarian intervention', *African Affairs*, 103(411): 211–26.

Holmqvist, Caroline (2005) *Private Security Companies: The Case for Regulation*, Policy paper no. 9. Stockholm: SIPRI.

Holt, Victoria, and Berkman, Tobias (2007) *The Impossible Mandate? Military Preparedness, the Responsibility to Protect and Modern Peace Operations*. Washington, DC: Henry Stimson Center; www.stimson.org/books-reports/the-impossible-mandate/ (accessed 24 February 2011).

Homer-Dixon, Thomas F. (1994) 'Environmental scarcities and violent conflict: evidence from cases', *International Security*, 19(1): 5–40.

Howell, Jude, and Pearce, Jenny (2001) *Civil Society and Development: A Critical Exploration.* Boulder, CO: Lynne Rienner.

HSRP (Human Security Report Project) (2009) *Human Security Report 2009/10*, Part II: *The Shrinking Costs of War*. Vancouver: Simon Fraser University.

Human Rights Watch (2003) *Basra: Crime and Insecurity under British Occupation*, www.hrw.org/en/reports/200306/02/basra (accessed 24 February 2011).

Huntington, Samuel P. (1996) *The Clash of Civilizations and the Remaking of World Order*. New York: Simon & Schuster.

Hutchful, Eboe, and Aning, Emmanuel K. (2004) 'The political economy of conflict', in Adekeye Adebajo and Ismail Rashid (eds), *West Africa's Security Challenges: Building Peace in a Troubled Region*. Boulder, CO: Lynne Rienner.

Huysmans, Jef, Dobson, Andrew, and Prokhovnik, Raia (eds) (2006) *The Politics of Protection: Sites of Insecurity and Political Agency*. London: Routledge.

Hyden, Goran (1999) 'Governance and the reconstitution of political order', in Richard Joseph (ed.), *State, Conflict, and Democracy in Africa*. Boulder, CO: Lynne Rienner.

Ibeanu, O. (1998) 'Exiles in their own home: internal population displacement in Nigeria', *African Journal of Political Science*, 3(2): 80–97.

ICG (International Crisis Group) (2002) *Belgrade's Lagging Reform: Cause for International Concern*, Balkans report no. 126, www.crisisgroup.org/~/media/files/europe/serbia%2019.ashx (accessed 24 February 2011).

ICG (2009) *Liberia: Uneven Progress in Security Sector Reform*, Africa report no. 148, 13 January, www.dyn-intl.com/media/3180/148_liberia_uneven_progress_in_security_sector_reform.pdf (accessed 24 February 2011); see Appendix E: 'The "dogs of peace"? Private companies in SSR'.

ICISS (International Commission on Intervention and State Sovereignty) (2001) *The Responsibility to Protect*. Ottawa: International Development Research Centre.

ICISS (2010) 'Learn about R2P', www.responsibilitytoprotect.org/index.php/about-rtop/learn-about-rtop (accessed 23 August 2010).

IDMC (Internal Displacement Monitoring Centre) (2009) *Internal Displacement: Global Overview of Trends and Developments in 2008*. Geneva: IDMC; www.internal-displacement.org/8025708F004BE3B1/(httpInfoFiles)/82DA6A2DE4C7BA41C12575A90041E6A8/$file/IDMC_Internal_Displacement_Global_Overview_2008.pdf (accessed 24 February 2011).

IRC (International Rescue Committee) (2007) *Mortality in the Democratic Republic of Congo: An Ongoing Crisis*, www.theirc.org/sites/default/files/migrated/resources/2007/2006-7_congomortalitysurvey.pdf (accessed 24 February 2011).

ISIS (International Security Information Service) (2006) *Developing an EU Strategy for Security Sector Reform*. Brussels: ISIS; www.ssrnetwork.net/uploaded_files/3279.pdf (accessed 9 March 2011).

ISS (Institute for Security Studies) (2005) 'Africa: the breeding ground for terrorism?', *African Terrorism Bulletin*, March, www.iss.org.za/Pubs/Newsletters/Terrorism/0205.htm#article12 (accessed 24 February 2011).

Jackson, Paul (2002) 'The march of the Lord's Resistance Army: greed or grievance in Northern Uganda', *Small Wars and Insurgencies*, 13(3): 29–52.

Jackson, Paul (2007) 'What does fourth generation warfare mean in Africa?', *Contemporary Security Policy*, 28(2): 267–85.

Jackson, Paul (2009a) 'Mars, Venus or Mercury: AFRICOM and America's ambiguous intentions', *Contemporary Security Policy*, 30(1): 1–4.

Jackson, Paul (2009b) 'Mission and pragmatism in US security policy in Africa', *Contemporary Security Policy*, 30(1): 45–9.

Jackson, Paul (2009c) '"Negotiating with ghosts": religion, conflict and peace in Northern Uganda', *The Round Table*, 98(402): 319–31.

Jackson, Paul, and Albrecht, Peter (2010) *Reconstructing Security after Conflict: Security Sector Transformation in Sierra Leone 1997–2007*. Basingstoke: Palgrave Macmillan.

Jackson, Robert (1990) *Quasi-States: Sovereignty, International Relations and the Third World*. Cambridge: Cambridge University Press.

Jackson, Robert (1992) 'Juridical statehood in sub-Saharan Africa', *Journal of International Affairs*, 46(1): 1–16.

Jacoby, Tim (2010) 'Emerging patterns in the reconstruction of conflict-affected countries', *Disaster*, 34(1): 1–14.

Jentleson, Bruce (2002) 'The need for praxis: bringing policy relevance back in', *International Security*, 26(4): 169–83.

Joseph, R. (ed.) (1999) *State, Conflict, and Democracy in Africa*. Boulder, CO: Lynne Rienner.

Kaarsholm, Preben (ed.) (2006) *Violence, Political Culture & Development in Africa*. Oxford: James Currey.

Kaldor, Mary (1999) *New and Old Wars: Organized Violence in a Global Era*. Cambridge: Polity; 2nd ed., 2006.

Kalyvas, Stathis (2001) '"New" and "old" civil wars: a valid distinction?', *World Politics*, 54(1): 99–118.

Kaplan, Robert (1994) 'The coming anarchy: how scarcity, crime, overpopulation, tribalism, and disease are rapidly destroying the social fabric of our planet', *Atlantic Monthly*, February; www.theatlantic.com/magazine/archive/1994/02/the-coming-anarchy/4670/ (accessed 25 February 2011).

Keen, David (1998) *The Economic Functions of Violence in Civil Wars*, Adelphi Paper no. 320. Oxford: Oxford University Press.

Keen, David (2000) 'War and peace: what's the difference', *International Peacekeeping*, 7(4): 1–22.

Keen, David (2008) *Complex Emergencies*. Cambridge: Polity.

Keen, David, and Wilson, Ken (1994) 'Engaging with violence: a reassessment of relief in wartime', in Joanna Macrae and Anthony Zwi (eds), *War and Hunger: Rethinking International Responses to Complex Emergencies*. London: Zed Books.

Kumar, Krishna (ed.) (1997) *Rebuilding Societies after Civil War: Critical Roles for International Assistance*. Boulder, CO: Lynne Rienner.

Kurtz, Christof (2007) 'Greed, grievance and atrocities', *Journal of Intervention and State Building*, 1(1): 132–49.

Le Billon, Philippe (2001) 'The political ecology of war: natural resources and armed conflicts', *Political Geography*, 20(5): 561–84.

Lewis, Peter (1992) 'Political transition and the dilemma of civil society in Africa', *Journal of International Affairs*, 46(1): 31–54.

Lindblom, Charles, and Cohen, David (1979) *Usable Knowledge: Social Science and Social Problem Solving*. New Haven, CT: Yale University Press.

Lischer, Sarah Kenyon (2003) 'Collateral damage', *International Security*, 28(1): 79–109.

Lischer, Sarah K. (2008) 'Security and displacement in Iraq: responding to the forced migration crisis', *International Security*, 33(2): 95–119.

Lujala, Päivi, Gleditsch, Nils Petter, and Gilmore, Elisabeth (2005) 'A diamond curse? Civil war and a lootable resource', *Journal of Conflict Resolution*, 49(4): 538–62.

McCartney, Clem, Fischer, Martina, and Wils, Oliver (eds) (2004) *Security Sector Reform: Potentials and Challenges for Conflict Transformation*. Berlin: Berghof Research Centre; www.berghofhandbook.net/dialogue-series/no.-2-security-sector-reform (accessed 25 February 2011).

Macfarlane, S. Neil, and Khong, Yuen Foong (2006) *Human Security and the UN: A Critical History*. Bloomington: Indiana University Press.

Macrae, Joanna (1998) 'The death of humanitarianism? An anatomy of the attack', *Disasters*, 22(4): 309–17.

Macrae, Joanna (2003) 'Coherence or cooption? Europe and the new humanitarianism', in Joanna Macrae, Emery Brusset and Christine Tiberghien (eds), *Europe in the World: Essays on EU Foreign, Security and Development Policies*. London: BOND.

Macrae, Joanna, and Zwi, Anthony (1994) *War and Hunger: Rethinking International Responses to Complex Emergencies*. London: Zed Books.

Macrae, Rob, and Hubert, Don (eds) (2001) *Human Security and the New Diplomacy: Protecting People, Promoting Peace*. Montreal: McGill–Queen's University Press.

Malan, Mark (2008) *Security Sector Reform in Liberia: Mixed Results from Humble Beginnings*. Carlisle, PA: Strategic Studies Institute, US Army War College.

Meertens, D. (2010) 'Forced displacement and women's security in Colombia', *Disasters*, 34(2): 147–64.

Menkhaus, Ken (2004a) *Somalia: State Collapse and the Threat of Terrorism*, Adelphi Paper no. 364, Oxford: Oxford University Press.

Menkhaus, Ken (2004b) 'Vicious circles and the security development nexus in Somalia', *Conflict Security and Development*, 4(2): 149–65.

Miall, Hugh, Ramsbotham, Oliver, and Woodhouse, Tom (1999) *Contemporary Conflict Resolution: The Prevention, Management and Transformation of Deadly Conflicts*. Cambridge: Polity.

Migdal, Joel (1988) *Strong Societies and Weak States: State–Society Relations and State Capabilities in the Third World*. Princeton, NJ: Princeton University Press.

Miskel, James, and Norton, Richard (2003) 'The intervention in the Democratic Republic of Congo', *Civil Wars*, 6(4): 1–13.

Moore, Jonathan (ed.) (2004), *Hard Choices: Moral Dilemmas in Humanitarian Intervention*. Oxford: Rowman & Littlefield.

Mueller, John (2000) 'The banality of "ethnic war"', *International Security*, 25(1): 42–70.

Muggah, Robert (2000) 'Conflict-induced displacement and involuntary resettlement in Colombia: putting Cernea's IRLR model to the test', *Disasters*, 24(3): 198–216.

Muggah, Robert (ed.) (2009) *Security and Post-Conflict Reconstruction: Dealing with Fighters in the Aftermath of War*. London. Routledge.

Münkler, Herfried (2005) *The New Wars*. Cambridge: Polity.

Munslow, Barry, and Brown, Christopher (1999) 'Complex emergencies: the institutional impasse', *Third World Quarterly*, 20(3): 551–68.

Musah, Abdul, and Kayodi Fayemi (eds) (2000) *Mercenaries: An African Security Dilemma*. London: Pluto Press.

Nathan, Laurie (2005) *'The Frightful Inadequacy of Most of the Statistics': A Critique of Collier and Hoeffler on Causes of Civil War*, Discussion paper no. 11. London School of Economics, Crisis States Research Centre.

National Intelligence Council (2004) *Mapping the Global Future: Report of the National Intelligence Council's 2020 Project*. Pittsburgh, PA, Government Printing Office; www.foia.cia.gov/2020/2020. pdf (accessed 27 February 2011).

Natsios, Andrew (1995) 'NGOs and the UN system in complex humanitarian emergencies: conflict or cooperation', *Third World Quarterly*, 16(3): 405–19.

Natsios, Andrew (1997) 'Humanitarian relief operations in Somalia: the economics of chaos', in Walter Clarke and Jeffrey Herbst (eds), *Learning from Somalia: The Lessons of Armed Humanitarian Intervention*. Boulder, CO: Westview Press, pp. 77–95.

Neack, Laura (2007) *Elusive Security: States First, People Last*. Lanham, MD: Rowman & Littlefield.

Neild, Rachel (2001) 'Democratic police reforms in war-torn states', *Conflict, Security and Development*, 1(1): 21–43.

Nel, Philip, and Righarts, Marjolein (2008) 'Natural disasters and the risk of violent civil conflict', *International Studies Quarterly*, 52(1): 159–85.

Newman, Edward (2004a) 'A normatively attractive but analytically weak concept', *Security Dialogue*, 35(3): 358–9.

Newman, Edward (2004b) 'The "new wars" debate: a historical perspective is needed', *Security Dialogue*, 35(2): 173–89.

Newman, Edward, and Richmond, Oliver (ed.) (2001) *The United Nations and Human Security*. Basingstoke: Palgrave.

OECD (Organisation for Economic Co-operation and Development) (2005) *Security System Reform and Governance*. Paris, OECD; www.oecd.org/dataoecd/8/39/31785288.pdf (accessed 27 February 2011).

Ofuatey Kodjoe, W. (1994) 'Regional organisations and resolution of internal conflict: the ECOWAS intervention in Liberia', *International Peacekeeping*, 1(3): 261–302.

Okechukwu, I. (1998) 'Exiles in their own home: internal population displacement in Nigeria', *African Journal of Political Science*, 3(2): 80–97.

Oucho, John (1997) 'The ethnic factor in the internal displacement of populations in sub-Saharan Africa', *African Journal of Political Science*, 2(2): 104–17.

Paris, Roland (2002) 'Human security: paradigm shift or hot air?', *International Security*, 26(2): 87–102.

Paris, Roland (2004) *At War's End*. Cambridge: Cambridge University Press.

Peluso, Nancy Lee, and Watts, Michael (eds) (2001) *Violent Environments*. New York: Cornell University Press.

Pentitilä, Risto (2002) *The Role of the G8 in International Peace and Security*, Adelphi paper no. 355. Oxford: Oxford University Press.

Perito, Robert M. (2005) *The Coalition Provisional Authority's Experience with Public Security in Iraq: Lessons Identified*. New York: United States Institute of Peace; www.usip.org/publications/coalition-provisional-authoritys-experience-public-security-iraq-lessons-identified (accessed 27 February 2011).

Pouligny, Beatrice (2006) *Peace Operations Seen from Below: UN Missions and Local People*. London: Hurst.

Prunier, Gerald (1997) 'The experience of European armies in Operation Restore Hope', in Walter Clarke and Jeffrey Herbst (eds), *Learning from Somalia: The Lessons of Armed Humanitarian Intervention*. Boulder, CO: Westview Press.

Pugh, Mike (1995) 'Peacebuilding as developmentalism: concepts from disaster research', *Contemporary Security Policy*, 16(3): 320–46.

Pugh, Mike (2005) 'The political economy of peacebuilding: a critical theory perspective', *International Journal of Peace Studies*, 10(2): 23–42.

Ramsbotham, Oliver, and Woodhouse, Tom (1996) *Humanitarian Intervention in Contemporary Conflict: A Reconceptualization*. Cambridge: Polity.

Reno, William (1998) *Warlord Politics and African States*. Boulder, CO: Lynne Rienner.

Reno, William (2000) 'Liberia and Sierra Leone: the competition for patronage in resource-rich economies', in E. Wayne Nafziger, Frances Stewart and Raimo Väyrynen (eds), *War, Hunger, and Displacement: The Origins of Humanitarian Emergencies*. Oxford: Oxford University Press.

Richards, Paul (1996) *Fighting for the Rain Forest: War, Youth & Resources in Sierra Leone*. Oxford: James Currey.

Richards, Paul (ed.) (2005) *No Peace, No War: An Anthropology of Contemporary Armed Conflicts*. Oxford: James Currey, pp. 1–21.

Rigby, Andrew (2001) 'Review article: Humanitarian assistance and conflict management: the view from the non-governmental sector', *International Affairs*, 77(4): 957–66.

Roberts, Adam (1999) 'NATO's "humanitarian war" over Kosovo', *Survival*, 41(3): 102–23.

Ross, E. (1998) *The Malthus Factor: Poverty, Politics and Population in Capitalist Development*. London: Zed Books.

Ross, Michael L. (2004) 'What do we know about natural resources and civil war?', *Journal of Peace Research*, 41(3): 337–56.

Rosser, A. (2006) 'Escaping the resource curse', *New Political Economy*, 11(4): 557–70.

Rossi, Simonetta, and Giustozzi, Antonio (2006) *Disarmament, Demobilisation and Reintegration of Ex-Combatants (DDR) in Afghanistan: Constrains and Limited Capabilities*. London: London School of Economics, Crisis States Research Centre.

Rostow, Walt William (1960) *The Stages of Economic Growth: A Non-Communist Manifesto*. Cambridge: Cambridge University Press.

Rupesinghe, Kumar (1998) *Civil Wars, Civil Peace: An Introduction to Conflict Resolution*. London: Pluto Press.

Sachs, J. D., and Warner, A. M. (2001) 'The curse of natural resources', *European Economic Review*, 45: 285–306.

Schecter, Darrow (2000) *Sovereign States or Political Communities? Civil Society and Contemporary Politics*. Manchester: Manchester University Press.

Schmeidl, Susanne (2002) '(Human) security dilemmas: long-term implications of the Afghan refugee crisis', *Third World Quarterly*, 23(1): 7–29.

Scholte, Jan Aart (2005) *Globalization: A Critical Introduction*, 2nd ed. London: Palgrave.

Schwartz, Moshe (2010) *Department of Defense Contractors in Iraq and Afghanistan: Background and Analysis*. Washington, DC: Congressional Research Service; www.fas.org/sgp/crs/natsec/R40764.pdf (accessed 6 March 20100).

Shawcross, William (2001) *Deliver Us from Evil: Peacekeepers, Warlords and a World of Endless Conflict*. New York: Simon & Schuster.

Shearer, David (1998) *Private Armies and Military Intervention*, Adelphi Paper no. 316. Oxford: Oxford University Press.

Sheehan, Michael (2005) *International Security: An Analytical Survey*. Boulder, CO: Lynne Rienner.

Sheffer, G. (2006) 'Diasporas and terrorism', in Louise Richardson (ed.), *The Roots of Terrorism*. London: Routledge, pp. 119–29.

Singer, Peter (2003) *Corporate Warriors: The Rise of the Privatized Military Industry*. Ithaca, NY: Cornell University Press.

Slim, Hugo (1995) 'Military humanitarianism and the new peacekeeping: an agenda for peace?', *Journal of Humanitarian Assistance*, September; www.jha.ac/articles/a003.htm (accessed 27 February 2011).

Slim, Hugo (1996) 'The stretcher and the drum: civil–military relations in peace support operations', *International Peacekeeping*, 3(2): 123–39.

Slim, Hugo (1997) *International Humanitarianism's Engagement with Civil War in the 1990s: A Glance at Evolving Practice and Theory*. Oxford Brookes University, Centre for Development and Emergency Practice; www.jha.ac/articles/a033.htm (accessed 27 February 2011).

Smillie, Ian (1997) 'NGOs and development assistance: a change in mind-set?', *Third World Quarterly*, 18(3): 563–77.

Smith, Chris (2001) 'Security-sector reform: development breakthrough or institutional engineering?', *Conflict, Security and Development*, 1(1): 5–20.

Smith, Hazel, and Stares, Paul (eds) (2007) *Diasporas in Conflict: Peace-Makers or Peace-Wreckers?* New York: United Nations University Press.

Smith, Merrill (ed.) (2004) *Warehousing Refugees: A Denial of Rights, a Waste of Humanity*. Arlington, VA: US Committee for Refugees and Immigrants.

Smith, Steve (2000) 'The increasing insecurity of security studies: conceptualizing security in the last twenty years', in Stuart Croft and Terry Terriff (eds), *Critical Reflections on Security and Change*. London: Frank Cass, pp. 72–101.

SNSFA (Subcommittee on National Security and Foreign Affairs) (2010) *Warlord Inc.: Extortion and Corruption along the US Supply Chain in Afghanistan*. Washington, DC: US House of Representatives.

Sörensen, Jens Stilhoff (2003) 'War as social transformation: wealth, class, power and an illiberal economy in Serbia', *Civil Wars*, 6(3): 77–8.

Spear, Jo (1999) 'The disarmament and demobilisation of warring factions in the aftermath of civil wars: key implementation issues', *Civil Wars*, 2(2): 1–22.

Stamnes, Eli (2004) 'Critical security studies and the United Nations preventive deployment in Macedonia', *International Peacekeeping*, 11(1): 161–81.

Stedman, Stephen (1995) 'Alchemy for a new world order: overselling "preventative diplomacy"', *Foreign Affairs*, 74, May/June.

Stein, Janice (2005) 'Humanitarianism as political fusion', *Perspectives on Politics*, 3(4): 741–4.

Stewart, Frances (2006) 'Development and security', in Robert Picciotto and Rachel Weaving (eds), *Security and Development: Investing in Peace and Prosperity*. Abingdon: Routledge, pp. 43–70.

Suhrke, Astri, Villanger, Espen, and Woodward, Susan L. (2005) 'Economic aid to post-conflict countries: a methodological critique of Collier and Hoeffler', *Conflict, Security and Development*, 5(3): 329–61.

Taylor, Christopher (1999) *Sacrifice as Terror: The Rwandan Genocide of 1994*. Oxford: Berg.

Thakur, Ramesh, and Schnabel, Albrecht (eds) (2001) *United Nations Peacekeeping Operations: Ad Hoc Missions, Permanent Engagement*. Tokyo: United Nations University Press.

Thomas, Caroline (2001) 'Global governance, development and human security: exploring the links', *Third World Quarterly*, 22(2): 159–75.

Thomas, J. (1981) 'Refugees: a new approach', *International Migration Review*, 15(1/2): 20–25.

Toole, M., and Waldman, R. (1997) 'The public health aspects of complex emergencies and refugee situations', *Annual Review of Public Health*, 18: 283–312.

Tripodi, Paolo, and Patel, Preeti (2002) 'The global impact of HIV/AIDS on peace support operations', *International Peacekeeping*, 9(3): 51–66.

UN (United Nations) (2000) *The Role of the United Nations Peacekeeping in Disarmament, Demobilization, and Reintegration: Report of the Secretary General*. New York, United Nations.

UN (2004) *The Rule of Law and Transitional Justice in Conflict and Post Conflict Societies: Report of the Secretary General*. New York, United Nations.

UN High Level Panel on Uncivil Society (2005) 'Civil society and global governance: contextual paper', www.unece.org/env/pp/ppif/Civil%20Society%20and%20Global%20Governance%20paper%20 by%20Cardoso.htm (accessed 2 March 2011).

UN OCHA (United Nations Office for the Coordination of Humanitarian Affairs) (1998) *Guiding Principles on Internal Displacement*, www.reliefweb.int/rw/lib.nsf/db900sid/LHON-65RDFJ/$file/ IASC_IDP_principles_1999.pdf?openelement (accessed 3 March 2011).

UNDP (United Nations Development Programme (2005) *Human Development Report 2005: International Cooperation at a Crossroads: Aid, Trade and Security in an Unequal World*. New York: UNDP.

UNHRC (United Nations High Commissioner for Refugees) (1995) *Sexual Violence against Refugees: Guidelines on Prevention and Response*. Geneva: UNHCR.

UNHCR (2001) *Protecting Refugees: A Field Guide for NGOs*, 2d ed. Geneva: UNHCR.

UNHCR (2003a) *Agenda for Protection*, 3ed ed. Geneva: UNHCR; www.unhcr.org/protect/ PROTECTION/3e637b194.pdf (accessed 27 February 2011).

UNHCR (2003b) *Framework for Durable Solutions for Refugees and Persons of Concern*. Geneva: UNHCR; www.unhcr.org/partners/PARTNERS/3f1408764.pdf (accessed 27 February 2011).

UNHCR (2004) *Protracted Refugee Situations*. Geneva: UNHCR; www.unhcr.org/statistics/ STATISTICS/40ed5b384.pdf (accessed 27 February 2011).

UNHCR (2008) *Protecting Refugees and the Role of the UNHCR 2008–9*. Geneva: UNHCR; www. unhcr.org/4034b6a34.pdf (accessed 27 February 2011).

UNRWA (United Nations Relief and Works Agency for Palestine Refugees in the Near East) (2010) 'Frequently asked questions', www.unrwa.org/etemplate.php?id=87 (accessed May 2010).

UNSG (United Nations Secretary-General) (2008) *Securing Peace and Development: The Role of the United Nations in Supporting Security Sector Reform*, A/62/659-S/2008/39. New York: United Nations.

USCRI (United States Committee for Refugees and Immigrants) (2009) *World Refugee Survey 2009*, www.refugees.org/resources/refugee-warehousing/archived-world-refugee-surveys/2009-world-refugee-survey.html (accessed 27 February 2011).

Vinci, Anthony (2005) 'The strategic use of fear by the Lord's Resistance Army', *Small Wars and Insurgencies*, 16(3): 360–81.

Vlassenroet, Koen, and Raeymaekers, Timothy (2004) 'The politics of rebellion and intervention in Ituri: the emergence of a new political complex?', *African Affairs*, 103(412): 385–412.

Waddell, Nicholas (2006) 'Ties that bind: DfID and the emerging security and development agenda analysis', *Conflict, Security and Development*, 6(4): 531–55.

Wallerstein, Immanuel (2004) *World-Systems Analysis: An Introduction*. Durham, NC: Duke University Press.

Walter, Barbara (1999) 'Designing transitions from civil war', in Barbara Walter and Jack Snyder (eds), *Civil wars, Insecurity, and Intervention*. New York: Columbia University Press.

Walter, Barbara, and Snyder, Jack (eds) (1999) *Civil Wars, Insecurity, and Intervention*. New York: Columbia University Press.

Watson, Charlotte, and Crozier, Rebecca (2009) *Security for Whom? Security Sector Reform and Public Security in Nepal*. Brussels: Initiative for Peacebuilding; http://www.international-alert.org/pdf/IfP_Security_Sector_Reform_and_Public_Security_in_Nepal.pdf (accessed 7 March 2011)

Wayland, Sarah (2004) 'Ethnonationalist networks and transnational opportunities: the Sri Lankan Tamil diaspora', *Review of International Studies*, 30(3): 405–26.

Weiss, Thomas (1996) *NGOs, the UN, and Global Governance*. Boulder, CO: Lynne Rienner.

West, Katarina (2001) *Agents of Altruism: The Expansion of Humanitarian NGOs in Rwanda and Afghanistan*. Aldershot: Ashgate.

Wheeler, Nicholas (2000) *Saving Strangers: Humanitarian Intervention in International Society*. Oxford: Oxford University Press.

White House (2006) *The National Security Strategy of the United States of America*, www.comw.org/qdr/fulltext/nss2006.pdf (accessed 24 February 2011).

Williams, Paul (ed.) (2008) *Security Studies: An Introduction*. London: Routledge.

Williams, Zack (2001) 'Child solders in the civil war in Sierra Leone', *Review of African Political Economy*, 28(87): 73–82.

World Bank (1989) *Sub-Saharan Africa: From Crisis to Sustainable Growth*. Washington, DC: World Bank.

World Bank (2011) *World Development Report 2011: Conflict, Security and Development*. Washington, DC: World Bank.

Wulf, Herbert (2004) 'Security sector reform in developing and transitional countries', in Clem McCartney, Martina Fischer and Oliver Wils (eds), *Security Sector Reform: Potentials and Challenges for Conflict Transformation*. Berlin: Berghof Research Centre, www.berghof-handbook.net/documents/publications/dialogue2_wulf.pdf (accessed 27 February 2011).

Yanacopulos, Helen, and Hanlon, Joseph (eds) (2005) *Civil War, Civil Peace*. Oxford: James Currey.

Zack-Williams, A. B. (2001) 'Child soldiers in the civil war in Sierra Leone', *Review of African Political Economy*, 28(87): 73–82.

Zartman, William (1995) *Collapsed States: The Disintegration and Restoration of Legitimate Authority*. Boulder, CO: Lynne Rienner.

Zolberg, Aristide, Suhrke, Astri, and Aguayo, Sergio (1986) 'International factors in the formation of refugee movements', *International Migration Review*, 20(2): 151–69.

Index

Taylor & Francis

eBooks

FOR LIBRARIES

ORDER YOUR FREE 30 DAY INSTITUTIONAL TRIAL TODAY!

Over 23,000 eBook titles in the Humanities, Social Sciences, STM and Law from some of the world's leading imprints.

Choose from a range of subject packages or create your own!

Benefits for you
▶ Free MARC records
▶ COUNTER-compliant usage statistics
▶ Flexible purchase and pricing options

Benefits for your user
▶ Off-site, anytime access via Athens or referring URL
▶ Print or copy pages or chapters
▶ Full content search
▶ Bookmark, highlight and annotate text
▶ Access to thousands of pages of quality research at the click of a button

For more information, pricing enquiries or to order a free trial, contact your local online sales team.

UK and Rest of World: **online.sales@tandf.co.uk**

US, Canada and Latin America:
e-reference@taylorandfrancis.com

www.ebooksubscriptions.com

ALPSP Award for BEST eBOOK PUBLISHER 2009 Finalist

Taylor & Francis eBooks
Taylor & Francis Group

A flexible and dynamic resource for teaching, learning and research.